Sustainable Development as Environmental Harm

In this in-depth analysis of First Nations opposition to the oil sands industry, James Heydon offers detailed empirical insight into Canadian oil sands regulation. The environmental consequences of the oil sands industry have been thoroughly explored by scholars from a variety of disciplines. However, less well understood is how and why the provincial energy regulator has repeatedly sanctioned such a harmful pattern of production for almost two decades. This research monograph addresses that shortcoming.

Drawing from interviews with government, industry, and First Nation personnel, along with an analysis of almost 20 years of policy, strategy, and regulatory approval documents, *Sustainable Development as Environmental Harm* offers detailed empirical insight into Canadian oil sands regulation. Providing a thorough account of the ways in which the regulatory process has prioritised economic interests over the land-based cultural interests of First Nations, it addresses a gap in the literature by explaining how environmental harm has been systematically produced over time by a regulatory process tasked with the pursuit of 'sustainable development'.

With an approach emphasizing the importance of understanding how and why the regulatory process has been able to circumvent various protections for the entire duration in which the contemporary oil sands industry has existed, this work complements existing literature and provides a platform from which future investigations into environmental harm may be conducted. It is essential reading for those with an interest in green criminology, environmental harm, indigenous rights, and regulatory controls relating to fossil fuel production.

James Heydon is a lecturer in Criminology at the University of Lincoln. He is also Chair of the British Society of Criminology's Green Criminology Research Network.

Crimes of the Powerful

Crimes of the Powerful encompasses the harmful, injurious, and victimizing behaviors perpetrated by privately or publicly operated businesses, corporations, and organizations as well as the state mediated administrative, legalistic, and political responses to these crimes.

The series draws attention to the commonalities of the theories, practices, and controls of the crimes of the powerful. It focuses on the overlapping spheres and inter-related worlds of a wide array of existing and recently developing areas of social, historical, and behavioral inquiry into the wrongdoings of multinational organizations, nation-states, stateless regimes, illegal networks, financialization, globalization, and securitization.

These examinations of the crimes of the powerful straddle a variety of related disciplines and areas of academic interest, including studies in criminology and criminal justice; law and human rights; conflict, peace, and security; economic change, environmental decay, and global sustainability.

Gregg Barak, *Eastern Michigan University, USA*
Penny Green, *Queen Mary University of London, UK*
Tony Ward, *Northumbria University, UK*

The Crime of Maldevelopment
Economic Deregulation and Violence in the Global South
María Laura Böhm

Sustainable Development as Environmental Harm
Rights, Regulation, and Injustice in the Canadian Oil Sands
James Heydon

For more information about this series, please visit: www.routledge.com/Crimes-of-the-Powerful/book-series/COTP

Sustainable Development as Environmental Harm

Rights, Regulation, and Injustice in the Canadian Oil Sands

James Heydon

Routledge
Taylor & Francis Group
LONDON AND NEW YORK

First published 2019 by Routledge

2 Park Square, Milton Park, Abingdon, Oxon OX14 4RN
605 Third Avenue, New York, NY 10017

Routledge is an imprint of the Taylor & Francis Group, an informa business

First issued in paperback 2021

Publisher's Note

The publisher has gone to great lengths to ensure the quality of this reprint but points out that some imperfections in the original copies may be apparent.

Library of Congress Cataloging-in-Publication Data
Names: Heydon, James, author.
Title: Sustainable development as environmental harm : rights, regulation, and injustice in the Canadian oil sands / James Heydon.
Description: 1 Edition. | New York : Routledge, 2019.
Identifiers: LCCN 2018058657 (print) | LCCN 2019004299 (ebook) | ISBN 9780429423536 (Ebook) | ISBN 9781138390089 (hardback)
Subjects: LCSH: Oil sands–Environmental aspects–Canada. | Sustainable development–Canada.
Classification: LCC HD9574.C22 (ebook) | LCC HD9574.C22 H49 2019 (print) | DDC 333.8/232150971231–dc23
LC record available at https://lccn.loc.gov/2018058657

ISBN: 978-1-138-39008-9 (hbk)
ISBN: 978-0-367-53079-2 (pbk)

Typeset in Bembo
by Wearset Ltd, Boldon, Tyne and Wear

To the people of Alberta.
For Thomas and his generation.

Contents

Acknowledgements

It is difficult to properly acknowledge the myriad of people who have informed the thinking on this project, not least because it is hard to pinpoint exactly where and when influences on an idea originate. Nevertheless, there are several individuals who have made a demonstrable impression on this work.

The most direct support for this research has come from Matthew Hall, whose input and support has been invaluable throughout. Similarly, Stephen Farrell and Nigel South provided helpful comments on an earlier iteration of this study, for which I am very thankful. Indeed, it was on the basis of their advice that this book was written.

I would like to thank the various green criminologists, established and upcoming, that have provided feedback on this research at various conferences over the past five years. I am immensely grateful for their words of advice and support. Similarly, I would like to thank the researcher who offered to act as a sponsor during the 2014 British Society of Criminology conference at the University of Liverpool. Much of the access gained can be traced back to this initial meeting, without which much of this would not have been possible.

I am also thankful to those who in Alberta who chose not to turn away a Caucasian, middle-class Englishman in the depths of the Canadian winter. I appreciate their participation in this research and am grateful for the opportunity to have listened to their views. Their voices have formed the foundation of this book.

I would also like to acknowledge the generous funding of the Economic and Social Research Council (Award No. ES/J500215/1), without which the research would not have been possible.

A special thank you goes to my wife, Laura. Providing unwavering support through periods of uncertainty and self-doubt, her encouragement and tireless faith in my abilities has been instrumental to the completion of this research.

Finally, I would like to thank my grandmother, Marjorie, parents, Mandy and Paul, and brother Dan. Without your efforts, none of this would have been possible.

Abbreviations

ACFN	Athabasca Chipewyan First Nation
ACO	Aboriginal Consultation Office
ACSREM	Alberta's Commitment to Sustainable Resource and Environmental Management
AENV	Alberta Environment
AER	Alberta Energy Regulator
AEUB	Alberta Energy and Utilities Board
AFL	Alberta Federation of Labour
AHF	Alberta Heritage Fund
AUC	Alberta Utilities Commission
BSC	British Society of Criminology
CAPP	Canadian Association of Petroleum Producers
CEEM	Cumulative Environmental Effects Monitoring Initiative
CEMA	Cumulative Environmental Management Association
CNRL	Canadian Natural Resources Limited
CT	Consolidated Tailings
DFO	Department of Fisheries and Oceans
EPL	End Pit Lake
ERCA	Energy Resources Conservation Act
ERCB	Energy Resources Conservation Board
ESRC	Economic and Social Research Council
ESRD	Alberta Environment and Sustainable Resource Development
FNIRD	First Nation industry relations departments
FPIC	Free Prior and Informed Consent
GDP	Gross Domestic Product
IFN	In-Flow Needs
JOSM	Joint Canada-Alberta Oil Sands Monitoring Plan
LARP	Lower Athabasca Regional Plan
LUF	Land Use Framework
LUS	Land Use Secretariat
MCFN	Mikisew Cree First Nation
MFT	Medium Fine Tailings

MRME	Muskeg River Mine
NAFTA	North American Free Trade Agreement
NEB	National Energy Board
NRTA	Natural Resources Transfer Agreement
NST	Non-Segregated Tailings
OECD	Organisation for Economic Co-operation and Development
PAH	Polycyclic Aromatic Hydrocarbons
PAI	Potential Acid Input
REDA	Responsible Energy Development Act
RSDS	Regional Sustainable Development Strategy
SCC	Supreme Court of Canada
UN	United Nations
UNDRIP	United Nations Declaration on the Rights of Indigenous Peoples
UNESCO	United Nations Education Scientific and Cultural Organisation
UNGP	United Nations Guiding Principles on Business and Human Rights
WBEA	Wood Buffalo Environmental Association

Part I

Background and Analytical Lens

Chapter 1

The Oil Sands and Their Discontents

In late September 2016, some 50 US Native American and Canadian First Nation leaders gathered in Musqueam Territory (Vancouver) and Mohawk Territory (Montreal). At this meeting, each of the representatives signed an agreement titled the Treaty Alliance Against Tar Sands Expansion (Treaty Alliance 2016a). Its text denotes a pledge by the signatory peoples to 'officially prohibit' and 'collectively challenge and resist … the use of our respective territories and coasts for the expansion of the production of the Tar Sands'. The pattern of industrial production to which this refers is the extraction of 'unconventional' oil, bitumen, that lies beneath the boreal forests of northern Alberta, Canada. As a commitment, the Treaty Alliance aims to halt all existing oil sands rail and tanker proposals, along with all five current pipeline proposals for moving the resource, including the Keystone XL, Northern Gateway, and Kinder Morgan projects. This Treaty therefore represents an unprecedented solidification of indigenous opposition to expansive oil sands production across the breadth of Canadian and American soil. Importantly, such extensive resistance is almost exclusively catalysed by the local and global environmental consequences engendered by this pattern of fossil fuel production. As the Treaty itself states:

> [Expanding transport routes for the oil sands resource] threaten[s] many Indigenous Nations' territories, waterways, shores and communities with the very real risk of toxic and hazardous oil spills. The expansion of the Tar Sands would also lead to increased destruction and poisoning of the lands, waters and air of the Indigenous Peoples … downstream of the Tar Sands.… [B]y leading to the expansion of the Tar Sands, such projects will unquestionably fuel catastrophic climate change … [which] has already started to endanger our peoples' way of life and now threatens our very survival.
>
> (Treaty Alliance 2016b: 1)

Both the Canadian and US federal governments responded to this Treaty with apathy, as did the industry bodies representing oil sands companies. The

Canadian Energy Pipeline Association (CEPA) promised to 'listen to aboriginal concerns' but reiterated its belief that more pipelines are needed (CEPA, quoted in Kennedy 2016), while the Canadian Association of Oil Producers noted that this would not alter the way it did business (McGuigan, quoted in McSheffrey 2016). Add to this the recent promise by the Government of Canada to nationalise one of the opposed pipelines, to ensure it gets built in the face of rising costs, and plans for a new, 'colossal' oil sands mine (Tuttle 2018), then the future relationship between indigenous environmental interests on the one hand, and those of state and corporate actors on the other, is likely to be characterised by antagonism and conflict for some time. However, while this Treaty represents a new, cross-national approach by indigenous peoples in their opposition to oil sands extraction, it must be understood as the contemporary manifestation of nearly 20 years of struggle against its growth.

The oil sands resource lies under 54,000 square miles of boreal forest, to the north of Alberta, Canada. It consists of three deposits, named the Athabasca, Peace River, and Cold Lake, which are generally referred to collectively as the Oil Sands. With the volume of proven reserves standing at 166 billion barrels, it is the third-largest oil reserve in the world, after Venezuela and Saudi Arabia. Consisting of a mixture of sand, clay, water, and bitumen, which is a semi-solid form of crude oil, the resource requires strip-mining or 'in-situ' techniques for its extraction. The latter of these inject steam and solvents into the deposit to reduce its viscosity, allowing it to be pumped to the surface. This is why it is known as an 'unconventional' oil source; the techniques for its extraction differ from the 'conventional' well-drilling methods used for crude oil. Although commercial bitumen production has occurred in the region since the 1960s, it was not until the mid-1990s that rising global oil prices made it more attractive to investors and rapid expansion began (Chastko 2007). Since this point, the high human and environmental costs of such 'unconventional' processes have become increasingly apparent, causing some to label oil sands extraction as 'the biggest environmental crime in history' (Milmo 2007).

While this is a dramatic label, it is not overly so. Extraction and processing of bitumen is between 12 and 24 per cent more carbon intensive than conventional oil production (Englander *et al.* 2013), generating waste-water ponds emitting levels of methane equivalent to half a million cattle per day (Timoney and Lee 2009: 66). Reserves also contain more than twice the total amount of oil burned in all of human history (Hansen 2012), meaning continued expansion of the operations will guarantee release of substantial quantities of emissions into the atmosphere for the foreseeable future. Indeed, extraction is expected to increase from a rate of one million barrels per day in 2000 to five million per day in 2040; a 400 per cent increase in fossil fuel production over a 40-year period (National Energy Board 2016: 52). In the context of the UN Paris Agreement, this is particularly problematic. Its target of maintaining global surface temperatures below 2°C requires 85 per cent of Canadian bitumen reserves to remain in the ground (McGlade and Ekins 2015: 190). Should even a 1.5°C warming threshold be breached, the risks of inland and coastal flooding, breakdowns in critical services due to extreme weather events, food insecurity, and widespread ecosystem collapse, among others, become increasingly likely characteristics of future existence on earth (Intergovernmental Panel on Climate Change 2018).

Yet, while the global consequences of oil sands expansion have attracted serious and popular consideration, they are inseparable from the more localised harms being experienced by those living in and around the oil sands deposit. Not only has industrial production of bitumen in the area been directly linked to hydrocarbon pollution in the Athabasca River watershed (Kurek *et al.* 2012), but airborne Volatile Organic Compounds, which contain carcinogens (Forrest *et al.* 2005; Cheng *et al.* 2007), have been found at levels 6,000 times higher than average in the surrounding area (Simpson *et al.* 2013). With the World Health Organization (2013) classifying air pollution as a leading cause of cancer deaths (see also Straif *et al.* 2013), evidence suggesting that the oil sands industry is not reporting all of its emissions (Simpson *et al.* 2013), and local doctors maintaining silence about the health implications of oil and gas operations for fear of reprisal (Edwards, 2014), the danger to the physical health of those in the vicinity is an obvious concern. One specific anxiety is tied to the rates of cancer seen in local indigenous communities. While the official position of the provincial government holds there to be no evidence of increased cancer rates or other illnesses (Talbot 2014), research by the Alberta Cancer Board (Chen 2009: 44) and the University of Manitoba (2014) suggests otherwise. It is this combination of global and local issues that has drawn increasingly critical attention towards the industry.

Over the last two decades some of the most vocal opposition has stemmed from the indigenous First Nation communities in and around the deposit, who have opposed unbridled expansion for much of this time. Their disapproval has been expressed through a variety of formal and informal channels since the turn of the century, but it is important to note that this has never been a uniform position. First Nations initially supported extractive operations as a means of tackling some of the socio-economic difficulties experienced by their communities, with industry investment providing opportunities for services and wage labour that were simply unavailable before (Taylor and Friedel 2011). To a certain extent this is still the case, with some First Nations being less resistant to industrial activity in the region than others. Indeed, many have developed successful enterprises providing services to the industry, such as the Fort McKay First Nation. Yet, as noted by Jim Boucher (quoted in Klinkenberg 2014), Chief of the First Nation and Director of its Group of Companies, this was born from necessity:

> I think our community is benefitting from oil sands development, but we do so because there are no other economic opportunities.... We were anti-development for a long time, but at the end of the day it came down to the point where government would approve the projects and our rights were diminished by virtue of what they were doing. Gradually, we came to recognise we had no other option but to develop an economy of our own.

More recently, this position has been echoed by the Chief of the Athabasca Chipewyan First Nation (ACFN), Allan Adam, and Archie Wacquan, of the Mikisew Cree First Nation (MCFN), who, after almost two decades of opposition, recently announced support for expansive pipeline infrastructure in the region (Thurton 2018). The reason for this is similar to that communicated by Boucher four years earlier; despite the best efforts of First Nations, they have been unable to successfully oppose expansion of the industry. As noted by Deranger (quoted in Toth 2018), a member of the ACFN and executive director for Indigenous Climate Action, '... [t]o be frank it's not surprising that it's come to this'. Despite many years of challenging oil sands projects, there has been 'little to no actionable recourse or change to the system'. Such fatigue is mirrored in Adam's justification for his pipeline support: '... [t]he fact is I am tired. I am tired of fighting' (quoted in Thurton 2018).

While this recent change in stance suggests support for the oil sands industry, it belies the fact that many of the local First Nations have actively opposed its expansion for almost two decades. Indeed, the announcement by the Chiefs provoked tension within their communities, as evidenced by one of several responses by ACFN elders: '... [i]t hurt. There's no such thing as a safe pipeline' (Rigney 2018, quoted in Toth 2018). This opposition is rooted in a concern for the impact of oil sands extraction on the health of those in the vicinity, their ability to engage in traditional land-based activities, such as hunting, fishing, and trapping, and its associated effect on the environment. Local First Nations are therefore in a difficult position. On the one hand, they rely on the industry for much-needed income, while, on the other, its continued growth threatens the very ecosystems upon which the more traditional aspects of their life depend. As such, their objections tend to be framed as a concern with the absence of compromise between expansion and environmental integrity. It is anchored to the observation that incremental environmental degradation has surpassed tolerable limits, degrading flora and fauna important to hunting, fishing, and trapping practices along with the confidence that they are uncontaminated. The resulting withdrawal from the land is recognised as a pattern of harm known as 'cultural loss' (see Berry 1999), and it is the purpose of this book to explain how and why it has been produced and reproduced over time by the regulatory mechanism responsible for sanctioning 'sustainable' industrial expansion in the region.

A variety of scholars have explored the environmental impact of oil sands development, but less well understood is how and why the provincial regulatory process has repeatedly sanctioned such an environmentally disruptive pattern of production. After all, the process is tasked with the 'sustainable development' of the resource, so an explanation for its manifestly unsustainable form warrants attention. Similarly, First Nations have substantive, constitutionally protected rights to hunt, fish, and trap on the land, in addition to a procedural right to be consulted and accommodated on any activity which may risk adversely affecting them. Collectively known as Treaty rights, understanding how and why the regulatory process has been able to routinely circumvent these protections on the way to ensuring industrial growth also demands an explanation. This book directs attention towards these two spheres as they are manifest within the regulatory process governing oil sands expansion, moving beyond descriptions of ecological disruption by shifting the gaze upwards, onto the policies, agencies, practices, and relations acting to produce and reproduce it. In doing so, the book aims to identify environmentally problematic aspects of the regulatory process and, by extension, highlight opportunities for pursuit of a less harmful pattern of development. Before explaining cultural loss as a form of harm and drawing out the content of the regulatory mechanism in more detail, the book will be situated in the field of green criminology.

Green Criminology and Environmental Harm

As a sub-field of criminology, green criminology covers a broad spectrum of environmental crimes and harms, ranging from climate change (White 2018) and wildlife trafficking (Wyatt 2016), through to deforestation (Boekhout van Solinge 2014) and the abuse of animal rights (Nurse 2017). Such diversity is reflected in the lack of a clear unitary label for the enterprise, with the terms 'environmental criminology' (White 2008: 6), 'eco-crime' (Walters 2010), 'eco-global criminology' (White 2011) and 'conservation criminology' (Gibbs *et al.* 2010), all being used in reference to its disparate but related areas of focus. Following Lynch's (1990) initial call for the sub-field, an early attempt to provide some delineation was made by South (1998: 220) in his justification for a 'green perspective', or 'rallying point' (ibid.: 212), able to accommodate issues pertaining to human, animal, and environmental justice. Lynch and Stretesky (2003: 231) built on this, defining the 'meaning of green [criminology]' as specifically entailing 'a political stance wherein it is acknowledged that various solutions to environmental degradation may require substantial economic and political reorganisation'.

This politicisation led Gibbs *et al.* (2010) to develop a focus on 'conservation criminology' over 'green criminology', citing as justification the risk of analytical myopia emerging from the prioritisation of economic determinants over the social. Indeed, Halsey's (2004: 844) critique focused on the same elements of Lynch and Stretesky's (2003) conception, dismissing its emancipatory ideal of socio-economic equality as a modernist 'hubris' and suggesting a post-structuralist approach in response. This unresolved debate is reflected in White's (2013: 30) concession, where green criminology is equated to a 'road wide enough for many travellers' and is symptomatic of Downes' (1988) broader characterisation of criminology as a 'rendezvous' subject, or Cohen's (1998: 4) labelling of it as 'somewhat like a parasite'. However, if considered a 'perspective' (South, 2014: 7), this is not necessarily a detrimental feature, because the flexibility built into it can 'be associated with any number of theoretical positions and schools' (ibid.). Accounting for this, and to acknowledge it as an area that 'is developing as an inclusive field of interest rather than a restrictive body of scholarship' (Hall 2014: 97), the term 'green criminology' will here be recognised in the broad manner suggested by White (2008: 8): 'to basically refer to the study of environmental harm, environmental laws and environmental regulation by criminologists'. It is therefore in the broadest sense that the focus of this book – the regulatory process acting to sanction environmental harm in the oil sands region – falls under the remit of green criminological scholarship.

With the boundaries of green criminology proving to be intentionally flexible, defining what is deemed to constitute an 'environmental crime' is even more ambiguous, having consequences for the terminology deployed here. Green criminology, much like its parent discipline, holds within it a tension surrounding what its 'rightful' subject matter should be. Representing a variation on a commonly recognised dichotomy, Halsey and White (1998: 345–346) differentiate between the 'legal-procedural' and 'socio-legal' approaches to defining 'crime', where the former refers to 'practices which are prescribed by the law' and the latter to 'damaging practices which may or may not be encapsulated under existing criminal law'. Although examples exist in which literature from the more legal-procedural approach has been associated with green criminology (see Gibbs *et al.* 2010), where an environmental crime tends to be equated with 'any act that violates an environmental protection statute' (Clifford and Edwards 2012: 33), the field is primarily situated on the 'socio-legal' side of the spectrum. Here it is 'harm' as opposed to 'crime' that is of primary concern, allowing green criminology to acknowledge that, ultimately, 'crime is a word, not a deed' (Nettler 1984: 16). Therefore, as Beirne and South (2007) argue, the discipline should problematise the nature of 'crime' to understand how its definitions are constructed – or not – by powerful interests. Such a position rests on the notion that '[m]uch depends on who is defining the harm and what criteria are used in assessing the nature of the activities so-described' (White 2013: 20). It is this reality that has led some to divorce 'crime' from the legal standards with which it tends to be defined; an approach favoured by those from within the harm perspective.

In recognising that '[c]rime has no ontological reality' the harm perspective generates an expansive field of view (Hillyard and Tombs 2004: 11), where 'crimes as well as non-criminal victimisations and experiences of injustice, unfairness and prejudice' become acceptable targets for study (Davies 2014: 207). By diverging from the more constrained definitions found in orthodox criminology, which tend towards legalism and a 'parochial obsession with the behaviour of poor people in rich countries' (Ward and Green 2000: 7), the harms-based approach was intended to overcome criminology's continued 'inattention' towards the ways in which economic and political elites cause harm outside definitions provided by criminal law (Michalowski and Kramer 2006: 5). As Hillyard *et al.* (2005: 64) note, 'despite decades of resistance' from within the discipline itself, 'criminology and criminal justice remain infected with individually-based analysis, explanation and "remedy"', proceeding to describe this as a feature from which criminology cannot escape 'because this is what it is, where it was born and how it has been constructed'. This characterisation, of a discipline unable to escape its orthodox foundations, led to the authors positing social harm as an entirely separate approach – one which 'starts from a different place ... [with] a focus upon the *social* origins of harm, upon the structures that produce and reproduce such harms' (Hillyard *et al.* 2005: 64, emphasis in original). It is in this sense that the regulatory process focused on in this book is deemed environmentally harmful. It is the primary mechanism through which the provincial government's 'sustainable development' agenda is given operational form, and through which ecological disorganisation in the region has been, and continues to be, produced by the expansive oil sands operations justified under its rubric.

First Nations, Cultural Loss, and Treaty Rights

Following confederation in 1867, one of the primary means through which the Government of Canada gained title to large tracts of indigenous land was through the system of so-called Numbered Treaties. Allowing for indigenous land rights to be extinguished without resorting to the costly forms of frontier conflict seen in the United States, these granted the government title to substantial tracts of territory in exchange for, among other things, formally acknowledged 'reserve' areas and guarantees that the traditional way of life maintained by indigenous peoples would not be adversely affected. Such concessions were not arbitrary; the government moved to clear an area only when it was found to have significant economic or political value. For instance, Treaty 8, of 11, which includes Alberta's oil sands, was only signed in 1899 after gold was found in the Yukon to the north. The influx of prospectors moving through the region increased the chance of settler conflict with indigenous peoples, raising a political issue, while the simultaneous expectation of mineral wealth in the area raised its economic equivalent. As the Under Secretary of State for the Provinces stated to the Lieutenant Governor for the Northwestern Territories in 1870 (quoted in Fumoleau 2004: 3):

> [W]hile assuring the Indians of your desire to establish friendly relations with them, you will ascertain and report to His Excellency the course you think most advisable to pursue, whether by Treaty or otherwise, for the removal of any obstructions that might be presented to the flow of population into the fertile lands that lie between Manitoba and the Rocky Mountains.

Alberta is completely covered by three such treaties, all of which were signed before it attained provincial status in 1905. Treaty 7, agreed in 1877, covers its southernmost region, Treaty 6, signed in 1876, covers its central area, and Treaty 8, agreed in 1899, covers the northern expanse. It is the latter of these Treaties that is of concern here.

Extinguishing Aboriginal Title to 840,000 square kilometres of territory, Treaty 8 covers most of the oil sands deposit in the province. Twenty-four indigenous groups, ancestors of the First Nations inhabiting what is now northern Alberta, signed the Treaty. However, they would not grant the government permission to 'take up' tracts of their territory 'from time to time for settlement, mining, lumbering, trading or other purposes' unless their hunting, fishing, and trapping practices were protected (Government of Canada 1899). In this sense a large part of the Treaty 8 negotiations were assurances of continuity in traditional socio-cultural and economic practices. As the original Report of Commissioners for Treaty No. 8 in 1899 made clear:

> [W]e had to solemnly assure them that only such laws as to hunting and fishing as were in the interest of the Indians and were found necessary in order to protect the fish and fur-bearing animals would be made, and that they would be as free to hunt and fish after the treaty as they would be if they never entered into it.... We assured them that the treaty would not lead to any forced interference with their mode of life....

Such hunting, fishing, and trapping rights, or 'Treaty rights' as they are collectively known, have been enshrined in Section 35 of the Canadian Constitution, which asserts that 'existing aboriginal and treaty rights ... are hereby recognized and affirmed'. Yet, despite appearing to afford protection from activities that may adversely affect the ability of First Nations to continue their traditional 'mode of life', for those groups in and around the oil sands industry these rights have failed to fulfil this purpose.

Each group of indigenous peoples are distinct. Collapsing their various cultural characteristics into an undifferentiated mass is a conceptual manipulation tied to the legacy of colonialism, where the 'Indian' label could 'stand for the whole' (King 2012: 83). Yet, one of the attributes shared by many of these groups is the 'deeply spiritual' relationship maintained with the land (Anaya, 2009: 69). As Cobo (1986/87) recognises in his capacity as a UN Special Rapporteur for Indigenous Peoples, this is 'basic to their existence ... and to all their beliefs, customs, traditions and culture'. Such a reality is true for First Nations in Northern Alberta, where the ecosystem is ontologically conceived as intrinsic to human life (Wheatley 1997). As Woolford (2009: 91) explains, their conceptions of nature and culture are not simply 'close' or 'reliant' on one another, but form an 'embodied inscription', where land and wildlife form a central component to their collective indigenous identities. For these peoples travel through the landscape is linked to the expression of oral traditions (McCormack 2012: 125), where 'history, culture and religion are both encoded and demonstrated in the geography of traditional territory'. Culture, in this sense, is 'reflected and embedded' in the interactions between people and the natural environment (Gibson 2017: 8). Indicative of a relational concept of place (Castree 2004), movement across the landscape has a recursive association with social relationships and interactions (Turnbull 2007), meaning that material engagement with the environment is essential for the preservation and development of the more immaterial aspects of collective indigenous identity.

It is precisely because of this nature-culture entanglement that a breakdown in the relationship results in the form of environmental harm known as 'cultural loss' (Berry 1999). It encompasses 'adverse impacts on a range of traditional activities, emotional well-being, or social relations engaged in by an individual and/or an Aboriginal community as the result of changes in the land' (Gregory and Trousdale 2009: 2470). These 'impacts' can result from less unwanted sources, such as willing participation in non-traditional practices, particularly by younger populations. Indeed, the two aspects of existence – the traditional and more contemporary – are not mutually exclusive and are often engaged with simultaneously. However, the cultural loss manifested in the oil sands has a more overtly coercive dimension, where the ecological disruption wrought by extractive projects is obstructing the ability of First Nations to continue with a myriad of traditional land-based practices, irrespective of their choice to do so or not.

First Nations in the region describe water as the 'life blood' of their culture (see ACFN 2016: 9; MCFN 2016: 9). This reflects the role of the river delta in facilitating travel by boat to hunting, fishing, and trapping locations, while also sustaining the culturally significant species that make up the surrounding ecosystem (MacDonald 2012). However, the oil sands industry requires a reliable supply of fresh water, drawn from the Athabasca River and its tributaries, to separate the sand from the bitumen. On average, every barrel of bitumen requires three barrels of water (Grant *et al.* 2013a). Even when accounting for natural fluctuations in the ecosystem, evidence suggests this withdrawal is contributing to low water levels across the delta system (Timoney 2013). This is detrimental for First Nations because the waterways underpin their ability to exercise many different land-based practices. Water-access by boat, along the web of waterways that exists in the delta area, is a preferred mode of exercising Treaty rights, allowing accessing to territories without disturbance from industrial traffic, opportunities for fishing, and providing a means of 'locating, shooting and carrying the many hundreds of pounds of meat that results from a successful kill' (Candler *et al.* 2010: 14). By rendering inaccessible areas in which hunting, fishing and trapping can occur, water withdrawal displaces First Nations from both the land *and* waterways (see MCFN 2016). With regulations governing water withdrawal being criticised as unfit for purpose (Sauchyn *et al.* 2015), and freshwater use in extractive operations expected to rise in accordance with projected industrial growth (Grant *et al.* 2013b: 3), this displacement is likely to become more pronounced in the future.

Water contamination is an associated concern, largely because of its degrading impact on the surrounding ecosystem and the health issues it engenders. In noting the elevated levels of contamination both upstream and downstream of the oil sands industry, one study described the amount of bitumen deposited on the land, via air and waterways, to be 'equivalent to a major oil spill, repeated annually' (Kelly *et al.* 2009: 4). Echoed by its companion study (Kelly *et al.* 2010), the 'explosive growth' of the oil sands industry 'poses risks to environmental and public health that demand immediate attention independent of provincial and industrial oversight' (Timoney 2007: 73). While industry is not allowed to discharge untreated waste water into the surrounding river delta, tailings ponds – which hold the waste water resulting from oil sands processing – contribute to unlicensed discharge. In 1998, these ponds contained around 250 billion litres of liquid; by 2037, this is projected to increase to over 1.5 trillion litres (McNeil 2017). With the content of tailings being acutely toxic to aquatic organisms and mammals (Gosselin *et al.* 2010), and unlicensed seepage from a single pond estimated to be 6.5 million litres per day (Frank *et al.* 2014), a concern for the health of the flora and fauna underpinning hunting, fishing, and trapping rights is not undeserved.

Such contamination has been evidenced in a range of culturally significant species. The avoidance of fish – a subsistence mainstay of First Nations – in certain areas is linked to observed deformities, with traditional users identifying 'lesions, internal and external tumours, and deformed skulls, skeletons and fins' (Timoney and Lee 2009: 77). Such abnormalities can result from natural causes, but increases in mortality rate, craniofacial irregularities, cardiac dysfunction, and stunted growth have all been observed in fish exposed to hydrocarbons from the Athabasca River (Colavecchia *et al.* 2006). Their concentration is now between 2.5 and 23 times greater than in 1960 as a direct result of oil sands developments (Kurek *et al.* 2012). This is compounded by the depleting effect low water levels are having on fish stocks. As a result, First Nations 'are running out of options for places to acquire fish that are considered safe to eat' (Larcombe 2012: 5–19). Similar conditions have been identified in moose, which are important for community dinners and creating visible markers of First Nation identity, such as moccasins, mitts, and jackets (Centre for Indigenous Environmental Resources 2010). Indeed, arsenic and mercury contamination of moose in the region, and the similarly important species of duck and muskrat, is high enough to be of concern for children, while selenium contamination is also a risk to adults (University of Manitoba 2014). Similar risks are visible in regard to migratory wildfowl because the bitumen deposits are located within the convergence zone of all four North American waterfowl flyways (Timoney 2013), with the total estimated bird mortality rate, from exposure to tailings, sitting between 458 and 5,029 birds per year (Timoney and Ronconi 2010: 1). Taken together, it is clear to see why the term 'ecocide' has been used to describe the environmental impact of the oil sands industry on the region (Rawlinson 2011).

Focus of the Book

A body of existing scholarship provides various explanations for the environmental harm documented. Some emphasise the enduring features of indigenous disempowerment inherent to settler-colonial societies, where cultural loss is the contemporary manifestation of a much older, industrial and ultimately structural pattern of 'cultural genocide' (Huseman and Short 2012: 221). Drawing attention to the way in which the indigenous–non-indigenous relationship established during the earlier, frontier-colonial period of the sixteenth to eighteenth centuries continues into the present, this specifically 'settler-colonial' relationship is one characterised by the following:

> [A] particular form of domination; that is, a relationship where power … has been structured into a relatively secure or sediment set of hierarchical social relations that continue to facilitate the dispossession of Indigenous peoples of their lands and self-determining authority.
>
> (Coulthard 2014: 6–7)

Others echo this position, where opportunities for public and First Nation engagement in decisions pertaining to extractives activity have been slowly dampened over the past 50 years (Slowey and Stefanick 2015; see also Mills 2017). This is exacerbated by the rise of neoliberal capitalism, where prioritisation of the 'indifferent, invisible hand of the market' has allowed industrial expansion to proceed uninhibited (Slowey and Stefanick 2015: 217). Even where there is little opportunity to oppose expansion from the offset, the historic dispossession of land and resources has left First Nations without sufficient stocks of natural, financial, and human capital to effectively mitigate its ensuing environmental effects (Parlee 2015). Other scholarship largely eschews the colonial dimension in favour of more dedicated economic analysis, where the pressure to expand production is rooted in the global political economy. Under such accounts, ineffective environmental protection results from government reluctance to regulate corporate misdemeanours in the context of the capitalist growth imperative (Stecyk 2017). Also implicated is the restrictive influence of the North American Free Trade Agreement on federal decision making in the expansion of oil sands extraction, along with government attempts at diverting popular attention away from environmental impacts using greenwashing (Smandych and Kueneman 2010). Such economistic explanations are taken to their furthest extent by Lynch *et al.* (2016), where ecological disorganisation in the oil sands is not seen as aberrant to the capitalist mode of production, but as an entirely normative and expected consequence.

Providing insightful explanations for the human and non-human consequences of oil sands extraction, these accounts tend to focus on nation-state or global actors and influences, or the structures of capitalism and settler colonialism. Drawing attention to these aspects highlights the importance of historical and global processes of production and exchange in producing and reproducing environmental harm, also implicating the mechanisms by which First Nations and members of the public can oppose or impede them. However, as these approaches emphasise influences at the more macro level of analysis, they exhibit two main shortcomings. First, the procedural role of First Nations in the regulatory process governing expansion is largely overlooked. There is certainly movement in this direction (see Mills 2017), but examinations, when they do occur, tend to centre on abuse of their substantive Treaty rights to hunt, fish, and trap. In doing so they forego analyses into why the procedural Treaty rights, to be consulted and accommodated by the provincial government on activities which risk such abuse, are proving ineffective at preventing such harm. These rights are triggered at very specific points in the regulatory process, so an understanding of how they are circumvented is necessary if a complete account of the situation is to be reached.

Second, existing macro-level explanations tend to obscure the provincial regulatory process governing industrial expansion, painting a situation in which federal political and international economic forces appear able to construct oil sands projects without opposition. This is not without good reason. The federal government has pursued an 'unprecedented' lobbying campaign against European Union oil regulations (Macalister 2011), and frequently supports efforts at expanding cross-province pipeline infrastructure. Furthermore, a letter leaked in 2013 shows that, two years earlier, an industry pressure group known as the Energy Framework Initiative (EFI) wrote to the federal Environment Minister. It asked for six pieces of federal environmental legislation to be diluted, for the purposes of advancing 'sustainable' economic growth (EFI 2011). One year later, each piece of legislation had been changed under the 2012 C-38 Omnibus Bill. However, while these influences are important to note, not all regulation pertaining to the oil sands falls under federal jurisdiction. On the contrary, the provincial government has had primary control over its natural resources since the introduction of the Natural Resources Transfer Agreement (NRTA) of 1930, instilling a long-held reluctance in the federal government to infringe on its authority (Bowness and Hudson 2013; Stefanick 2015). Consequently, despite federal involvement in oil sands regulation, '... [b]y far the largest scope of power falls to the province of Alberta' (Vlavianos 2007: 4). As such, while it is important to observe federal and international pressures, attention also needs to be directed at the regulatory apparatus within Alberta itself. This is starting to occur, particularly in the field of law (see Olszynski 2017, 2018), but it is an area requiring further exploration.

In light of this, the precise intersection at which the book focuses its analytical lens is where the pressure for 'sustainable' extraction of the resource meets the Treaty rights afforded to First Nations. This is justified for two reasons. First, the 'sustainable development' of the oil sands has been a strategic objective of the provincial government since the mid-1990s, when rapid expansion of the industry began. As such, there is a need to explain how and why industrial development has been consistently permitted under this rubric despite very clear and credible evidence that it is anything but 'sustainable'. Second, while the substantive and procedural Treaty rights of First Nations are supposed to guard against this very reality, they are failing to do just that. This book therefore serves a dual purpose; not only does it explain how ecologically disruptive oil sands production has been repeatedly prioritised under the guise of 'sustainable development' in provincial policy and practice, but it also explores the means by which historical Treaty protections have been circumvented in the process of doing so.

To fulfil this purpose, the operational point of focus is the provincial regulatory mechanism responsible for repeatedly sanctioned industrial growth since the mid-1990s. This process is comprised of two key stages: that of 'planning', where consultation occurs with First Nations on proposed oil sands projects, and 'approval', which references a subsequent stage in which quasi-judicial public hearings are called (see Chapter 2). This latter stage allows the energy regulator to decide whether approval of a given oil sands project would be in the 'public interest', a determination which depends on a balance of social, economic, and environmental impacts. Taken together, these two phases represent the operational sites of social conflict between interests pertaining to the expansion of bitumen production and those to Treaty rights. Examining how this relationship has developed within these specific stages since the mid-1990s, in the incremental sanctioning of industrial growth, provides a detailed account of how, and to what extent, the regulatory process has prioritised economic production over the land-based interests of First Nations for almost two decades.

To examine this process as a 'site' of social conflict (see Tombs 2017), an exploratory lens loosely structured around Kramer and Michalowski's (2006) state-corporate analytical model is used. This structuring is in alignment with the attention given by the model to the 'catalysts' contributing to a pattern of harm and the mechanisms present for its 'control'. The actual content of the analytical lens is informed by the literature on 'sustainable development'. As

Chapter 2 illustrates, running through this concept is a tension between the imperative to pursue 'sustainable' economic expansion using technology, demonstrating the presence of eco-modernist environmental philosophy, and efforts aimed at slowing it down through opportunities for 'non-elite' participation in decision making by actors outside of government and industry. This latter position is affiliated with 'eco-socialism'. The operational stages of the regulatory process map onto this broad dichotomy. The initial 'planning' phase can be conceived of as the point at which First Nations can decelerate or even relocate productive operations, as there is a legal duty for them to be consulted and accommodated on any activity that may adversely affect their substantive Treaty rights. The subsequent 'approval' stage is that in which the Government of Alberta's policies for the 'sustainable development' of the oil sands resource are given operational form, as the hearing Panels are required to balance its conceptual trio of social, economic, and environmental concerns in pursuit of a 'public interest' deliberation. This second stage is where the government policy objective of 'sustainable development' becomes operationalised in practice, in the sanctioning of expansive production. As such, the 'catalysts' for environmental harm centre on government objectives for 'sustainable development' in policy and their operationalisation within the 'approval' stage of the public hearings, while the mechanism for its 'control' is conceptualised as the 'planning' stage, where First Nations are consulted and accommodated on adverse impacts to the hunting, fishing, and trapping rights. Chapter 2 draws out this process in more detail.

Data Collection and Methods

The data gathered in this book was based on a multi-methods approach of purely qualitative orientation. This involved the thematic analysis of provincial government policy and strategy documents, along with the hearing documents which record the deliberations underpinning provincial regulatory approvals of major oil sands projects. These documents stretch from 1997, around the point at which rapid expansion of the contemporary industry began, through to 2013, when the latest open-pit oil sands mine triggered a public hearing. This was accompanied by a similarly thematic analysis of interview transcripts from 33 semi-structured interviews. Conducted with senior personnel involved with various points of the regulatory process, these centred on two areas: first, the issues and tensions encountered during consultation with First Nations; and second, the influences exerted upon regulatory personnel when deciding whether to approve an oil sands project.

Six government policies and strategies directing the 'sustainable development' of Alberta's oil sands resource were chosen for analysis (see Table 1.1). These were specifically determined by the 2012 Lower Athabasca Regional Plan (LARP), a high-level strategy providing direction on resource

Table 1.1 Government of Alberta Policies and Strategies Relating to Oil Sands Expansion

Year introduced	*Year replaced*	*Document title*	*Designation*
1999	2008	Alberta's Commitment to Sustainable Resource and Environmental Management	Policy
1999	2008	The Regional Sustainable Development Strategy	Strategy
2008	Ongoing	Launching Alberta's Energy Future	Policy
2008	Ongoing	Alberta's Land Use Framework	Strategy
2009	Ongoing	Responsible Actions	Policy
2012	Ongoing	Lower Athabasca Regional Plan	Strategy

use in the oil sands region. The LARP describes these six documents as the 'key … policies and strategies' informing its core environmental management frameworks. They have been in place for the entire period in which the contemporary oil sands industry has existed. While other agreements, acts, and authorisations are relevant, these six were chosen for their level of detail with regard to overarching government objectives and the methods by which they are expected to be achieved. It should also be noted that while 'policy' and 'strategy' can be referred to interchangeably, this book defines them according to their position in relation to government decision-making. There is some overlap, but in broad terms 'policy' is taken to refer to documents outlining broad government aims and objectives, whereas 'strategy' refers to those detailing the actions designed to achieve these goals.

To understand how projects have been sanctioned during the quasi-judicial hearings at the 'approval' stage of the regulatory process, 12 public hearing records for all large-scale oil sands mines and their related projects were examined (see Table 1.2). These were specifically chosen for three reasons. First, although in-situ projects are larger in number, open pit mines have historically accounted for a greater proportion of bitumen production than in situ (AER 2015). Second, the size of open pit projects means their operation involves a greater degree of ecological disruption, particularly in the immediate area. As such, the public hearings triggered by such risks, and the concomitant socio-economic benefits that accompany them, provide a more exemplary record as to how the regulatory Panels seek to balance these issues in pursuit of the 'public interest'. Finally, the decision-making process around in-situ operations is less transparent than that for open-pit mines, meaning the lack of publicly available data restricts the extent to which they can be examined. As the public hearing documents are of considerable size, the sections pertaining to water quantity and quality and to the broader category of cumulative environmental effects were selected for analysis. These were

Table 1.2 Public Hearing Documents for Oil Sands Projects

Year of approval	*Project title*	*Project type*
1997	Steepbank	Open-pit/surface mine
1997	Aurora	Open-pit/surface mine
1999	Millennium	Open-pit/surface mine
1999	Muskeg River	Open-pit/surface mine
1999	Mildred Lake	Expansion of bitumen upgrader
2004	Horizon	Open-pit/surface mine
2004	Jackpine	Open-pit/surface mine
2006	Steepbank Expansion	Expansion of Steepbank open-pit/ surface mine and Voyageur bitumen upgrader
2006	Muskeg River Expansion	Expansion of Muskeg River open-pit/ surface mine
2007	Kearl	Open-pit/surface mine
2011	Josylin North	Open-pit/surface mine
2013	Jackpine Expansion	Expansion of Jackpine open-pit/ surface mine

chosen because of their centrality to First Nation culture, relationship with hunting, fishing, and trapping rights, and tensions between cumulative effects and environmental thresholds.

The third component, the interviews, encompassed participation from those involved with each stage of the regulatory process. For this, chain-referral sampling was used because of its suitability for locating information-rich key informants (Patton 2002). Given the difficulty in gaining access to powerful institutions, a need to gather information from actors with specific knowledge of the regulatory process and its capacity for 'identifying policy-makers and specific elites, and understanding networks and processes' (Williams 2012: 17), chain-referral sampling ensured a close fit between methods and research focus. Furthermore, these 'chains' tended to be created within and between government agencies, allowing for creation of a detailed, process-specific data set. Using this technique, 33 participants were interviewed in 2015 at the relevant locations in Alberta, including Calgary, Edmonton, and Fort McMurray. These included personnel from the Aboriginal Consultation Office (ACO), Land Use Secretariat (LUS), Department for Environment and Sustainable Resource Development (ESRD), oil sands industry, and First Nation industry relations departments (FNIRD). Most participants were in senior organisational positions and had responsibility for managing different aspects of the regulatory process. Other interviewees were drawn from groups peripheral to the regulatory process, here labelled 'Consultants' and 'Research Organisations'. Their inclusion was unexpected but welcome, providing nuanced information on different aspects of the research process and proved to be instrumental in establishing 'chains' of participants across different stages of the process. Furthermore, some of these were retired from official positions, meaning they were less guarded in their assessment of what had been happening.

Book Structure

Following this introduction, Chapter 2 provides the justificatory basis for examining oil sands growth using the concept of 'sustainable development'. This also incorporates brief discussion of the environmental philosophies which underpin use of the term in policy and practice, eco-modernisation, and eco-socialism, and their parity with the language of 'catalyst' and 'control' from the criminological literature. Demonstrating how different interpretations of 'sustainable development' are anchored to different philosophical schools, this allows for specific traits associated with each to be drawn out, providing a framework for the analysis of 'sustainable development' in policy and practice. The chapter then goes on to detail the regulatory process in focus. It explains the features that have remained constant since the mid-1990s, when rapid oil sands expansion began, and presents a functional model towards which the analytical lens can be directed. Taken together, this chapter outlines the regulatory process and the analytical lens through which it is to be analysed.

Chapters 3, 4, and 5 are concerned with each separate stage of the regulatory process, foregrounding the interview and document analysis data. Chapter 3 focuses on the provincial policies and strategies driving oil sands growth since 1999, establishing the dominant objectives forwarded by these documents and the purported means for their realisation. It is here where the governmental 'push' towards an eco-modernist form of 'sustainable development' first becomes visible. Chapter 4 moves into the more operational realm of the regulatory process, drawing from interviews with those involved at the 'planning' stage to explain how substantive and Treaty rights have been circumvented. It is here where the systematic marginalisation of First Nation voices and misrecognition of their specific rights becomes apparent, along with the accounts used by regulatory personnel to justify such treatment. Chapter 5 presents an analysis of the 12 decision documents pertaining to oil sands projects at the 'approval' stage of the process, illustrating the extent to which the ecological modernisation advocated in policy and strategy has been operationalised in practice, during the quasi-judicial hearings. It is here where the absolute faith in techno-scientific mitigation, and the role it plays in fulfilling the economic imperatives outlined in policy and strategy, comes to the fore.

Whereas the previous three chapters are concerned with explaining 'how' oil sands projects have been approved despite intensifying environmental impacts and First Nation Treaty protections, Chapters 6 and 7 focus on the regulatory process as a whole to explain 'why' it operates in this manner. Chapter 6 concentrates on the 'catalyst' for environmental harm: 'weak' ecological modernisation and its emphasis on narrow, techno-scientific methods for mitigating adverse environmental impacts. Situating this in the context of the provincial government's broader neoliberal economic reforms, which have failed to diversify revenue streams for over two decades, Chapter 6 also demonstrates how perceptions of the oil sands industry as a provincial 'social good' influences regulatory decisions to repeatedly sanction its expansion. Chapter 7 follows this with a focus on the mechanism for 'control': the legal duty to consult and accommodate First Nations on any issue that may adversely affect their Treaty rights. More specifically, it demonstrates that the Government of Alberta is using a diluted interpretation of this duty, limiting the extent to which Treaty rights can protect against cultural loss. Permitting the systematic marginalisation of First Nation voices throughout the regulatory process, it is this that allows for the operationalisation of 'weak' ecological modernisation in practice. Collectively termed a 'compound denial', a host of justifications rooted in settler-colonial assumptions and disavowals underpin this marginalisation, demonstrating the active influence of context within the process itself. Taken together, these two chapters explain why the 'sustainable development' of the oil sands resource has produced the environmental harm of cultural loss over almost two decades. The book concludes by considering the implications of this analysis for policy, practice, and green criminology as a field of study.

Chapter 2

Regulating 'Sustainable Development' of the Oil Sands Resource

In outlining '[t]he future of green crime', Stretesky *et al.* (2013: 148) propose that 'green criminologists [should] identify those situations where production is central to the economy, and then examine how economic production is prioritised over ecological production'. Implying a need to examine not only the principles upon which a system of production rests, but also the organisational characteristics through which its material consequences are realised, this statement directs analyses towards the mechanisms and justifications which actually enable industrial expansion. Indeed, it is not enough to condemn a system of production for its consequences alone, particularly if a detailed explanation of a particular pattern of harm is being sought. Instead 'a full understanding of environmental crime requires an analysis of ... practices pursued by legitimate actors and political representatives' (Ruggiero and South 2013: 370). It is to these calls for a contextualised analysis of the processes acting to produce and reproduce the environmental harm described in the previous chapter that this chapter now turns. More specifically, considering that the First Nations are experiencing a form of cultural loss tied to environmental effects, the analytical lens will be trained towards the institutional junctures at which industrial growth is prioritised over First Nation concerns. In this case, it is the regulatory process governing the 'sustainable development' of the oil sands resource that is pulled into focus. Here, before outlining the specific elements internal to the regulatory process, the analytical lens of 'sustainable development' through which it is to be examined will be both justified and clarified. This includes a brief exposition of the two duelling philosophies internal to the concept: eco-socialism and ecological modernisation.

The Conceptual Contours of 'Sustainable Development'

As the environmentally harmful expansion of the oil sands industry has been repeatedly permitted over two decades, the idea of 'sustainability' becomes central to the inquiry. Increasingly adopted by nation-states since the late

1980s, due in no small part to its acceptance by the UN General Assembly, this notion is formally manifested as the concept of 'sustainable development'. Initially posited by the UN World Commission on Environment and Development (WCED) in the 1987 Brundtland Report, it defined 'sustainable development' as 'development that meets the needs of the present without compromising the ability of future generations to meet their own needs' (WCED 1987). While many still use this definition, the concept has come to increasingly denote efforts at balancing a trio of interests: social justice, economic growth, and environmental limits (Sachs 2015). Enshrined within the Millennium Development Goals of 2000 and its 2015 successor, the Sustainable Development Goals, the indicators used to identify progress on these frameworks correspond to this trio of concerns (UN 2015: xi). With progress on these objectives subject to evaluation up until at least 2030, the relevance of 'sustainable development' to global environmental challenges is unlikely to diminish any time soon.

The influence of this concept has long been visible in Canada. When the Brundtland Commission released its report in 1987, the federal government enthusiastically endorsed it only a year later (Boyd 2012). Subsequent federal administrations have expressed similar support, leading to the adoption of a dedicated sustainable development strategy in 2010. This was echoed at the provincial level by the Government of Alberta, where 'sustainable development' of the oil sands resource has been advocated since at least 1999 (Government of Alberta 1999). Moving beyond policy and into the realm of regulatory operations, the legislation governing quasi-judicial hearing Panels also mirrors this focus, where deliberating personnel are required to balance social, economic, and environmental factors in the process of making a 'public interest' decision on whether to approve an oil sands project. As such, closer inspection of 'sustainable development' as a concept is needed if the form advocated in policy and actualised through regulatory practice is to be fully understood.

Despite being defined in the Brundtland Report and increasingly formalised by the UN, over time it has been variously criticised as 'contestable' (Jacobs 1991: 5), '[f]raught with contradictions' (Redclift 1987: 438), 'misunderstood' (Mawhinney 2002: 5), and 'distracting' (Foster 2015: 12). This is because 'sustainable development' can be interpreted in several different ways. The most dominant of these equates 'sustainable development' with 'green economic growth', where it denotes 'in essence … a form of "green capitalism"' (Halsey and White 1998: 350). This is rooted in the socio-economic benefits perceived to emerge from neoliberal economic 'development', growing out of earlier modernist efforts to replicate the 'progress' experienced by Western centres after World War Two in the peripheries (see Blaustein *et al.* 2018). Acting to justify 'business-as-usual', attempts are made to lessen the environmental impact of economic growth instead of seeing growth in and of itself as an issue. This interpretation acknowledges that 'sustainable development' has been widely adopted by dominant political and economic forces since its inception, conceptually anchoring it to the dominant mode of production.

Although mirroring a reality where 'commitment to sustainable development *can* be entirely hollow, often cynically manipulated, often meaningless' (Hay 2002: 217, emphasis added), such a position surrenders the concept to terms defined by interests pertaining to capital. This overlooks the fundamental difference between 'sustainable development' and 'sustainable growth', mistaking the former, which Daly (1990: 1) refers to as the 'qualitative improvement or unfolding of potentialities', for the latter, which is defined as the 'quantitative increase in physical scale'. The need for this conceptual distinction is reinforced by Burkett (2005: 94), who separates the notion 'sustainable capitalism' from 'sustainable development'. Accounting for the subtleties and tensions inherent to this difference allows for a more incisive examination of the environmental policies and regulatory practices pursued in the oil sands.

The ambiguity inherent to the concept evokes Elliot's (2013: 19) argument that it may be more appropriate to instead define what 'sustainable development' is not: unbridled economic expansion. Forming another dominant, but less normative, interpretation, this tends to associate 'sustainable development' with various notions of 'balance', 'equality', and 'justice'. Such a view is echoed in the green criminological work of Benton (2007: 10, emphasis in original), who notes that the concept means more than accelerated economic growth, and that 'justice is a part of the *content* of "sustainable development" as a social, economic, and political strategy'. This close affinity with environmental justice is mirrored by Lowe (1999) and Walker (2012), with Sands (1995) suggesting that the concept exhibits four aspects of justice: inter-generational equity, sustainable use, intra-generational equity, and environmental protection. Under these formulations, expansionary economic imperatives are given less priority in the face of socio-environmental interests. In this sense, the difference between the two perspectives hinges on whether 'sustainable development' is interpreted from a 'narrow economic' or a 'holistic' perspective (David 1988: 153), where the former is synonymous with economic growth and the latter with environmental justice.

When taken as a whole, the body of work underpinning the concept ultimately represents a non-consensus – a reality which appears problematic when attempting to evaluate policies and regulatory practices making use of the term. Kates *et al.* (2005: 20) speak to this reality when cautioning that 'if anyone can redefine the term to fit their purposes, it becomes meaningless in practice, or worse, can be used to disguise or greenwash socially or environmentally destructive activities'. Although correct to a certain extent, this implies that a widely accepted, shared meaning of the term is achievable or even desirable; a position that is recognisably ideological when considering the difficulties with establishing a singular conception over the last three decades. However, despite such discord, Hay's (2002: 217) words are instructive:'we should not throw the concept out just because it is contestable'. On the contrary, Connelly (2007: 260) considers the conceptual ambiguity and subsequent tensions over the 'true' meaning of the term to be 'inevitable', recognising it as an 'inherently political concept'. This position builds on the work of Haughton and Counsell (2004: 72–73), who acknowledge a 'multiplicity of sustainabilities', directing attention towards 'the ways in which these are shaped and mobilised' instead of searching for a definitive meaning of the term. Accepting this disparity provides a means to interpret the policy objectives and regulatory justifications serving to accelerate oil sands production in the face of local concerns, providing a more defined and detailed platform from which to develop an explanation for the environmental harm being produced.

Considering arguments over the meaning of 'sustainable development' to be not only 'semantic disputations', but also to conceal substantive political arguments with which the term is connected, Connelly (2007: 262) notes the importance of paying attention to how the ideals inherent to the concept, i.e. of compromise between social, economic, and environmental concerns, are given concrete meaning. This, it is suggested, 'avoid[s] the pitfalls of conflating opposing positions that are cloaked within [its] comforting rhetoric' (ibid.: 259). Shifting the underlying image from that associated with recent UN frameworks, where 'sustainable development' sits at the confluence of three overlapping circles representing social justice, environmental protection, and economic development, Connelly conceives of a model in which each of these are situated at points perpendicular to one another, also positioning the three dominant eco-philosophies with which they are aligned along their axis (see Figure 2.1).

Most important, for present purposes at least, are the three dominant eco-philosophies visible in and through the particular configuration of factors prioritised in any given scenario. For instance, the philosophy known as ecological modernisation tends to underpin interpretations of 'sustainable development' which emphasise balance between economic growth and environmental protection (see Mol and Spargaaren 2000). This places less emphasis on social justice and is considered the contemporary 'theoretical adversary' of positions affiliated with eco-socialism (Buttel 2004: 332). In a similar vein, the philosophy of eco-socialism can be seen to result from the prioritisation of balance between environmental protection and social justice. As expected, there is less emphasis placed here on economic growth. The third and final philosophical spectrum refers to those positions which de-emphasise environmental issues – an area associated with the more traditional political-economic sphere. In an era of global climate change, this latter position is becoming rarer, at least in rhetoric.

Taken together, the suitability of this model allows for the philosophies underpinning the language of 'sustainable development' to be identified at

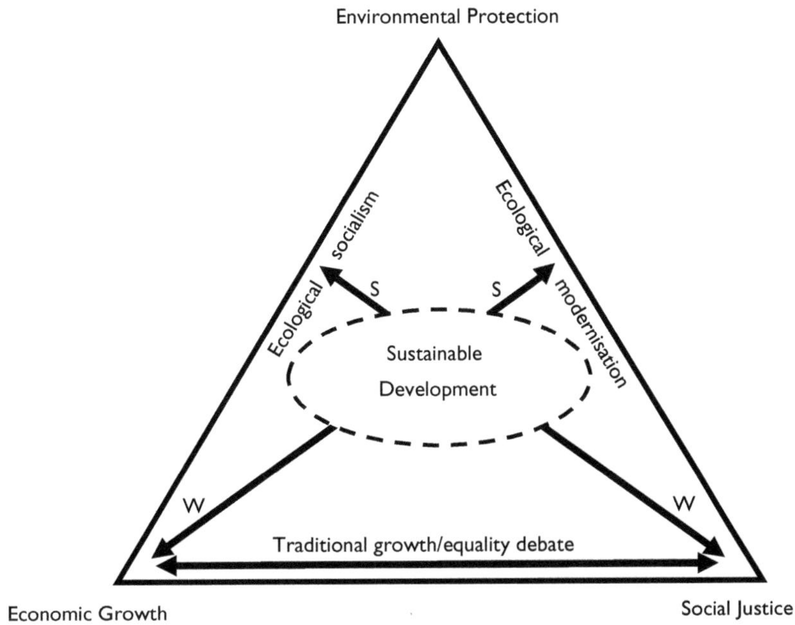

Figure 2.1 'Sustainable Development' and Its Underpinning Eco-Philosophies*.

Source: Adapted from Connelly (2007: 270).

Note

* 'S' and 'W' denote the 'strong' and 'weak' dimensions of the respective eco-philosophy, according to its priorities.

the level of regulatory policy and practice. In doing so, it recognises that 'advocating sustainable development … in principle does not commit governments or international organisations to its achievement in practice' (Redclift 1987: 34). Drawing out the philosophies underpinning the language used serves to direct inquiry to a number of more specific characteristics which would otherwise remain hidden. This enables features of policy and procedure to be crystallised and analysed according to the philosophical category to which they bear relevance and from which they garner support. As such, proceeding from the recognition that ecological modernisation and eco-socialism are the two dominant and duelling paradigms underpinning the language of 'sustainable development', it is important to briefly outline their central tenets.

Ecological Modernisation

The term 'ecological modernisation' can refer to either a social theory or an environmental reform programme (Hayden 2014). With regard to the former, ecological modernisation is considered the most contemporary and dominant social theory on environment. Indeed, Mol (2001: 49) views it as the latest in three historical 'waves of environmental concern and reform'. The 'first wave' of 'nature conservation' existed around 1900 and had a focus on protecting reserves and species, the 'second wave' emerged around 1970 and centred on minimising environmental additions and withdrawals, and the 'third wave', which emerged in the late 1980s and includes ecological modernisation, has a focus on 'sustainable development' (ibid.). Rudel *et al.* (2011) depict a similar transition, noting the dominance of theories concerned with the political economy of environmental decline in the 1970s and 1980s, and their succession by the more institutional responses of the 1990s and beyond. Different reasons are posited as the catalyst for this shift. Cohen (1997) links it to the emergence of Beck's (1992) 'risk society', Mol (1995) associates it with the more recent restructuring of industrial production processes along ecological lines, and Fisher (2002) relates it to a Habermasean 'legitimation crisis', where the shift from liberal to advanced capitalism has encouraged a search for crisis solutions in areas beyond economics. Although Buttel (2000: 62) considers a more pragmatic reason for the emergence of ecological modernisation, where it has gained traction because it provides alternatives to the idea that patterns of ever-expanding production need to slow, the fundamental message is the same: ecological modernisation essentially aims to address 'environmental crises without leaving the path of modernisation' (Spaargaren and Mol 1992: 334).

With industrial sectors making greater use of precautionary, risk-based approaches to the environmental management of their resource use and waste streams, as opposed to the more reactive approaches used prior to the 1990s, the theory of ecological modernisation is an attempt to account for the nature of this transformation. However, as noted above, the term itself also refers to a discourse or reform programme. Throughout this book, unless specific reference is made to 'eco-modernisation' as a theory of social change, it is in the sense of the latter that the term is being used. That said, the discourse and reform programmes tend to operate in tandem, pointing to the reality that operational efforts at 'greening' capitalism are often buttressed by an accompanying 'rhetoric of reassurance' which suggests capitalism can be made compatible with environmental protection (Dryzek 2013: 159). This is reflected in its 'core' philosophical assumption, which is that eco-efficiency gains can be achieved without radical structural change (Buttel 2000). Indeed, eco-modernist reforms tend to signal apolitical, techno-centric and rational elitist approaches to environmental management, mirroring the 'win-win' characteristics associated with the 'compliance school' of more general regulation (see Tombs 2017). Here, negotiation and compromise between regulators and regulated belie the consensus assumed to exist between public and private interests.

Although eco-modernist reform programmes advocate 'cleaner' technologies, the various means by which this is achieved belies a tension at the heart of the philosophy, and one which maps onto the spectrum established by Connelly (2007) above. For instance, while some approaches advocate large-scale transitions to renewable sources of energy, others tend to favour narrow alterations to existing industry by calling for developments in sustainable fossil fuels. This reflects the tension between 'strong' and 'weak' forms of the philosophy. The notion of structural conditions being unchangeable is most visibly reflected in Christoff's (1996: 490) description of 'weak' ecological modernisation, which is not only 'technocratic', 'neo-corporatist' and 'closed' to broader forms of democratic participation, but also primarily concerned with making 'narrow' technological adjustments to address environmental issues. Indeed, Christoff (ibid.) explains that, in deliberating over whether to use 'weak' as a descriptor, 'one is tempted to write, false'. Having greatest parity with the 'oxymoron' of 'sustainable growth' (Daly 1990: 401), this strain of the philosophy tends to pursue narrow efficiencies of production and techniques aimed at 'decoupling' economic growth from adverse environmental effects (Sezgin 2012). It is this 'weak' variant that has attracted substantial policy and financial support across Europe and North America, despite repeated warnings over their ineffectiveness (Hayden 2014).

Juxtaposed against this 'weak' form is Dryzek's (1997: 172) '[r]adicalised' ecological modernisation. Corresponding with Christoff's (1996: 490) 'strong' conceptualisation, this advocates a 'restructuring of political and economic life, rather than a mere re-tooling of industry' (Dryzek 1997: 172). Under this variant such 'restructuring' occurs along more ecological lines, has more open and democratic channels for decision-making, and approaches environmental issues from a position acknowledging their international dimension (Christoff 1996). Berger *et al.* (2001: 62) augment this macro level of analysis with 'regional and local level[s]', recognising the necessity of holism in addressing ecological disorganisation. It is these features that imbue the 'strong' approach with a transformative potential, enabling Gleeson (2006) to position it as a transitional strategy towards more sustainable practices which are 'decoupled' from economic growth on a macro scale. However, owing to its tendency to advocate extensive social change, this 'strong' manifestation of the philosophy has been less influential in mainstream politics (Hayden 2014).

It should also be noted that, by virtue of its focus on making techno-scientific adjustments to operational activities, eco-modernisation is also affiliated with environmentally specific forms of risk-based reasoning such as the precautionary principle. Not only does this relationship exist because the technology so central to eco-modernist philosophy 'creates as many uncertainties as it dispels' (Lee and Stokes 2005: 104), but also because '[u]ncertainty is the unifying hallmark of environmental and natural resource regulation' (Doremus 2007: 548). While it has a number of different interpretations (see Martuzzi 2007), the precautionary principle is generally seen as a response to potential threats to human and environmental well-being, requiring official protective action to be taken where there is scientific uncertainty as to the likelihood of damage or risk (White 2008). Put another way, the concept operationalises the notion 'better safe than sorry', supporting regulatory action in response to an actual or perceived risk to human beings or the environment. However, it is the spectrum of approaches taken towards this uncertainty or risk that is key. Much like eco-modernisation more generally, the precautionary principle has 'weak' and 'strong' forms, with designation similarly depending on the extent to which it has the potential to alter existing structural conditions. For instance, the former variation references precautionary measures permitting continuation of an activity, but only under intense scrutiny and at risk of potential, albeit narrow, alteration. This differs from the latter, 'strong' form, which involves the prohibition or phasing out of a particular activity in the face of uncertainty or risk (Tickner and Raffensperger 2003). It is because of this that the latter, 'strong' variant poses a challenge to existing patterns of expansive production, leading Sunstein (2002) to criticise it as the 'paralyzing principle'. Nevertheless, these two features essentially correspond to the broader variants of 'strong' and 'weak' ecological modernisation, providing insight into the type of precautionary measures present at each pole of the philosophy.

Eco-Socialism

Within green political thought there are a number of socialist positions, which Hay (2002) categorises as three core traditions: 'democratic socialism', 'Marxism', and 'classical anarchism'. The first emphasises the role of trade-union-based parliamentary parties in prioritising environmental quality (ibid.: 255). The second tradition, Marxism, contains a variety of sub-categories which vary according to their integration with environmental scholarship. Emerging from Marx's recognition that human labour is contingent on prior products of nature, this tradition subsumes ecological considerations within its remit while recognising that the capitalist mode of production requires transformation if socio-environmental issues are to be addressed (ibid.: 262–276). Finally, the anarchist strain of eco-socialism operates from the standpoint that 'small is beautiful because small is natural', being associated with the observation that 'small, non-hierarchical social unit[s] … corresponds to what is to be found in nature' (ibid.: 279). As expected, positions affiliated with this tradition tend to advocate a shift away from centralised and state-led social arrangements (see Bookchin 1982). While these are only very brief outlines of the central tenets associated with one typology of traditions, which are contested even within their respective categories, the point is that eco-socialism does not denote a monolithic or broadly unified philosophy, at least not to the extent of eco-modernism. As such, in order to provide some delineation, the literature within the arguably dominant Marxist tradition will form primary focus.

Much like eco-modernisation, eco-socialism can be read as a social theory, albeit one that is far more historical and class-based in its analysis. At the root of its explanation for contemporary ecological degradation is Marx's understanding of the interdependent relationship between human and non-human nature. He considered the raw materials provided by nature to be an essential, a priori ingredient to all human labour:

> Labour is, first of all, a process between man and nature.... He confronts the materials of nature as a force of nature. He sets in motion the natural forces which belong to his body ... to appropriate the materials of nature in a form adapted to his own needs.
>
> (Marx 1976: 283)

He described this relationship as an 'interdependent process of social metabolism', in which the capitalist mode of production causes an 'irreparable rift' (Marx 1981: 949). Foster (1999: 383) uses this environmental aspect of Marx's work to label the severing of the human/non-human relationship as the 'metabolic rift', defining it as 'the material estrangement of human beings in capitalist society from the natural conditions of their existence'. Its essential elements can be distilled as follows:

> ... capitalism's uncoupling of production from the solar budget constraint, and its tremendous acceleration of matter-energy throughput, had led to an entropic degradation of natural conditions – a metabolic rift between human reproduction and the conditions needed for this reproduction to be healthy and sustainable.
>
> (Burkett 2005: 204)

This situation has its origins in the commons enclosures in Britain between the fifteenth and eighteenth centuries (Foster 2009). Prior to this, farming occurred within a relatively localised religious, political, and environmental context, but the transference of common land to private ownership helped facilitate emergence of the capitalist mode of production. Resulting in the commodification of labour, land, and tools, this enabled a new 'science' of economics to be applied to the process of alienating workers from the products of their own labour (Burkett 2005). The concurrent movement of workers from the country into the urban population centres also generated oppositions between 'town' and 'country', and global North and South – points which came to denote the origins and final destinations of commodities. Precipitating the emergence of large-scale capitalist agriculture, this unidirectional movement of products made using the soil's 'constituent elements' essentially leads to the 'squandering' of its 'vitality' (Marx 1981: 949). Even industrial, techno-scientific attempts at replenishing this nutrient base furthers the degradation as it is not part of a broader process in which original nutrients are returned to the ground, thus belying the unsustainability of the capitalist system a whole. Indeed, it is for these two conjoined reasons that

Marx ultimately viewed capitalism as 'simultaneously undermin[ing] the original sources of all wealth – the soil and the worker' (Marx 1976: 638).

In explaining what eco-socialism would look like in practice, Kovel (2007: 243) follows the above diagnosis and describes a society 'in which production is carried out by freely associated labour and with consciously eco-centric means and ends'. Implying a societal regard for environmental thresholds and limits, he notes that markets will be 'hemmed in' and made to function 'according to eco-centric ethics rather than profiteering' (ibid.). This poses a challenge to the 'win-win' regulatory approaches affiliated with ecological modernisation. Indeed, Kovel (ibid.) goes on to argue that use value and quality would be 'valorized over exchange value and quantity', with an economy 'embedded within society rather than, as under capitalism, standing over it' (ibid.). Foster (2009: 7) speaks similarly of the need for deep structural change:

> … there is little real prospect for the needed global ecological revolution unless these attempts to revolutionise social relations in the struggle for a just and sustainable society, now emerging in the periphery, are somehow mirrored in movements for ecological and social revolution in the advanced capitalist world. It is only through fundamental change at the centre of the system, from which the pressure on the planet principally emanates, that there is any genuine possibility of avoiding ultimate ecological destruction.

This predisposition to brevity when forwarding solutions is echoed by Gould *et al.* (2004: 305), who suggest that a more sustainable political-economic system 'would entail the state's substantial control over ecosystems without regard to issues of profitability and wages/employment'. Similarly, Malm (2018: 228) argues for an end to two centuries of capitalist rule, noting that humankind needs to live 'with the autonomous sun and wind and waves without any more solid energy to expand on'. A characteristic of eco-socialism more generally (Somerville 2018), those affiliated with the perspective tend to give little theoretical attention to the institutional forms needed to guarantee the sustainable outcomes of which they speak. Indeed, beyond revolutionary praxis, little detail is provided on how the fundamental role of the state in maintaining the capitalist mode of production is to be overcome. This ultimate focus, on awaiting some revolutionary point in time when socio-ecological values will be prioritised over those pertaining to capital, is a high expectation in the context of global capitalism. Furthermore, when the state is invoked as a way of controlling markets there is an overestimation as to the extent to which regulatory agencies are impervious to the influence of interests pertaining to capital (see Tombs and Whyte 2009). The lack of attention given to solutions that are attainable within existing institutional parameters means that the choice posited by eco-socialist philosophy appears stark: between rapid structural changes brought about by revolutionary praxis or ecosystem failure.

Despite this, O'Connor (1996: 205), working within the same philosophical tradition, notes how the 'loose', 'flexible', and historically contingent fit between the forces and relations of production opens up opportunities for different social movements to force concessions from interests pertaining to capital. It is in this space where the importance of participation by 'non-elite' groups in environmental decision-making comes to the fore. While differences exist among eco-socialists as to the extent to which production processes can be 'greened' without breaching environmental thresholds, the primary role of 'non-elite' participants in environmental decision-making is broadly agreed upon across the literature. This does not require indigenous peoples to be categorised as part of the working class, either. Although Widdowson and Howard (2008) take this view, it is disputed by Kulchyski (2012), who notes that this conception eviscerates First Nations from the land by requiring them to support capital projects to attract income and better conditions as workers. Indeed, indigenous peoples were never a structurally significant part of the broad working class in Canada. Their relationship was one primarily orientated around economics – due to their 300-year involvement in the fur trade – and only recently shifted to one organised around politics and state apparatus. This allowed them to stay apart from the major confrontations between capital and labour throughout Canada's history, leading to another set of equally important confrontations, but between capital and the natural environment:

> [A]lthough increasing numbers of aboriginal people have joined the labour force in the past few decades, and although aspects of working class culture are embraced by aboriginal people … the defining struggles of aboriginal people have been over land use.
>
> (Kulchyski 2012: 29)

Manifest in the numerous land-orientated protections afforded by the various Treaties, and the Aboriginal Title intermittently but progressively elaborated on by the Supreme Court of Canada, the very specific consequences of these conflicts are qualitatively different from those more traditionally associated with the labour movement. Nevertheless, eco-socialist philosophy can accommodate both, as demonstrated by the Treadmill of Production theory recently adopted by green criminology (see Stretesky *et al.* 2013). Broadly falling within the 'Marxist' bracket of eco-socialism (Buttel 2004), it identifies the contemporary political-economic imperative to accelerate production as the basis for ecological disruption. This is seen to arise from the activities of three groups of social actors: agents of capital, labour organisations, and the state. Although not absolute, each of these has an incentive to continually accelerate production. Corporations do so because of the growth imperative, labour does so because it seeks improved living conditions through the medium of job creation, wage increases, and reduced unemployment, and the state does so because of its need for additional tax revenue and political contributions from wealthy benefactors.

Importantly, treadmill theories refer to a fourth group of influential social actors, that of 'environmental groups'. While it is not ideal to associate First Nations with classifications generated without accounting for colonialism, this theoretical construct has parity with their land-based interests and does not require their categorisation as 'working class'. Given the label of 'non-elites', Gould *et al.* (2004) note that such participants can pressure private capital and/or state decision-makers to make more pro-environmental decisions in the production process. Stretesky *et al.* (2013: 132–138) separate this overarching group further, sub-categorising these 'environmental enforcement organisations' as having a preoccupation with either 'advocacy' or 'operations'. With the former pursuing the creation or greater enforcement of environmental laws through lobbying and awareness-raising, and the latter pursuing similar goals via legal procedures or monitoring efforts, the theory essentially positions environment-orientated groups as 'creators rather than creatures of social change' (Schnaiberg 1980: 364). First Nations can be seen as spanning both of these sub-categories, but the legal power they wield, by virtue of their Treaty rights, edges them closer to the latter of the two. As such, their procedural right to be consulted and accommodated, when a proposed activity has the potential to adversely affect their hunting, fishing, and trapping practices, grants them greater access to operational decision-making procedures than other 'non-elite' groups. As such, if eco-socialist philosophy was to be mapped onto Connelly's (2007) model of 'sustainable development' above, its 'strong' and 'weak' variations correspond to the extent to which the socio-environmental interests of First Nations are prioritised over those of capital.

The Regulatory Process in Focus: Irregularity of Form, Consistency of Function

As noted above, explaining the environmental harm occurring in the oil sands region demands attention be focused on the provincial regulatory process governing industrial growth. This is justified on several grounds. First, considering that 'producer decisions are influenced by the regulations imposed by the state' (Gould *et al.* 2004: 302), and that 'regulation is the manifest empirical link between apparently distinct and separate state and corporate sectors' (Tombs and Whyte 2009: 107), directing the analytical lens towards the regulatory process responsible for managing the expansion of oil sands production is the logical point of progression. Second, this regulatory mechanism has permitted rapid expansion of the industry since the mid-1990s, meaning that the environmental harm witnessed originates in the approvals it has sanctioned. Third, the process is mandated to pursue 'sustainable development' through its regulatory review and approval functions. Fourth, the records of the hearing Panels, which are initiated when stakeholders or First Nations refuse to withdraw their concerns about a proposed project, afford access to the detailed deliberations made in pursuit of 'sustainable development'. Finally, the regulatory process contains aspects that can be conceived of as both 'catalysts' and 'controls' for environmental victimisation, as it not only operationalises government policy but also functions as a forum through which First Nations can have their concerns heard and associated risks mitigated.

The regulatory process itself can be separated into three key stages: 'planning', 'approval', and 'oversight' (see Figure 2.2). The 'planning' stage refers to the process by which a corporation designs a project, consults with First Nations on how environmental effects detrimental to their Treaty rights may be mitigated, and submits an application for said project, which includes an environmental impact assessment, to the provincial energy regulator for review. Should any outstanding concerns remain among First Nations, or other directly and adversely affected stakeholders, a quasi-judicial hearing may be called. This is the transition to the 'approval' stage. Here, various forms of evidenced argument are presented to a quasi-judicial regulatory Panel, or 'hearing Panel', in a formal setting, enabling the energy regulator to make an informed decision on whether or not to approve a project. Should approval be granted, the process shifts to the final regulatory stage, that of 'oversight'. This phase refers to the mechanisms by which state and corporate agencies attempt to mitigate the environmental effects of the project while in operation.

A standalone analysis of the latter phase of 'oversight' will be excluded from the inquiry. This is because the mechanisms operating at this stage share space with the precursor 'approval' phase, as they are referred to during the quasi-judicial reviews as a means of mitigating environmental risks. Put another way, independent analysis of the 'oversight' phase risks unnecessary duplication, obscuring the way in which the very presence of monitoring mechanisms plays a fundamental role in sanctioning industrial growth at the

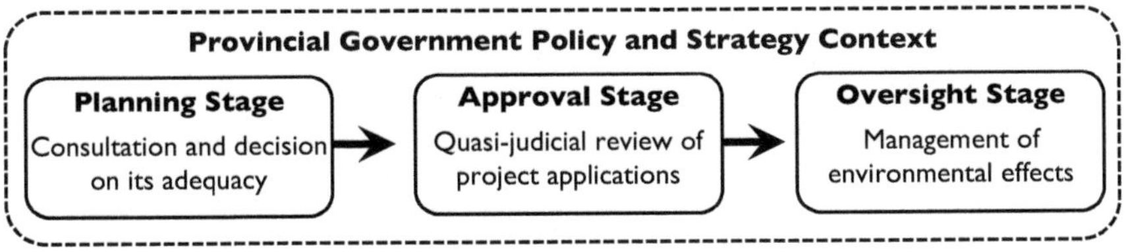

Figure 2.2 Government Regulatory Model for Oil Sands Project Development.
Source: Adapted from Lambrecht (2013: 6).

precursor 'approval' stage. The analytical lens will instead be trained upon the policy and strategy context in which the regulatory process sits. Echoing Spangenberg's (2010: 561) call to examine the 'driving forces' and 'pressures' for industrial growth enshrined in such documents, the content of which exerts influence upon the regulatory process, this will draw attention to the priorities underpinning the objectives of 'sustainable development' and the advocated measures for its acquisition, as directed by the provincial government.

Rapid oil sands development began in the mid-1990s, and the agencies and legislative frameworks involved at each stage have changed over the subsequent period. This time frame has seen three different regulatory agencies made responsible for sanctioning oil sands expansion at the 'approval' stage, and under equally varying pieces of legislation. While complicating matters, such alterations are unproblematic because they are characteristics of 'form' rather than 'function'. The subsequent sections draw out these differences in greater detail, with respect to both the 'planning' and 'approval' stages of the regulatory process, before highlighting the consistencies that run through each. Indeed, despite the various changes in 'form' there are fundamental aspects of each stage that have remained constant over this 20-year period, allowing for the key elements of the process to be crystallised in preparation for analysis and evaluation.

The 'Planning' Stage and the Duty to Consult and Accommodate

Lambrecht (2013: 7) views the regulatory process through a prism of functionality, interpreting the 'planning' stage broadly to include activities which 'inform a government decision whether to "approve" [a] project, and to identify appropriate conditions of approval if any' (ibid.). While a range of activities could be included under this conception, it will here be taken to reference consultation with First Nations on applications for individual oil sands projects. The 'adequacy' of this consultation must be confirmed before a project can be approved. For much of the period in which the contemporary oil sands industry has existed, First Nations have had little input into where the industry should expand, at what pace, and if it should do so at all. This is because they were only included in a much narrower stakeholder engagement process as 'directly and adversely affected' persons. However, since the 2005 *Mikisew Cree First Nation* v. *Canada (Minister of Canadian Heritage) [2005] 3 SCR 388* (hereafter *Mikisew*) decision at the Supreme Court of Canada (SCC), oil sands projects within the remit of a Treaty area can no longer be sanctioned before the proponent has consulted with First Nations beforehand. This requires a government agency to decide on the adequacy of this consultation. Between 2005 and 2013 responsibility for this determination stood uneasily between the Land Use Secretariat (LUS) and the Energy

Resources Conservation Board (ERCB), with neither the ERCB nor the hearing Panels ever directly addressing the issue (Passelac-Ross and Buss 2011: 45). However, creation of the Aboriginal Consultation Office (ACO) in 2013 saw it imbued with the sole responsibility for 'upholding the honour of the Crown' with respect to First Nation consultation (Government of Alberta 2013a: 3). This effectively removed responsibility from the ERCB and LUS. The ACO is therefore the most recent government agency tasked with making decisions on the adequacy of proponent consultation.

The Crown duty to consult with First Nations emerges from a number of judgments issued by the SCC, with the duty evolving in detail at the issuance of each. The most important in this regard is the *Mikisew* judgment as it expanded the duty to those parts of Canada subject to Treaty agreements – a decision particularly relevant to Alberta, which is wholly covered by Treaties 6, 7, and 8. In such cases the duty to consult is anchored to the language of the Treaty in question and, with regard to *Mikisew*, it was the language of Treaty 8. Upon signing this Treaty in 1899, the Mikisew Cree were among the First Nations that 'surrendered' their title to land. Leaving aside fundamental and lingering questions about the legitimacy and accuracy of its agreements (see Fumoleau 2004), the text contains a 'lands taken up provision' which stipulates restrictions on these rights and establishes conditions in which they may be infringed upon:

> And Her Majesty the Queen Hereby Agrees with the said Indians that they shall have right to pursue their usual vocations of hunting, trapping and fishing throughout the tract surrendered as before described, subject to such regulations as may from time to time be made by the Government of the country, acting under the authority of Her Majesty, and saving and excepting such tracts as may be required or taken up from time to time for settlement, mining, lumbering, trading or other purposes.
>
> (Government of Canada 1899)

As outlined in *Mikisew*, the Crown had intended to build a winter road through the First Nation's Peace Point Reserve, with their decision being informed by public comment only and not by consultation with the First Nation. Referring directly to the Treaty text, and acknowledging the stated agreement that surrendered lands 'from time to time' would be 'taken up', the Supreme Court noted the absence of detail by which this process is supposed to occur. Deciding that 'the Crown was and is expected to manage the change honourably' (*Mikisew* para 31), the SCC filled this procedural gap with the duty to consult and accommodate.

The trigger for this duty was set at a low threshold in a previous judgment, *Haida Nation* v. *British Columbia (Minister of Forests) [2004] 3 SCR 511* (hereafter *Haida*). Here, the SCC found the duty to arise when 'the Crown has knowledge, real or constructive, of the potential existence of Aboriginal right or title and contemplates conduct that might adversely affect it'. *Mikisew* (para 34) built on this, stating that in a Treaty context government is presumed to be aware of the presence of any rights, thereby shifting the trigger from determining the potential existence of a right to determining the 'degree to which conduct contemplated … would adversely affect those rights'. Once triggered, the extent and depth of the ensuing consultation depends on either the strength of the claim to title or rights, or the seriousness of the harm that may result from the proposed activity (ibid.). In the case of Treaties, the specific agreements outlined in their text have a bearing on the depth of consultation required. This is determined by a range of factors, including the clarity of promises made under the particular Treaty; the seriousness of impact resulting from proposed Crown actions; the history of dealings between the two parties; and whether the Treaty provides a framework to manage foreseen changes in land use (*Mikisew* para 63). Finally, the adequacy of this consultation is determined by what the Court refers to as the 'informational' and 'response' components of the duty (ibid.: para 64). This ultimately renders government responsible for not only providing Aboriginal peoples with the relevant information in a timely way, to allow them time to express their interest and concerns with proposals, but also for ensuring that their representations are seriously considered and, if possible, integrated into the proposed plan of action (ibid.).

This obligation, to conduct a recursive process of consultation which can effect change in the original plans, brings attention to the second part of the duty: to accommodate. This is key because, as noted in *Mikisew* (para 54), 'consultation that excludes from its outset any form of accommodation would be meaningless'. Although *Haida* (para 48) stated that consultation 'does not give Aboriginal groups a veto over what can be done with the land', this judgment was referring to a situation in which Aboriginal claims were asserted but unproven. In contrast, the substantive rights conferred by Treaty 'requires a higher duty of accommodation on part of the Crown than in a pre-proof context' (Laidlaw and Passelac-Ross 2014: 8). As the SCC acknowledged in *Mikisew* (para 48):

> If the time comes that in the case of a particular Treaty 8 First Nation, 'no meaningful right to hunt' remains over its traditional territories, the significance of the oral promise that 'the same means of earning a livelihood would continue after the treaty as existed before it' would clearly be in question, and a potential action for treaty infringement, including the demand for a Sparrow justification, would be a legitimate First Nation response.

This recognition leads Laidlaw and Passelac-Ross (2014: 8) to conclude that, in a Treaty context, consultation and accommodation should be framed by the principles of the 'Sparrow Test'. This refers to dual criteria in the *Sparrow [1990] 1 SCR 1075* (hereafter *Sparrow*) judgment, which determines whether a right has been infringed upon and, if so, whether it can be justified. As a necessary corollary, the Crown's obligation to protect the rights conferred therein would expand, as would the range and 'depth' of consulting and accommodating measures. Ultimately, this is because 'only demonstrably compelling and substantial objectives can trump Treaty rights' (Laidlaw and Passelac-Ross 2014: 8). Sparked by the *Mikisew* judgment, and in an attempt to ensure that its agencies operate in accordance with these cases, the Government of Alberta published its first policy on First Nation consultation in 2005 and released a later one in 2013. As such, since 2005, proposed oil sands projects which risk adversely affecting First Nation Treaty rights trigger the duty to consult, requiring said consultation to have been conducted 'adequately' before applications can proceed to the 'approval' stage of the regulatory process.

The 'Approval' Stage and the Content of the 'Public Interest Test'

Following consultation with First Nations and engagement with public stakeholders at the 'planning' stage, there is further opportunity for 'non-elite' participation in decision-making at the subsequent 'approval' stage of the regulatory process. This refers to the point at which public hearings are called by the energy regulator, being triggered by a First Nation or interested party submitting a 'statement of concern' about a particular project. Indeed, these concerns may have been carried over from the previous 'planning' phase if a proponent failed to sufficiently mitigate those originally raised. These hearings allow for the energy regulator to judge an application 'on a case-by-case basis, taking into account the specific facts and circumstances of each application in addition to any statements of concern received' (AER 2016a). There are issues around whom the energy regulator permits into these hearings, which is based on an increasingly narrow determination of whether parties are 'directly and adversely affected' (see Fluker 2015). This has made participation 'subject to an exclusionary process of filtration, in which potential opponents of development are defined as illegitimate participants' (Bowness and Hudson 2013: 71). While this can be an issue for First Nations, they have participated in all of the hearings under examination here. As such, it is the means by which these concerns have been dealt with once inside the hearings that is of primary concern.

Within the 'approval' stage, the overarching body in charge of regulating oil sands expansion through public hearings is the provincial energy regulator. As a government agency, it has undergone several changes over the last 20 years, much like those responsible for determining the 'adequacy' of consultation at the 'planning' stage of the process. Although the regulation of energy resources dates back to 1932, with the creation of the Turner Valley Conservation Board, of initial focus here is the Alberta Energy and Utilities Board (AEUB), which entered into being in 1995, under the Alberta Energy and Utilities Board Act (Government of Alberta 2016a). This merged the previous functions of the ERCB and the Public Utilities Board (PUB) into a single entity. According to Doern and Gattinger (2003: 136), 'The lion's share of the AEUB mandate originates from the ERCB, which had regulatory authority over virtually all aspects of energy resource development.' This holds significance because, as Low (2009a: 3) notes, 'The overarching policy objective for the ERCB has always been the orderly development – with the emphasis on development – of the province's petroleum resources.' Indeed, the purpose of the merger was to 'provide a more streamlined and efficient regulatory process' (Government of Alberta 2016a).

In 2008, the Alberta Utilities and Commission Act split the AEUB into the Alberta Utilities Commission (AUC) and the ERCB. The former undertook the responsibilities of the PUB while the latter regulated fossil fuel development and pipelines unrelated to gas utilities (Low 2009a). This created a single body with a consolidated mandate to 'promote efficiency in Alberta's energy regulatory system', and to ensure that it 'can effectively manage growth pressures and provide all Albertans with a robust regulatory authority … that can make timely decisions to capitalize on opportunities that are in the public interest' (Alberta Ministry of Energy, quoted in Low 2009b: 32). Between 2008 and 2013 the ERCB approved the Total E&P Joslyn North project (ERCB 2011), also being involved in the approval process for the expansion of Shell's Jackpine mine in 2013. However, before this latter approval could be issued the energy regulator underwent another substantive change. This resulted from a number of provincial government reports on improving competitiveness, particularly in the natural resources sectors. As a consequence, the Regulatory Enhancement Taskforce was established in 2010 with the purpose of providing guidance towards this goal. One of the six recommendations made to government in its final report was to '[e]stablish a single regulatory body with unified responsibility for policy assurance (regulatory delivery) of upstream oil and gas development activities' (Government of Alberta 2011a: 14). This led to the creation of the AER in 2012, under the Responsible Energy Development Act (REDA) of the same year (Government of Alberta 2012b).

The AER replaced the ERCB in 2013, taking over all its regulatory functions whilst heralding 'a new governance structure that will achieve the benefits of strong corporate oversight and independent adjudication of energy applications throughout the hearing process' (AER 2013a). Entirely funded by industry, the AER is 'responsible for all projects from application to reclamation', turning it into a 'one-stop shop' by also giving it jurisdiction over the mineral and surface right disposition, water permit and investigatory responsibilities previously maintained by the Ministry of Environment and

Sustainable Resource Development (ESRD) (Canadian Association of Petroleum Landmen 2013: 1). While the consultation responsibilities of the ESRD were moved instead to the ACO, the AER was essentially made responsible 'for all projects from application to reclamation' (ibid.). As these changes began during Shell's application for expansion of its Jackpine Mine the eventual public hearing was conducted by the AER and, as such, considered the requirements outlined under both the ERCA and its replacement, the REDA (see AER 2013b). This was done according to the 'transitional provisions' outlined under Section 83 (2) of the latter legislation, which noted that 'any approval issued or any order, declaration made or issued by the former Board before coming into force of this section continues to have effect … until it expires or is amended or terminated …' (Government of Alberta 2012b: 37). Alongside the continuity of staffing seen between the regulatory agencies (see AER 2014), this demonstrates additional continuity among some of the key legislative features of public hearings across the entirety of large-scale, open-pit oil sands approvals over the past two decades.

Despite these organisational changes the structure of the regulatory process has remained consistent over this time, as has the 'public interest test' deployed by the regulatory Panels within the hearings. Between 1995 and 2000, one of the AEUB's 'primary roles' was to 'adjudicate and regulate energy developments and utility rates in the public interest' (Alberta Ministry of Energy 1999: 22). At this point direction was provided by the subsequently amended Oil Sands Conservation Act Regulation 76/88, with its requirement to 'ensure orderly, efficient and economical development in the public interest of the oil sands resources of Alberta' (Government of Alberta 2000a: Sec. 3(a)). Between 2000 and 2008, before the AEUB was replaced by the ERCB, the primary piece of legislation governing hearing Panel decisions was the Energy Resources Conservation Act (ERCA) (Government of Alberta 2000b). This legislation continued to direct Panel decision-making processes towards the 'public interest' (ibid.: Sec. 3):

> Where by any other enactment the Board is charged with the conduct of a hearing, inquiry or other investigation in respect of a proposed energy resource project, it shall, in addition to any other matters it may or must consider in conducting the hearing, inquiry or investigation, give consideration to whether the project is in the public interest, having regard to the social and economic effects of the project and the effects of the project on the environment.

The period 2008–2012 saw this same piece of legislation govern the ERCB at the hearings, despite there being no definition of 'public interest' or 'the public' in either the ERCA (ibid.) or the Alberta Interpretation Act (Government of Alberta 2000c). Despite this, the phrase 'public interest' is deployed throughout other legislation administered by the ERCB, including the Oil

Sands Conservation Act (Government of Alberta 2000a: Sec. 3(b)) and the Pipeline Act (Government of Alberta 2000e: Sec. 4(a)). This was the case until 2012, when the REDA replaced the ERCA, leading to the concurrent replacement of the ERCB by the AER. This was a noteworthy modification because the REDA also removed the 'public interest' mandate from the regulatory hearing Panels. However, as this is a relatively recent development, all the open-pit mines in the oil sands have been approved under the justificatory rubric of the 'public interest'.

Due to its role in the expansion of the large oil sands mines, and its apparently mercurial quality, use of the 'public interest test' within the 'approval' stage has attracted a small degree of scholarly attention. Writing in 2008, just after the AEUB split into the ERCB and the AUC, Hierlmeir's (2008: 4) analysis of hearing decision documents leads her to the conclusion that the public interest has 'become shorthand' and 'replac[ed] the reasoning for decisions'. Observing that '[i]f the public interest was mentioned, it was often as a brief comment which justified approval of a project' (ibid.), Hierlmeir (ibid.: 5) goes on to conclude 'some may argue' that operator acquisition of mineral rights prior to the hearings generates an economic interpretation of the 'public interest'. Three years later Low (2011) conducted a larger study aimed at identifying how the hearing Panels both interpret the 'public interest' and address those concerns seen as encompassed by its remit. In noting that the hearing Panels tend to 'presume that Albertans as a whole are interested in having the province's energy resources developed without interpretation to reap the attendant economic benefits' (ibid.: 29), Low describes a situation in which 'public interest' determinations are contingent on those issues submitted within statements of concern by intervening parties.

While providing important information on the flexibility built into the 'approval' stage of the regulatory process, this literature is largely concerned with distilling the meaning of the 'public interest' as interpreted by the hearing Panels and in accordance with occasionally competing legislative requirements (see Low 2011: 29). As such, comparably little attention is given to the deliberative 'balancing act' which leads up to and underpins these eventual decisions, nor the way in which prioritisation of economic interests may be the routine manifestation of a broader, institutionalised environmental philosophy blind to the tensions between industrialisation and conservation. A response to this is made possible by identifying the parity between the primary legislation governing hearing Panel deliberations and the concept of 'sustainable development' outlined above. Taking the ERCA as the point of departure, the considerations underpinning the 'public interest' mandate are present in its requirement to 'give consideration to whether the project is in the public interest, *having regard to the social and economic effects of the project and the effects of the project on the environment*' (Government of Alberta 2000b: Sec. 3, emphasis added). The implied need to balance this trio of factors is also visible in the latest mandate granted by the REDA, despite much being written on its apparent removal of the 'public interest test' from its text (see Nikiforuk 2015). As stated in the Section 3 of the REDA General Regulation:

> For the purposes of section 15 of the Act, where the Regulator is to consider an application or to conduct a regulatory appeal, reconsideration or inquiry in respect of an energy resource activity under an energy resource enactment, the Regulator shall consider
>
> (a) the social and economic effects of the energy resource activity,
> (b) the effects of the energy resource activity on the environment,
> (c) the impacts on a landowner as a result of the use of the land on which the energy resource activity is or will be located.
>
> (Government of Alberta 2012b: Sec. 3)

Although this latest legislation adds a fourth factor for consideration, landowners, to the deliberation process, the essential requirements remain the same. As such, all contemporary oil sands projects have been approved within a hearing process that seeks to balance social, economic, and environmental factors in pursuit of a 'public interest' determination – the trio of factors central to the concept of 'sustainable development'. This consistency, across hearing Panel deliberations and overarching oil sands policies and strategies, provides a point upon which the analytical lens can be directed to examine the environmental philosophy cutting across institutional-organisational forms, to permit oil sands expansion at the 'approval' stage of the regulatory process.

Conclusion

The fundamental tension inherent to the concept of 'sustainable development', between an eco-philosophy that pursues accelerated industrialisation through techno-scientific efficiencies and another that advocates its deceleration via 'non-elite' participation in decision-making, mirrors the two operational stages of the regulatory process governing oil sands expansion. With the 'planning' stage representing the point at which First Nations may exert control over the push for industrialisation, the subsequent 'approval' stage provides insight into how social, economic, and environmental considerations have been weighed in the process of its repeated sanctioning. While entailing a degree of simplification, this approach provides a suitable lens through which to analyse the regulatory process in terms of the form of 'sustainable development' it has been tasked with pursuing, and the extent to which First Nations have been able to influence those oil sands projects that have passed through its stages. In the ensuing chapters this is used to establish the eco-philosophy underpinning provincial policies and strategies for the 'sustainable development' of the resource, the 'driving forces' and 'justifications' for economic growth spoken of by Spangenberg (2010: 561), and the ways in which these materialise at the level of operations. This approach is also used to explain how the duty to consult and accommodate First Nations has been interpreted and implemented within the regulatory process, allowing for the identification of factors which allow for these interpretations to be operationally accepted. It is to the first of these tasks that the next chapter turns.

Part II

The Regulatory Process

Chapter 3

The Directing Features of Policy and Strategy

As outlined in the previous chapter, the regulatory process under investigation consists of three stages: 'planning', 'approval', and 'oversight'. While subsequent chapters present data on the first and second of these, this chapter presents findings from the thematic analysis conducted into the six overarching policies and strategies governing oil sands extraction since 1999. Taken together these contextualise the decisions and deliberations made within the regulatory process, illustrating the overarching priorities driven by the provincial government in its pursuit of 'sustainable development' of the oil sands resource.

This chapter establishes the dominant objectives forwarded by these policies along with the purported means for their realisation, describing the imbalance of priorities inherent to the 'sustainable development' approach and the fixation with science and technology as providing the means for mitigating environmental impacts. Also outlined in the post-2008 policies is an apparently high degree of support for greater First Nation consultation on individual oil sands projects, in addition to the similarly apparent inclusion of their input into some of the policies themselves. Taken together, these characteristics are largely consistent across the time frame in which the policies and strategies have been issued. In this sense, a prescient statement was made in the earliest policy document analysed, setting the scene for all those to follow: 'A vision should endure. Its implementation may change and vary depending on the demands of a particular time or situation, but the vision should remain constant. This is the case in Alberta' (Government of Alberta 1999: 2).

Throughout the documents the consistent 'vision', or objective, has been a form of 'sustainable development' interpreted through the philosophical lens of ecological modernisation. As such, the approach advocated is one that sees 'sustainable technology, sustainable consumption, and market-based solutions as providing the answers [to environmental problems]' (Foster *et al.* 2010: 19). It was explained in the previous chapter that eco-modernist philosophy operates on a spectrum between 'strong' and 'weak' positions, with each approach recommending a different set of techniques for addressing environmental issues. This chapter demonstrates that the advocated approach throughout policy and strategy is largely that of the 'weak' strand, being visible in the consistent pursuit of economic growth and reliance on techno-scientific means of environmental mitigation. However, 'strong' ecological modernisation was also visible in the 'open' and 'democratic' way government purported to include First Nations in both policy and regulatory practice. Such a combination is not entirely unusual, as 'it is essential to note that weak and strong features of EM [ecological modernisation] are not always mutually exclusive binary opposites' (Christoff 1996: 491). That said, the sheer extent of the environmental victimisation illustrated in Chapter 1 suggests that the techno-scientific methods of environmental mitigation are not fulfilling the purpose intended. A similar discrepancy is visible when such harm is compared to the consultation claimed to have occurred with First Nations at the level of strategy and operations. Chapters 4 and 7 examine this difference in greater detail. For present purposes, however, this chapter outlines the environmental philosophy underpinning the Government of Alberta's plans for the 'sustainable development' of the oil sands resource.

The chapter is divided into three sections. Each centres on the dominant objective posited in each of the policies and strategies analysed – environmentally sustainable economic growth. The first describes the presentation of this objective in greater detail, explaining its positioning within a particularly eco-modernist interpretation of 'sustainable development' and its consistent association with the notion of inter-generational justice. The second section explains the dominant means by which these objectives are to be realised at the level of operations – a form of precautionary adaptive management which seeks to mitigate risk through optimistic recourse to techno-scientific innovation. The third and final section explores the purported level of First Nation involvement in the creation and execution of the various policies and strategies. While this was subsumed into broader stakeholder engagement in the documents published prior to the 2005 *Mikisew* decision at the SCC, those released following this decision support the provision of First Nation-specific consultation at the level of both policy and operations. Finally, the chapter summarises the findings in preparation for Chapter 6, where data from interviews with those involved at the 'planning' stage of the regulatory process will be presented, illuminating, among other things, the discrepancy that exists between First Nation consultation in policy and practice.

The Pursuit of Growth and the Universalisation of Its Benefits

The dominant philosophy to which the policy and strategy objectives have adhered for almost two decades is that of 'weak' ecological modernisation'. Creating a space in which the conflict between economic growth and environmental protection is nullified, largely because realisation of the latter is rendered contingent on the former, the term 'sustainable development', and its associated conceptual faculties, has been widely deployed in place of the term 'sustainable growth', which would actually be more accurate. With resource extraction posited as a fundamental priority for the Government of Alberta, and repeatedly presented as a key means by which the provincial population at-large maintain their quality of life, 'sustainable development' is here anchored to the extraction and exchange of non-renewable resources more generally, and of the oil sands in particular. This is an unquestioned aspect of each policy document, representing, in part, the historical prominence of the oil industry in Alberta. However, when this is coupled with the concurrent pursuit of growth in the enterprise, for the very purpose of providing province-wide 'social goods', not only is 'sustainable development' tied to an industry which is, by its very nature, unsustainable, but an assumption is being made that incremental resource extraction is in the universalised interests of the provincial population. Indeed, when this position is associated with the notion of inter-generational justice, as visible throughout the documents, it has the effect of expanding the universalising assumption onto the broad 'publics' of the future. As a consequence, the provincial social 'goods' and 'interests' are premised on ever-expanding resource extraction, while the more situated and localised environmental concerns of First Nations become absorbed, and therefore nullified, by this narrative.

The first policy of relevance was published in March 1999, titled 'Alberta's Commitment to Sustainable Resource and Environmental Management' (ACSREM) (Government of Alberta 1999). It outlines a 'vision' for 'sustainable development' which establishes resource extraction as both an unquestioned priority for the province and the dominant means by which provincial societal interests are to be met (ibid.: 2). This 'vision' is clarified using five points intended to outline its content, providing insight into the environmental philosophy underlying the interpretation of the term. Although the need to balance multiple interests in the final three of these is emphasised, the dominant consideration in the first two is of economics. The first point requires government agencies to ensure that '[t]he use of Alberta's natural resources shall be sustainable', which is taken to mean that '[n]on-renewable resources shall be managed in a manner to maximize benefits to Albertans' (ibid.: 3). The objective of this is made clear in the second, subsequent point of clarification, where the explicit purpose of such management is to 'support and promote the Alberta economy' to ensure 'the optimum value for the resource is obtained and there will be a fair return to Albertans' (ibid.). This economic valuation is also framed in more social terms, with the clarification that 'support[ing] and promot[ing] the Alberta economy' also encompasses 'Alberta's ability to provide Albertans with health, education and other social and economic benefits, now and in the future' (ibid.). Visible here is a theme which becomes increasingly dominant as new policies are released – that the quality of life enjoyed by existing and future inhabitants of Alberta is premised upon resource extraction. Environmental protection is absent from these initial points of clarification.

The remaining three points place heavy emphasis on integrated resource management, giving broad recognition to the interconnectedness of various aspects within and between both society and environment. In substantiating the policy vision for 'sustainable development', the third point focuses entirely on the latter of these, stating that 'Alberta's environment shall be protected' (ibid.). This is taken to mean 'Alberta's air, land and water shall be protected and maintained for the health and enjoyment of Albertans', and that '[s]pecies diversity shall be protected and maintained' (ibid.). Although this is clearly anthropocentric, directed at 'Albertans' generally, the protection encompasses both animate and inanimate aspects of the environment. Recognition of this ecological multiplicity is extended into point four, where 'sustainable development' is taken to include managing resources 'on an integrated basis' (ibid.). This is further demonstrated in the accompanying explanation of this term, where recognition is given to the need to manage environmental effects in a regional capacity:

> Resources such as trees, minerals, wildlife, water, fish, range, public land and plants, shall be managed in a manner that addresses their interdependence and recognizes that the use of one resource can affect other users and other resources....
>
> (Ibid.)

The fifth and final point clarifying the 'vision' for 'sustainable development' expands on this inter-related view, explaining the need for resource management 'to provide a range of products and values' for 'multiple benefits' (ibid.: 4). When discussing this in direct regard to minerals, which explicitly includes oil (ibid.: 1), again a relationship is established between the flow of revenue from resource extraction and the social aspects of 'provid[ing] education, health care and social services' (ibid.: 4). Taken together, this early conceptualisation of 'sustainable development' renders social goods contingent on resource extraction, positioning environmental interests secondary to these priorities.

The subsequent Regional Sustainable Development Strategy (RSDS) was published in 1999 (Alberta Environment 1999), three months after the ACSREM document. In operation for nine years, until it was replaced with the Provincial Energy Strategy in 2008, this strategic document informed eight of the 12 hearing decisions on large-scale oil sands projects analysed in Chapter 4. Tasked with providing operational direction for ACSREM's 'vision', the RSDS was introduced 'on anticipation of further oil sands resource development in northern Alberta' (ibid.: 1). Despite reiterating the text communicated in the previous ACSREM policy, the document goes on to place a greater emphasis on the economic growth of the oil sands in particular. Indeed, it is here posited as a primary strategic target for the province and anchored to the concept of inter-generational justice:

> The eventual development of most of the surface mineable oil sands … will be guided by the need to maximise the benefits for future generations, and the requirements to maintain the quality of the environment. (Ibid.: 6)

With the policy continuing to deploy the assumption that extraction of oil sands is in the best interests of 'future generations', a modification is reflected in a subtle change to its interpretation of 'sustainable development'. Whereas the previous ACSREM document adopts a more conciliatory position with regard to the conceptual centrality of economic growth, in the sense of there being a need to 'balance' growth with environmental protection (Government of Alberta 1999: 1), the RSDS views 'sustainable development' as 'based on integrating environmental protection with economic growth and resource use, and making full use of the available management tools and resources' (Alberta Environment 1999: 4). Whereas the former suggests that possibilities for economic growth may be avoided to protect the environment, the latter suggests that environmental protection is actually contingent on such growth. The term 'sustainable growth' would therefore be a more appropriate descriptor for the objectives of this strategy, belying the particularly 'weak' form of ecological modernisation to which the concept is aligned.

The notion of inter-generational justice is also communicated throughout the document, adopting language similar to that used by the Brundtland Report in its original definition of 'sustainable development'. It finds form within the policy 'vision' itself where, as a 'leader in 'sustainable development', the province is to ensure that the social, environmental, and economic benefits of resource management are realised 'in the present and future' (ibid.: 2). Similar language is encountered in the second point clarifying the content of the 'vision', where it is stated that '[n]atural resources will be managed to continue to support Alberta's ability to provide Albertans with health, education and other social and economic benefits, now and in the future' (ibid.: 3). As the concept is used alongside the notion that resource extraction acts as the foundation for the acquisition of provincial social interests, it has the effect of expanding this universalising, unquestioned interpretation across time, concealing those interests which may disagree with or diverge from this position in both the present and future.

The next policy of relevance, Launching Alberta's Energy Future, was not released until 2008. Here, the term 'sustainable development' is referenced only once, with 'sustainable prosperity' being used instead to describe the goal of Alberta's updated 'Energy Vision' (Government of Alberta 2008a: 19). Interpreted alongside the concept of inter-generational justice, this approach is seen to 'pave the way to sustained wealth creation, while safeguarding our environment and our social advantages for future generations of Albertans' (ibid.). As outlined in the document, 'This is the path that allows Alberta to not only respond to "issues" but take full advantage of the opportunities' (ibid.) – an approach indicative of the 'win-win' concept of 'sustainable growth'.

The philosophical dominance of eco-modernisation feeds into the six 'Critical Assertions' taken to represent the 'fundamental guideposts', providing a less abstracted direction for this 'sustainable prosperity' 'vision'. There are several assumptions underpinning all of these assertions, dominant among which is the continued and unquestionable primacy of resource extraction as the basis for economic growth. This is most prominent in the first and second assertions, where '[t]he development of clean hydrocarbons is essential to Alberta's energy future', and '[o]ngoing development of Alberta's energy resources will be a platform for continued economic growth and success', respectively (ibid.: 20). The underpinning message, that economic growth based on resource extraction is a priority for the province, takes on additional justificatory characteristics in the text accompanying these assertions. Notwithstanding the continued and unquestioned pursuit of economic growth premised on resource extraction, the policy goes on to present a dual justification for such a goal: its positive contribution to levels of national and provincial employment and the unexplained inadequacy of alternative renewable sources. Again, social goods are anchored to non-renewable resource extraction, which, apparently, cannot be substituted for by renewable alternatives.

These overarching 'critical assertions' within the 'sustainable prosperity' vision are given more operational form via the three explicit outcomes of the policy, i.e. '[c]lean energy production, [w]ise energy use, and [s]ustained economic prosperity' (ibid.). Throughout each of these the presence of 'weak' ecological modernisation is visible in their communicated pursuit of a growth in productive output. In the explanation for the first outcome – 'clean energy production' – concerns around 'clean' fossil fuel consumption are assuaged by recourse to a form of techno-scientific optimism, where innovation will lead to economically feasible gasification processes and carbon capture (ibid.: 23). This focus on rendering expansive production 'sustainable' by 'greening' consumption is also mirrored in the second and third policy outcomes of 'wise energy use' and 'sustained economic prosperity' (ibid.: 25–28). Suggesting a reduction in per-capita consumption as a means of limiting harmful emissions, the second outcome is entirely focused on consumption patterns. However, it is important to make clear that this is not advocating a concurrent reduction in production, which would indicate a break with 'weak' ecological modernisation. Instead, the policy is fixated on modifying consumption patterns so as to maintain production output and ensure continued economic growth:

> Energy that companies and individuals do not consume is energy that can be upgraded or sold to further benefit Alberta. So 'saving' energy not

> only reduces heating or lighting costs, but offers the potential to create more wealth for Albertans.
>
> (Ibid.: 25)

The underpinning primacy of economic growth contained within this justification is confirmed in the third and final policy outcome, 'sustained economic prosperity'. Here, among the 'number of steps to derive greater wealth over the longer term and in a more sustainable way through its energy industry' (ibid.: 27), an expected and desired increase in energy production is communicated. Indeed, the policy goes on to recommend pursuing such prosperity by 'optimizing the recovery of our energy resources' (ibid.). Importantly, this includes 'tapping more of what we are currently leaving in the ground … reaching our oil sands resource potential … [and] broadening the markets for our energy resources' (ibid.). This desire to increase production is coupled with an expectation that it will occur, forming the basis for a plan to send a greater range of bitumen products to market. The given purpose of this is to create 'long-term jobs' and increase tax revenues 'on top of the royalties the province already receives from bitumen' (ibid.). As communicated in precursor policies, the notion of social goods being derived from both employment and non-renewable royalties continues to be used as justification for expanding bitumen production.

Published in the same year, 2008, the province-wide Land Use Framework (LUF) was introduced as the operational means of implementing the Provincial Energy Strategy, much like the RSDS providing operational direction for the ACSREM policy. Having the express goal of 'manag[ing] public and private lands and natural resources to achieve Alberta's long-term economic, environmental and social goals' (Government of Alberta 2008b: 7), it continues to communicate the three core elements inherent to 'sustainable development'. Indeed, this concept is recognised as part of the LUF's 'vision', 'desired outcomes', and 'guiding principles', all of which are intended to 'guide and inspire' Alberta's 'collective journey' in pursuit of the overarching policy goal (ibid.: 15). With respect to the 'vision' to which the LUF is contributing, it 'confirms the principles of sustainability and inter-generational responsibilities' (ibid.), echoing previous policies in its use of the characteristics inherent to the Brundtland Commission's early definition of 'sustainable development'. Similarly, to 'translate … vision into reality' the LUF identifies three outcomes, which any attempt to implement its central tenets 'must contribute … to', 'directly or indirectly' (ibid.). Again, these mirror the conceptual social, economic, and environmental triad within 'sustainable development', being posited as the pursuit of a '[h]ealthy economy supported by our land and natural resources', '[h]ealthy ecosystems and environment', and '[p]eople-friendly communities with ample recreational and cultural opportunities' (ibid.). Finally, ten 'guiding principles' are outlined, which have the intended purpose of aligning practical decisions 'with our vision and desired outcomes' (ibid.).

The first and foremost of these 'guiding principles' is '[s]ustainable [d]evelopment', which is again explained using terms provided by the Brundtland Commission. The first page of the executive summary clarifies just how far this is to be interpreted through the lens of 'weak' ecological modernisation:

> The purpose of the Land-use Framework is to manage growth, not stop it, and to sustain our growing economy, but balance this with Albertans' social and environmental goals. This is what the Land-use Framework is about – smart growth.
>
> (Ibid.: 2)

This is expanded on further in the LUF, where it is noted that the 'Government of Alberta rejects the simplistic view that to save the environment we must stop development' (ibid.: 6). Although it would be more accurate to replace the term 'development' with 'growth', as with the majority of the documents, the message is clear: the interpretation of 'sustainable development' in this policy is incompatible with positions advocating a stable or decreasing rate of production. The presence of 'weak' ecological modernisation therefore continues here, too. This is particularly important as the values, outcomes, and principles contained within this LUF operate as the basis for the 2012 LARP (ibid.: 3), the localised manifestation which specifically directs industrial activity in the oil sands area.

With the explicit purpose of 'build[ing] on the vision outlined in the Provincial Energy Strategy' of 2008 (Government of Alberta 2009a: 5), Responsible Actions: A Plan for Alberta's Oil Sands was subsequently published in 2009. As the name implies, this more specific policy targeted the oil sands region in particular. Continuing the drive to increase production visible in its precursor policies, the 'sustained growth' of the oil sands industry is explicitly advocated in the first paragraph of the introduction (ibid.: 4). Going on to note the 'significant role Alberta's oil sands reserves will play in meeting the world's demand for energy' (ibid.), after recognising that 'demand for oil is expected to continue to rise' (ibid.: 2), a growth in production is clearly not an objective this policy sets out to oppose. Indeed, the associated and continued interpretation of 'sustainable development' as 'sustainable growth' is recognisable in the introductory text (ibid.: 4):

> The Government of Alberta's long-term vision for the oil sands is that development occurs responsibly, sustains growth for industry and the province over the long term, and is done in a manner that enhances Albertans' quality of life.

This pursuit of 'sustainable growth' is repeated in the 'guiding principles', which provide the 'foundation for the development of this strategic plan and … the basis for implementation' (ibid.: 9). Based on '[h]ealthy environment and communities', '[c]ollaboration', '[b]alanced growth' and '[p]ublic interest and accountability', it is the latter two that most reflect the dominance of growth and influence of ecological modernisation. Indeed, the former of this couplet includes '[m]aximising long-term value and benefits from Alberta's oil sands while considering the economic, environmental, and social factors of development' (ibid.). Here, the central interest is in increasing the exchange value obtained from the oil sands resource, with social, economic, and environmental factors being recognised as peripheral considerations. This principle also aims to '[b]uild on our strengths in developing our energy resources, and further increase our competitiveness within integrated North American and global markets' (ibid.). Recognising that this document uses 'development' interchangeably with 'growth', it is clear that expansion of production is a central pillar in the direction provided to oil sands management.

The policy goes on to translate these four guiding principles into three outcomes, which are 'aligned with the three broad outcomes of the Provincial Energy Strategy' (ibid.: 10). These include 'optimized economic growth', 'reduced environmental footprint', and 'increased quality of life for Albertans today and in the future' (ibid.). The contradiction between the first and second of these outcomes is a further indication of 'weak' ecological modernisation, as it sees no conflict between growth and environmental protection. Moreover, as seen in previous policies, the focus on 'quality of life for Albertans' emphasises the relationship between provincial 'social goods' and resource extraction, meaning that although the social, economic, and environmental considerations continue to be presented as a triad of equal interests, the environment is implicitly positioned on a lesser footing.

The most recent strategy developed to guide expansion in the oil sands is the 2012 LARP (Government of Alberta 2012a). Despite being introduced as part of the Government of Alberta's commitment to manage cumulative environmental effects (ibid.: 3), it continues to interpret 'sustainable development' as 'sustainable growth'. This is immediately visible in the introduction, where the stated purpose of the LARP is to 'set the stage for robust growth, vibrant communities and a healthy environment within the region over the next 50 years' (ibid.: 2). This focus on growth is also reflected in its outcomes, which are 'consistent with and support the province-wide outcomes set out in the Land-use Framework' (ibid.: 24). Indeed, the first outcome for the region is that '[t]he economic potential of the oil sands resource is optimized' (ibid.: 37), with the strategies deployed to ensure its success including '[c]ontinue[d] implementation of the Alberta Provincial Energy Strategy and Responsible Actions: A plan for Alberta's Oil Sands' (ibid.: 37). Outlined as the third objective of this outcome, it is made clear that policies need to be 'developed that promote new investments in energy, mineral and coal development', with its accompanying explanation noting that '[g]rowth of all energy sub-sectors is crucial for the regional and provincial economy' (ibid.:

41). Taken together, the focus on expanding production is still present, even here, in the plan introduced to tackle the specific issue of cumulative environmental effects emerging from the now-substantial oil sands industry.

The Facilitation of Growth Using Techno-Scientific Mitigation

The means of facilitating the 'sustainable growth' consistently advocated throughout policy and strategy takes the form of an adaptive managerialism premised on expected future advances in science and technology. Communicated using the business-orientated language of markets, innovation, and competition, this approach is the supposed method by which pursuit of economic growth can continue alongside environmental protection. Indeed, the conservation–efficiency duality, which underpins the idea that economic growth can be 'decoupled' from its material inputs and outputs, is a cornerstone of ecological modernisation. The techno-scientific optimism accompanying this narrative is portrayed with more certainty in the earlier documents, where industrial expansion and economic growth are seen as complementary because adaptive management premised on technological innovation is still understood to be effective. This begins to break down, however, as the material ecological consequences of industrial expansion are gradually realised – a pattern evidenced by the confused and contradictory messages that begin to emerge in later documents. Yet, despite this, repeated recourse to techno-scientific methods of environmental mitigation is referred to throughout and, as indicated by the previous chapter, this – along with the objective of 'sustainable growth' – is the hallmark of a particularly 'weak' strand of eco-modernist philosophy.

The ACSREM policy, published in 1999, contains no mention of the role for science and technology in ensuring environmental protection. Instead, it makes extensive reference to the need for 'integrated' forms of planning in '[a]ll provincial initiatives with significant implications for resource and environmental management' (Government of Alberta 1999: 5). As this is the underpinning direction document for the subsequent RSDS, this approach is visible throughout both policies. Yet, owing to the more operational nature, the RSDS contains greater clarity on how such management is to be deployed. Having the purpose of reducing uncertainty and concern over time via systematic monitoring and knowledge production, scientific and technological advances have a key role in this strategy.

The techno-scientific orientation of the ACSREM policy is mirrored in one of the principles upon which the subsequent RSDS is based, which states that '[l]earning will continue'. Referring to a form of adaptive management, advocated here is a 'learning-based process involving the fundamental features of learning [the accretion of understanding through time] and adaptation [the adjustment of management through time based on this learning]' (Williams

2011: 1347). Considering that such a techno-scientific solution is tasked with facilitating the ultimate policy aim of 'sustainable growth', and that its 'fixes' are equated with the precautionary principle and eco-modernisation (see Hajer 1995), largely because technology and science operate as the medium through which ecological issues are addressed, the philosophy underpinning the objective for 'sustainable growth' is here also present in the techniques deployed to achieve it.

The role of adaptive management within the RSDS is further communicated throughout its 'focus', which is explained as 'address[ing] the need to balance resource development and environmental protection' (Alberta Environment 1999: 5). Here the environmental management framework is seen to be based on 'a strong foundation of environmental information and science to assist in making decisions', 'a method to identify priority regional environmental issues', and a means to 'organize the science and monitoring work that is needed to understand these issues' (ibid.: 5). Through consultation with various stakeholders, including Aboriginal communities, this management system is directed at 'only 72' issues of environmental concern (ibid.: 11). Subsequently grouped into 14 themes, these issues are categorised according to their 'urgency' and 'gaps'. The former of these is 'based on the combination of timing, risk and uncertainty for each issue', and the latter on 'identifying the information and systems needed to manage each issue' (ibid.: 11–12). Echoing the 'adaptive management' visible in the underlying principles of the RSDS (ibid.: 16), these 14 themes of concern are grouped according to their priority so that various agencies and organisations can develop solutions. In adopting this approach, the document communicates an awareness of the uncertainty present and a need to gather more data on potential environmental impacts. Together this signifies an apparent precaution with regard to the environmental issues expected to arise through continued growth, particularly as no fewer than eight organisations, including the Cumulative Environmental Effects Management Partnership (CEEMP) and the Regional Aquatics Monitoring Program (RAMP), were tasked with providing the monitoring information for their resolution. As such, the RSDS, and to a lesser extent its precursor ACSREM document, relies on a form of precautionary managerial optimism, where it is assumed that the expected environmental effects of industrial growth can and will be mitigated by recourse to future advances in science and technology.

By 2008, with the introduction of the provincial energy strategy, Launching Alberta's Energy Future (Government of Alberta 2008a), the focus on technology became more extensive and explicit with regard to its role in ensuring sustainability. Environmental problems are recognised as 'critical issues that must be addressed in the years to come by industry, government and the research and technology sector' (ibid.: 9), demonstrating the presence of rational elitism within the policy. Here technology is more explicitly granted the dual role of not only protecting the environment but also increasing efficiencies of production:

> We must move the results of our research through technology development and commercialization to full-scale commercial deployment in order to see our energy research investments pay economic and social dividends.... We need technology more than ever today to keep our energy industry competitive and sustainable.
>
> (Ibid.: 16)

This conservation–efficiency duality is further enshrined in two of the policy's 'critical assertions', which provide the 'fundamental guideposts' for its vision for 'sustainable development'. In assertion 4, it is stated that 'Alberta will invest in energy infrastructure, including policy development and energy research', having the aim of 'promot[ing] and ensur[ing] the development of new technologies that increase efficiency and reduce environmental impact' (ibid.). Similarly, assertion 5 suggests that 'Government will encourage energy efficiency and conservation at all levels', recognising that '[e]nergy resources should be consumed with an emphasis on efficiency, conservation and wise use' (ibid.: 21). As such, there is a continuing tendency to perceive the technology needed to protect the environment as identical to that which can increase rates of production and growth – a relationship rooted firmly in 'weak' eco-modernist philosophy.

The specific means by which environmental thresholds are to be overcome while increasing production is also visible in this policy, a process known as 'decoupling'. Aiming to delink economic development from environmental deterioration, this process is targeted at 'reducing the amount of resources such as water or fossil fuels used to produce economic growth' (UN Environment Programme 2011: xi). The term 'decoupling' is here mentioned explicitly for the first time:

> There is real hope that a combination of wise energy use and appropriate technology development can begin to decouple emissions from energy consumption. In other words, we can begin to create a world where the carbon associated with our living patterns is captured and sequestered, or not even produced in the first place.
>
> (Government of Alberta 2008a: 25)

Without detailing how fossil fuels are to be decoupled from emissions, the policy then goes on to outline a number of technological and managerial 'levers' through which the three central outcomes are to be achieved. Importantly, these continue to mirror the central tenets of eco-modernist philosophy, where environmental protection becomes synonymous with economic growth through a process mediated by science and technology.

Of the seven levers, the three focusing on 'Addressing Environmental Footprint', 'Change Energy Consumption Behaviour', and 'Innovate' hold the most relevance to the oil sands (ibid.: 31). The remaining four are applicable but are of a more general orientation. Of the three, the first continues to advocate a managerial approach to environmental protection, where the LARP is confidently presented as containing a 'series of comprehensive targets, outcomes and actions that have been set for the region to protect the air, land and water' (ibid.: 32). These, it is suggested, are 'specifically designed to address environmental and growth pressures from the pace of development in the region' (ibid.). As will be seen in Chapters 4 and 5, the optimism with which this has been presented is, at the very least, misplaced. The rest of this 'lever' deals with development technologies aimed at minimising the environmental footprint (ibid.). One of the two priorities for the second of these three 'levers', 'Change Energy Consumption Behaviour', is titled 'Carbon Charges'. It is here where the influence of ecological modernisation can be seen in relation to the 'cap and trade' mechanism for controlling emissions. This unilaterally places an upper limit on the amount of pollution an economy can emit each year:

> Alberta is wary of the 'cap and trade' mechanisms being advocated by others. Their requirements would be onerous and targeted disproportionately at energy producing jurisdictions....
>
> (Ibid.: 39)

This aversion demonstrates a broader reluctance to deviate away from 'win-win' modes of regulation, which tend to rely on negotiation and compromise between public and private bodies to develop regulatory standards (see Tombs 2016). Not only is the disproportionate influence exerted by a 'cap and trade' mechanism on emissions-producing jurisdictions deemed unfair, as if this is both unreasonable and not its fundamental purpose, but its subsequent demand for a carbon pricing mechanism that '*must* be market-based', '*must not* redistribute wealth from Alberta', and '*must not* impede our competitiveness', clearly illustrates the Government of Alberta's aversion to regulation which risks decelerating production (Government of Alberta 2008a: 39, emphasis added). Instead, a fluid approach is preferred which 'can evolve as needs evolve, and it should be time-limited, with its purpose and impact periodically reviewed' (ibid.). This is essentially referencing adaptive management, with the information on this 'lever' finishing with the statement 'Alberta's energy future relies heavily on technology', and the final 'lever', 'Innovate', only embodying the managerial and techno-centric ethic further. Consistent with previous policies, and when coupled with the techno-scientific solutions posited in other areas of this provincial energy strategy, the philosophy underpinning acquisition of the 'sustainable development' objective here continues to be 'weak' ecological modernisation.

The subsequent 2008 LUF also advocates use of techno-scientific adaptive management with specific regard to cumulative environmental effects. Of its seven 'Strategies', 'Strategy 3' states that '[c]umulative effects management will be used at the regional level to manage the impacts of development on land, water and air' (Government of Alberta 2008b: 3). Despite its interchangeable use of 'development' with 'growth', recognition of which would contradict its statement that '[o]ur watersheds, airsheds and landscapes have a finite carrying capacity' (ibid.) were it not for the philosophy of ecological modernisation operating at its base, visible here is a techno-scientific managerial optimism with respect to all dimensions of ecological disorganisation. However, the optimism is expressed in a rather confused manner. This is largely because the principle of growth so central to the philosophy of ecological modernisation comes into conflict with recognition of cumulative breaches to environmental thresholds:

> Cumulative effects cannot be managed as an 'add-on' to existing management approaches; nor is it about shutting down development. It is about anticipating future pressures and establishing limits; not limits on new economic development, but limits on the effects of this development on the air, land, water and biodiversity of the affected region. Within these limits, industry would be encouraged to innovate in order to maximize economic opportunity.
>
> (Ibid.)

Appearing as an attempt to acknowledge the existence of environmental thresholds while at the same time assuaging concerns surrounding the security of any potential future investments in the region, the managerialism deployed appears conflicted, despite the final sentence placing it firmly within the context of ecological modernisation. Indeed, the potential danger posed to industrial growth by such a system of management is real, in terms of it being sensitive to, and requiring productive operations that are in accordance with, environmental 'limits'. As such, this threat is tempered by a 'final caveat', '[c]umulative effects management is an emerging practice, an art not a science. Accordingly, it should be used pragmatically not dogmatically' (ibid.). The managerialism takes on a scientific and technological dimension when coupled with 'Strategy 6', where the purpose of the LUF is to '[e]stablish an information, monitoring and knowledge system to contribute to continuous improvement of land-use planning and decision-making' (ibid.: 4).

The subsequent 2009 policy, Responsible Actions (Government of Alberta 2009a), was targeted at the oil sands in particular, and advocates further use of adaptive management premised on advances in science and technology. Within the six 'strategies' designed to implement its 'vision' for 'sustainable development', the first, to '[d]evelop Alberta's oil sands in an environmentally responsible way' (ibid.: 17), references the previous LUF as the means by which cumulative effects will be managed (ibid.: 18). Building on this, 'Strategy 6' aims to '[m]aximize research innovation to further support sustainable development and unlock the deposit's potential' (ibid.: 33), imbuing such practices with the techno-scientific conservation–efficiency duality made explicit in the overarching provincial energy strategy, Launching Alberta's Energy Future. As noted in the accompanying explanation, this strategy is intended to:

> … increase long-term and stable investments in research, promote world-class innovation, leverage technology to address development of the resource, and proactively address environmental challenges.
>
> (Ibid.)

The three 'goals' and ten 'objectives' which further operationalise this approach are similarly focused on pursuing adaptive management based on science and technology. Ultimately, although this policy is far more detailed than those previous with regard to the way it seeks to pursue research-based management to fulfil both efficiency and conservation goals, the essential characteristics of an adaptive approach to management premised on a techno-scientific optimism remain unchanged.

As part of its seven 'Strategic Directions', the final and most recent document, the 2012 LARP, ensures continuation of the techno-scientific approach seen previously. It even begins with the guarantee to 'continue implementation of … The Alberta Provincial Energy Strategy and Responsible Actions: A Plan for Alberta's Oil Sands' (Government of Alberta 2012a: 25). These 'Strategic Directions' include various management-orientated goals, including: 'improving integration of industrial activities', to 'better co-ordinate industrial activities … reduce land disturbance of the productive forest land base … and reduce environmental impacts' (ibid.); the 'strengthening [of] infrastructure planning', to 'attract and retain skilled workers [which] will be essential to enable the region's future economic growth' (ibid.: 31); and 'managing air, water and biodiversity, and minimizing land disturbance' through the use of 'management frameworks'. This latter strategy is particularly important, not only because of its relevance to environmental protection, but also because its explanation acknowledges the existence of ecological thresholds and describes the responses, known as 'management frameworks', should they be encountered (ibid,: 27):

> Limits in these frameworks are intended to be clear boundaries in the system not to be exceeded. Triggers are to be used as warning signals to allow for evaluation, adjustment and innovation on an ongoing basis.

Displayed here is an apparent contradiction between the overarching goal of 'sustainable growth' and the strategic recognition of 'clear boundaries in the system not to be exceeded', much like the rather confused explanation of cumulative effects management found in the overarching 2008 LUF. Indeed, recourse to 'adaptive' and 'innovative' mitigation measures, in the space between social awareness of a material limit and the material limit itself, is indicative of ecological modernisation's 'win-win' philosophy underpinning the notion of 'sustainable growth'.

The only other environment-orientated 'strategy' within the LARP is that targeted at 'creating new conservation areas'. Posited as a 'significant aspect of the LARP' by virtue of 'the balance it strikes between development and conservation in the region' (Government of Alberta 2012a: 29), this strategy states that '[n]o new oil sands, metallic and industrial minerals or coal tenure will be sold in conservation areas designated under the LARP' (ibid.: 30). With '[a]pproximately 16 percent of the region's land base … to be managed as new conservation areas' (ibid.: 29), this appears to be a largely precautionary, environment-orientated measure. Indeed, as these must be '[a]reas that support aboriginal traditional uses … representative of the biological diversity of the area … [and] of sufficient size [i.e. roughly 4,000–5,000 square kilometres]', according to the key criteria for their creation (ibid.: 30), the conservation areas appear to be a rare instance where interests pertaining to the environment are prioritised over those relating to economics. This said, operationalisation of this policy goal in practice suggests a very different reality (see Chapter 4).

The Legitimation of Growth via Aboriginal Participation in Environmental Decision-Making

The early 1999 ACSREM document supports 'non-elite' participation in the decision-making process, subsuming such input into a broader category of 'public interest' (Government of Alberta 1999: 6). The document does not mention First Nations specifically, or even Aboriginal groups more broadly. This is likely because it was published prior to the 2005 *Mikisew* decision and the first Government of Alberta policy on First Nation consultation. Nevertheless, the need for '[e]ffective [d]ecision [m]aking' within environmental management is based on the notion that '[d]ecisions should be made after consultation with Albertans, giving particular attention to people and industry that are directly affected by the decision' (ibid.: 5). Explaining that '[r]esource and environmental management decisions shall include consultation' (ibid.), the document presents an interpretation of the 'public interest' that goes beyond the more specific and environmental interests of First Nations:

> [Consultation includes] [e]nsuring decisions on resource and environmental management are taken in a provincial context, considering broad public interest, and involve input from those communities and industries that will be most directly affected by them. A role for provincial and national interests through consultation must also be provided.
>
> (Ibid.: 6)

As this consultation is subsumed under a broader heading explanation stating that '[i]nterests must be balanced. Projects must be assessed. Disputes must be resolved' (ibid.: 5), the advocated conception of 'public interest' appears weighted against the more localised environmental, cultural, and Treaty concerns of First Nations. This is particularly visible when coupled with the assumed and unquestioned pursuit of resource-based economic growth seen throughout the same documents, being situated as a basis for the acquisition of provincial social interests and concurrently demonstrating a predetermined weighting inherent to the pursuit of such 'balance'.

There is more recognition of the specific needs of First Nations and Aboriginal communities in the subsequent 1999 RSDS document (Alberta Environment 1999), where a greater degree of 'non-elite' participation is exhibited. Here First Nations are specifically recognised as not only contributing to the creation of the policy, but viewed as a necessary stakeholder in its execution. With regard to the former, First Nations and Aboriginal groups are hailed as providing 'an essential voice in developing the strategy, which includes recognition of their existing rights and uses in the region' (ibid.: 4). Subsequently mentioned as part of the strategic focus of the document, they are guaranteed a form of inter-generational justice specific to their hunting, fishing, and trapping rights:

> First Nations and Aboriginal communities requirements for a traditional lifestyle – Land, plants and animals will continue to be available to support a traditional lifestyle for current and future generations.
>
> (Ibid.: 6)

Although mention of Aboriginal peoples only occurs once more in the policy, with regard to their input in creating the 72 environmental issues to be addressed by the RSDS, reference is also made to 'regional stakeholders' throughout, of which they are one. In this sense their role in the execution of this strategy finds greater articulation within its founding 'Principles', where environmental '[s]tewardship will be shared' (ibid.: 5). Going on to note that, 'in all cases', regional stakeholders 'will continue to share in strong environmental stewardship of the land and resources', the medium through which such participation is to be realised is made clear:

> Regional stakeholders will contribute their time, expertise and knowledge, and take part in multi-stakeholder initiatives. In turn, this gives them a greater voice in resource and environmental management in the region.
>
> (Ibid.: 5)

During the period this document was active, between 1999 and 2008, the primary multi-stakeholder initiatives for addressing regional environmental issues associated with the oil sands were the CEEMP and the RAMP. The former of these later became the Cumulative Environmental Effects Monitoring Initiative (CEEM) and subsequently the Cumulative Environmental Management Association (CEMA). There are therefore two forms of First Nation participation being communicated here: participation in the creation of the strategy itself, and participation in the multi-stakeholder mechanisms deployed to achieve these protections. This is despite Aboriginal interests being broadly subsumed under the more generic rubric of 'regional stakeholders'. As such, the policy displays characteristics associated with 'strong' ecological modernisation, exhibiting 'deliberative democratic' and 'open' decision-making with respect to the participation and involvement of 'non-elites' (Christoff 1996: 490).

Within the 2008 provincial energy strategy, Launching Alberta's Energy Future (see Government of Alberta 2008a), the ideas of consultation and public participation are notable by their absence. Instead, with specific regard to the environmental issues resulting from oil sands extraction, it states that 'critical issues … must be addressed in the years to come by industry, government and the research and technology sector' (ibid.: 9). No mention is made of either stakeholders or First Nations having a role in decision-making, communicating a form of rational elitism at odds with the 'non-elite' participation advocated by the other policies and strategies.

In contrast, this rational elitism is absent from the subsequent 2008 LUF, where '[t]he ideas and opinions of Albertans have played a vital role in developing the framework' (Government of Alberta 2008b: 8). Indeed, from this point on there is explicit reference to First Nations in all of the policies of relevance, largely due to the provincial policy on consultation published in response to the 2005 *Mikisew* decision. Between May 2006 and October 2008 there were five separate stages of consultation involving numerous stakeholder, First Nation, and Aboriginal groups (ibid.). This signals a departure from the more general participation of 'stakeholders' communicated in previous documents to a more specific process of consultation with individual First Nations. This resulted in a compilation of seven desired areas for improvement in land management, of which the most relevant here is '[i]ncreased consultation with First Nations and Metis communities, stakeholders and the public to ensure a fair opportunity to influence new policies and decisions' (ibid.). Building on this, the seventh and final strategy of the LUF is to pursue '[i]nclusion of aboriginal peoples in land-use planning' (ibid.: 4), where its recognition of First Nation hunting, fishing, and trapping rights is clearly articulated alongside the then-recently-established duty to consult:

> The provincial government will strive for a meaningful balance that respects the constitutionally protected rights of aboriginal communities and the interests of all Albertans. The Government of Alberta will continue to meet Alberta's legal duty to consult aboriginal communities

> whose constitutionally protected rights, under section 35 of the Constitution Act, 1982 (Canada), are potentially adversely impacted by development. Aboriginal peoples will be encouraged to participate in the development of land-use plans.
>
> (Ibid.)

The explanation accompanying this strategy goes on to note that 'First Nation and Metis communities that hold constitutionally protected rights are uniquely positioned to inform land-use planning' (ibid.: 41), again demonstrating a change compared to their lack of specific mention in earlier policies. However, despite this, the LUF only reiterates the dominance of the 2005 First Nation Consultation Policy on Land Management and Resource Development, which First Nations actually rejected when it was initially released (ibid.: 41). In this sense, the LUF does not attempt to add anything not already present in the original consultation policy. This is despite consultation on its content resulting in First Nation requests for 'increased consultation … to ensure a fair opportunity to influence new policies and decisions' (ibid.: 4). Nevertheless, the LUF still expresses an interest in consulting First Nations on land use plans, which includes the LARP, advocating a form of 'non-elite' participation that echoes the democratic participation of 'strong' ecological modernisation.

The subsequent 2009 policy, Responsible Actions: A Plan for Alberta's Oil Sands (Government of Alberta 2009a), builds on the results of three extensive stakeholder consultations published in 2007. The most relevant of these for present purposes is that titled 'Oil Sands Consultations: Aboriginal Consultation Final Report' (Government of Alberta 2007). In this document 61 recommendations are forwarded by First Nations, 22 of which relate to environmental protection and 17 to consultation (ibid.: 9–11). Even the six pertaining to 'First Nation Rights and Interests' are directly related to the procedural duty to consult or the Treaty rights to hunt, fish, and trap on the land (ibid.: 10). Building on this input, 'Strategy 4' of the six outlined states that '[w]e will strengthen our proactive approach to Aboriginal consultation with a view to reconciling interests' (Government of Alberta 2009a: 11). However, immediately visible in the first sentence of the explanation given for 'Strategy 4' is the unquestioned and effectively unilateral prioritisation of 'sustainable growth' for Aboriginal communities:

> Building relationships and sharing knowledge and experiences through dialogue will enable Aboriginal communities, industry, government, and other stakeholders to make informed decisions that will further support sustainable growth in their communities.
>
> (Ibid.: 29)

Although this underpinning expansionary assumption clearly defines the boundaries of any dialogue, it does suggest the possibility to at least displace production. Indeed, the goals established as the markers by which effective dialogue can be said to have been achieved appear to seek greater First Nation involvement, aiming to '[p]romote clarity and consistency in consultation processes' and '[e]nhance collaborative government-to-government relationships' (ibid.: 30). Within these two goals, seven objectives are outlined which aim to improve various aspects of consultation with regard to oil sands development, five of which aim to improve the procedural dimension of this process. Although coloured by the underpinning expansionary assumption, this desire to deepen First Nation participation in the decision-making process is again a feature inherent to the more 'open' and 'democratic' aspects of 'strong' ecological modernisation.

The final document of relevance, the 2012 LARP (see Government of Alberta 2012a), is one of the seven land-use plans translating the 2008 LUF into strategic directions for the more operational levels of government. Having its primary jurisdiction over the oil sands area in particular, the document was devised following what appears to be the most extensive consultation with First Nations, and other stakeholder groups, seen in any of the policies or strategies. As noted by the Government of Alberta (2018a), the LARP 'is a product of more than three years of consultations with Albertans, First Nations and experts on social, economic and environmental issues'. This is communicated on the very first page of text (Government of Alberta 2012a: 2). In a similar manner to other policies, First Nations are seen here as integral to the creation of the LARP. Indeed, one of the seven regional outcomes for the policy is dedicated to the '[i]nclusion of aboriginal peoples in land-use planning' (ibid.: 37), the objective of which is made clear further in the document:

> To encourage aboriginal peoples' participation in land-use planning and input to decision-making in recognition of the cultural and economic importance of land use to those aboriginal communities with constitutionally protected rights. This will provide both aboriginal communities and the Government of Alberta with a basis for better addressing current and potential land-use conflicts, in a manner supportive of aboriginal traditional uses, such as the exercise of treaty rights.
>
> (Ibid.: 63)

In the explanation of this outcome it is affirmed that 'the Alberta government will look for opportunities to engage these communities and invite them to share their traditional ecological knowledge to inform land and natural resource planning in this region' (ibid.: 34). This continues to echo the 'strong' ecological modernisation seen throughout the more recent documents, where First Nations are involved in both the creation and subsequent execution of the policies and strategies as an independent group of stakeholders with specific rights.

Conclusion

This chapter has demonstrated that, over almost two decades, the policies and strategies relating to oil sands development exhibit some fundamental and largely unchanged characteristics associated with the philosophy of ecological modernisation. Across the spectrum of those examined, three features are particularly visible. First, and most fundamentally, the primary objective being pursued is 'sustainable growth'. Although couched in the language of 'sustainable development', where balance and compromise is sought between social, economic, and environmental considerations, it is quite clear that economic growth takes precedence over the other interests. More specifically, it is positioned in opposition to the thresholds invoked by the environmental dimension and as the basis for acquisition of the social dimension. This is tied to the unquestioned and omnipresent idea that such provincially beneficial economic growth must be based on resource extraction. When coupled with the repeated deployment of inter-generational justice under these terms, the suitability of such an approach is universalised across space, ignoring dissenting opinions, and time, assuming parity with the interests of future generations. Both aspects of this assumed consensus appear at odds with the more situated existence associated with the traditional cultural practices of the First Nations in the region.

The dominance and consistency with which 'sustainable growth' is pursued throughout the policies pulls the other two features, techno-scientific managerialism and First Nation participation in decision-making, in line with its purpose. Facilitating this dominant objective, the various forms of adaptive management premised on techno-scientific advances are consistent with eco-modernist philosophy, with the lack of attention given to the problems of growth in and of itself positioning this on the 'weak' side of the spectrum. As made clear, the documents consider the solutions to environmental issues to be rooted in further economic growth. Although the optimism with which this is pursued is more clearly articulated in the earlier policies, where the material ecological consequences of expansion are yet to be fully realised, the tools of science and technology common to this philosophy are consistently deployed as the means by which 'sustainable growth' is to be achieved.

The role of First Nations in the decision-making process appears to be similarly bound by this particular and dominant consideration. However, there is a shift in the policy and strategy documents following the 2005 *Mikisew* decision, where First Nations are increasingly recognised as an independent group of stakeholders with specific rights and needs. As such, their participation in the creation and execution of policies from 2008 onwards is more specific and extensive than that in precursor policies. Indeed, such participation is more closely associated with 'strong' ecological modernisation, making it appear at odds with the 'weak' form exhibited by the concurrent pursuit of 'sustainable growth' and regular recourse to techno-scientific mitigation. The following two chapters provide detail on how these overarching policy objectives have been operationalised in sanctioning material expansion of the oil sands industry. This clarifies the form of eco-modernist philosophy deployed, demonstrating how this has been possible when faced with intensifying First Nation opposition and increasing evidence as to the disruptive environmental effects occurring.

Chapter 4

Issues with the 'Planning' Stage of the Regulatory Process

The previous chapter demonstrated how the policy context in which the regulatory process sits is defined by key tenets of eco-modernist philosophy. 'Sustainable growth' of the oil sands industry has been the dominant objective since at least 1999, with its promise of 'green' industrialisation being facilitated by techno-scientific advances aimed at 'decoupling' production from its environmental consequences. However, the previous chapter also illustrated that policies and strategies, or at least those published following the 2005 *Mikisew* decision, tended to suggest that their content had been devised through extensive processes of consultation with First Nations. Even those prior to the *Mikisew* decision painted a picture in which 'non-elite' stakeholders had been engaged with in order to reach the given policy position. As a feature of 'strong' eco-modernist philosophy, this sits uneasily with those of its 'weak' counterpart, which are visible in both the growth objective and techno-scientific means for rendering it 'sustainable'. This chapter is the first of two that provides insight into the disparity between these policy claims and their operationalisation, which are given form through the regulatory process. While this chapter explores the reality of consultation at the 'planning' stage, the next explores that pertaining to techno-scientific mitigation of 'sustainable growth' at the 'approval' stage.

As outlined in Chapter 2, the regulatory process consists of three stages: those of 'planning', 'approval', and 'oversight'. Here, data from interviews with regulatory personnel involved at the initial 'planning' phase is presented. This explores three key clusters of process-specific tension surrounding First Nation consultation, all of which are premised on an underpinning provincial, paternalistic justification which serves to legitimate decisions made during this stage of the process. The first key area of conflict sits outside the regulatory process but intersects heavily with it, centring on the extent to which First Nations were consulted on the Lower Athabasca Regional Plan prior to its introduction in 2012 – a strategic tool which is supposed to inform regulatory decision-making to ensure development does not exceed environmental thresholds. The second area of conflict focuses on the delegation of consultation responsibilities to individual proponents following the disposition of land leases. The third area centres on the Government of Alberta's narrow interpretation of Treaty rights relative to that maintained by First Nations. Although this 'planning' phase could encompass other, more specific sub-stages, focus on these three in particular has been dictated by the dominant themes identified by the involved personnel. The final section of the chapter describes the role of the underpinning paternalistic justifications for decisions pertaining to expansion, along with the associated tension between the Government of Alberta and the Supreme Court of Canada.

The Marginalisation of First Nation Voices in the Lower Athabasca Regional Plan

As explained in Chapter 1, First Nations are not absolutely opposed to the oil sands industry, but support its existence in accordance with the capacity of the surrounding environment to withstand the changes it incurs. As Participant A from FNIRD 1 explained,

> [Our First Nation is] in no way against economic development, it's very supportive, but we don't want to hurt anybody. We don't want to kill the economy, but we also want to have a viable ecosystem that can hold true in a certain time.

Participant C from Industry, who was also member of a First Nation, echoed this position but from a different angle, rhetorically asking: 'How are we [First Nations] going to survive if industry leaves?' One of the ways in which the Government of Alberta has attempted to achieve the balance implicit to such comments is via the implementation of land use plans, which map out the more strategic direction and rate of oil sands development on a macro scale prior to the submission of any individual applications. Essentially, they outline what can and cannot be done on the land. As noted above, the specific framework governing the oil sands region is the 2012 LARP, which is supposed to inform the regulatory process to ensure development does not breach environmental thresholds on a cumulative scale. Before 2012 no land use plan existed to guide industrial expansion in the oil sands; their introduction followed increased recognition of the detrimental environmental effects of collective industrial activity in northern Alberta.

In development since 2008, the LARP is a significant undertaking, involving engagement with a variety of public and private interest groups. Following its conception many First Nations were consulted on its content by the LUS, including those interviewed. FNIRD 2 was 'heavily involved', meeting with this secretariat 'every month for about three years' prior to its finalisation (Participant A, FNIRD 2). As a result of this process, six dominant requests were made by indigenous peoples more broadly, including that they be granted: greater influence in land use planning processes; explicit recognition within the LARP of their constitutional rights; inclusion of traditional ecological knowledge in land use monitoring and management decisions; a request to slow the pace of extraction until a better understanding of the current ecological impact is achieved; development of cumulative effects management thresholds; and provision of economic development opportunities for aboriginal communities (Government of Alberta 2013b). Despite this, the First Nations considered the consultation process to have been superficial, with the final plan being characterised instead by the exclusion of their input. According to Participant A from FNIRD 2, there is a difference here between rhetoric and reality:

> There's a lot of good merit, and good ideas and good principles, behind what they are trying to establish. World class environmental monitoring? Absolutely. Multi-stakeholder engagement, real consultation, land management, economic prosperity for the province? All of those require us to get supportive, but it's just unfortunate that [how] it's being spoken about [and] how it's being delivered are actually very different.

Both First Nations stated that the primary factor undermining this narrative was the economic prerogative of the LARP, noting that such an emphasis was achieved by marginalising their voices. In effect, the growth objective established the parameters of consultation even before consultation on its content began, serving to narrow the opportunities available for the concessions needed to develop a plan that found agreement among the various stakeholders.

One of the key criticisms raised by First Nations was the omission of their input on conservation areas – land where development is barred but which permits its occurrence on adjacent parcels. Representing an example of First Nations trying to balance traditional land-based practices with the need for wage labour, recommendations for the location of these areas, their size, proximity to communities, and suitability for supporting the ecosystem and Treaty practices were submitted during consultation. However, the outcome of this expensive and labour-intensive exercise was the subordination of their input in relation to the economic value of bitumen: '[T]he major driver for deciding conservation areas, that had to be considered at the table with Alberta, was location of resources' (Participant A, FNIRD 2). The primacy of economic reasoning underpinning such decisions was confirmed by Participant B from the LUS:

> [I]f you look at the leases that have been sold by the Department of Energy on that landscape, then you look at the regional plan and the conservation areas that have been set out … it probably doesn't take a rocket scientist to figure out where the conserved land was in relation to the economic driver, right?

Figure 4.1 clearly supports this view, with the map on the left indicating conservation areas requested by a First Nation during consultation on the LARP and, on the right, those that were ultimately approved. The areas in grey denote recoverable oil sands deposit. Although initially appearing that some minor concessions were made here by the provincial government, this is incorrect. The shaded area marked '1' is the Birch Mountains Wildland Provincial Park and those marked '2' form the Marguerite River Wildland Provincial Park, both of which were established in 2000 under the Provincial Parks Act, creation of which had nothing to do with consultation on the LARP (Griffiths *et al.* 2001: 7).

The extent of this rejection of input appeared to depend on which First Nation was being consulted, or, more specifically, which part of the landscape they inhabited. As Participant A from the LUS noted, '[I]t depends on where you are in the Lower Athabasca'; and 'closer up to where [the northern First Nations are] there's quite a few conservation areas'. This is true; the Kazan and Richardson Wildland Parks were introduced into the northernmost area of the LARP following consultation with First Nations. For instance, in relation to a request by the ACFN to establish conservation areas covering key parts of their traditional territory (see ACFN 2010: 20), the Government of Alberta extended Richardson Wildland Park to cover only that area not intersecting with the oil sands deposit (see Government of Alberta 2012a: 92–93). Ultimately, although the Government of Alberta established some conservation areas following consultation with First Nations, these were subordinated to a perception of oil sands as the priority source of value in the region. With the unwavering commitment to the realisation of this value being made visible in the placement of these protected spaces, it would be mistaken to speak of the Government of Alberta accommodating First Nation input in this regard.

While it is quite clear that First Nation concerns have been excluded from the part of the land use plan dealing with conservation areas, it is important to

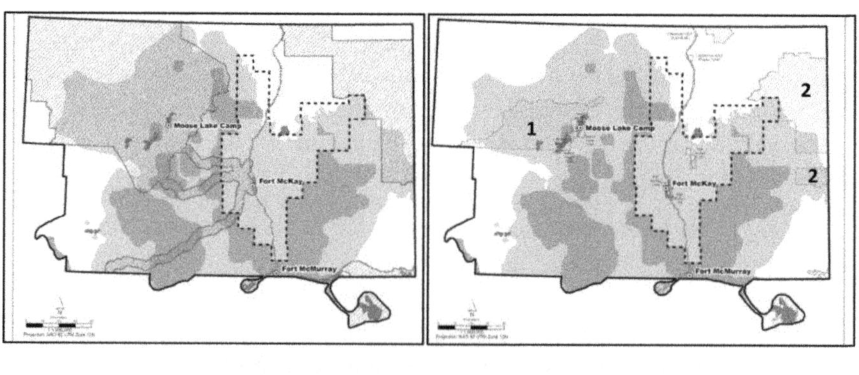

Figure 4.1 Requested Conservation Areas vs. Granted Conservation Areas.
Source: Nishi *et al.* (2013: 50–51).

note where such decisions originate. Without this consideration it may appear that the operational staff of the LUS was responsible for limiting implementation of First Nation requests, which is not wholly true. Ultimate responsibility lies higher in the chain of decision-making. As Participant A from the LUS explained:

> [T]he government didn't do as much as maybe was being recommended [by the Land Use Secretariat following consultation with First Nations] because the best thing we can do, and other government agencies can do, is put recommendations forward showing pros and cons. But one of the disadvantages is that when it goes out of our process into the Assistant Deputy Minister level, or to the Deputy Minister level, because they have committees some Deputies might say 'well, no, we're not supporting of that', and if enough Deputies agree with it, it's gone. So it … might be toned down, or the strong recommendation is not to go that way.

Such tension, between the economic prerogatives of government officials and the operational dynamics within the semi-autonomous departments over which they preside, was considered problematic by many participants. Indeed, despite attempts at finding viable areas for balance and compromise with First Nations, the process of passing recommendations upwards constrained any possibility of achieving a more co-operative, concessionary approach. It served to impose the overarching priorities of government at a point beyond which further consultation could occur, retracting any possibility for compromise and rendering the mediation process ineffective relative to its potential. The material consequences of this were discussed by participants from the LUS in direct relation to the conservation area requests submitted by a First Nation:

> [W]here it looked like from our perspective, us being more neutral, that there was more potential … not huge, don't get me [wrong], but I think we could have done a little more over in that area, because there seemed to be some land that was vacant. You know, [it] wasn't a lot, maybe a 6–8 km zone around their reserve, but it would have given them a little bit of buffer. But it was deemed to be potential oil sands, and so those departments on the economic side ruled the day and it didn't go through.
>
> (Participant A, LUS)

This official opposition to non-economic interests is in alignment with the LARP and its associated documents, which continue the emphasis on 'sustainable growth' seen in its precursor policies and strategies. The LARP's Terms of Reference clearly state that 'regional plans are designed to integrate and achieve – not hinder – the Government of Alberta's environmental, economic and social objectives over the long term' (Government of Alberta 2009b: 3). Indeed, the LARP describes one of its key purposes as ensuring that '[o]pportunities for the responsible exploration, development and extraction of energy, mineral and coal resources are maintained' (Government of Alberta 2012a: 41), also noting that the management intent of conservation areas is 'not considered compatible' with the land disturbance associated with such activities (ibid.: 30). Ultimately, official opposition to the creation of conservation areas on potential deposits of bitumen has its basis in levels of government much higher than those actually engaged in the consultation process, and it is the primacy of economic growth at these levels that restricts the opportunities available for a more conciliatory approach at the operational level, where consultation is actually conducted.

Mirroring comments made by Participant F from FNIRD 1, that '[t]he government want to go full steam ahead, but First Nations are asking them to do it in stages', this implicit congruence, between the government's desire to exploit oil sand deposits and the associated tendency to veto recommendations which may inhibit or slow down acquisition of this goal, is further illuminated by the consultation that occurred on the South Saskatchewan Regional Plan (see Government of Alberta 2014a). This was developed after the LARP, for the geographical area south of the oil sands deposit. As Participant A from the LUS noted:

> [W]e think our South Saskatchewan Plan is a better plan because more was heard and approved. I think there were opportunities in the Lower Athabasca where we could have maybe done something, and that's just strictly from my understanding of what was out there, and some of those opportunities have been lost. It doesn't mean that there isn't some still left, but it all depends; if the government says 'well, we're willing to slow down some of the mineable stuff because you're really in marginal stuff', then that could really change the equation.

This not only reflects the variable depth of consultation and accommodation conducted with First Nations throughout Alberta, but also further demonstrates the direct association between such variability and the economic value of the land on which First Nations hold their traditional territories. The same participant went on to note that 'we have done a pretty good job consulting and engaging [as the Land Use Secretariat]', but '[w]here the Government of Alberta may not meet a test of, say, the Supreme Court … is how did we accommodate that information, that desire to have these lands set aside' (Participant A, LUS). As can be seen, the answer to such a question relates in no small part to the location of a First Nation in relation to recoverable oil sands.

One frequently suggested way of overcoming this impasse was through the co-management of resources – an approach which sees government share

decision-making power over a specific area with other relevant stakeholders. This would allow multiple interested parties, and not only the Government of Alberta, to direct oil sands extraction at the more strategic level. However, the First Nations noted that 'government have declined. [Their] argument is: '[I]f we do it for you we'd have to do it for all First Nations' (Participant A, FNIRD 1). Although this was followed by the comment '[w]ell, so what? That shouldn't make a difference' (ibid.), industry participants disagreed with such an argument, asserting that 'the worry is if each company had to do a separate agreement on each project, with a separate First Nation, you're going to end up with a dog's breakfast of a development' (Participant A, Industry). Members of the LUS were more sympathetic. Indeed, their efforts to move towards some of the ideas within a co-management model have been blocked by higher level officials in the past, with the difficulties encountered being described as tied to context. According to Participant B of the LUS:

> I've put in proposals. I've sent position papers up to say, you know, if the Minister, if the NRTA and all those other things prohibit us from handing over decision making could we make some sort of advisory system beneath, where the Minister could still hold onto the ultimate decision making power, but we could enhance the consultation process, or sort of enhance the deliberation to make … the collaborative recommendation. If I submitted that four years ago … I'd get laughed out of government. But now I've got a Premier who's hinting around those five First Nations in the Lower Athabasca Region that he wants to set [up] a, what he's calling an 'issues table' with them. So I went up with the premier back in November to meet with those Chiefs and he sat down with them and he said 'listen, the way we're doing business isn't working … we end up in Court all the time, this isn't a way to continue working together'. He said that it's his priority to set up an issue table with them to start to work on some things like co-management. He actually said the word and I almost fell off my chair.

And Participant A of the ACO noted:

> I think we could make some headway if government … if we were open to having discussions we traditionally have not been willing to enter into. Things like co-management … or something akin to revenue sharing. Right now, in our current market, that discussion would be very difficult to even broach, let alone possibly heading into an election.

The fundamental element shared by these two perspectives is not simply the influence of context in inhibiting achievement of more effective consultation arrangements, although it could be broadly categorised as such. Instead, a far more specific characteristic is demonstrated: an aversion to regulatory change which could instil systemic uncertainty into the process governing industrial operation and expansion. Indeed, the specific references made to the problematic nature of court cases in the first quote, and the political-economic constraints imposed by the drop in the price of conventional crude in the second, suggest that giving greater decision-making power to First Nations, through the introduction of co-management in particular, would risk compounding the economic consequences of such circumstances by introducing into the regulatory system another potential barrier to expansion. Indeed, one participant, who had spent decades in government prior to undertaking their role at the time of interview, regarded Treaties and their associated rules surrounding land access to be one of '[t]he big impediments to the growth of our economy' (Participant A, Research Organisation 1). Such a position echoes the reality that '[w]ith oil and gas, time is of the essence. Time is money, so to speak' (Participant A, ESRD). As co-management introduces another layer into the regulatory framework, and one which produces not only time delays but also the possibility of project relocation or even veto, it is clear why such an aversion exists, particularly in a policy context where growth of the oil sands industry is defined as the primary objective.

Despite government reluctance, Participant B from the LUS considered political support to be 'edging that way', in the direction of an overarching strategy more closely aligned to the principles of co-management. Alienated from other evidence, such a shift seems to signal a sudden and uncharacteristic benevolence on behalf of the provincial government. This, however, is misplaced, particularly in light of the provincial and federal historical record in dealing with First Nations. Indeed, the real reason for this change of approach was described by Participant D from the Energy Regulator:

> [I]t's all court cases … this is what you'll find out about Canada. They'll (government) say we want to negotiate, we prefer to negotiate than litigate, but any changes that have come to First Nations have come through litigation, have been through litigation, and I don't think it's going to change for a while yet.

The consequences of such trials were visible in almost every interview, where discussions touched upon the influence of the then-recent case of *Tsilhqot'in Nation* v. *British Columbia [2014] 2 SCR 257* (hereafter *Tsilhqot'in*). A landmark decision by the Supreme Court of Canada, the Tsilhqot'in First Nation was granted Aboriginal Title to 680 square miles of the land on which it had historically occupied. Despite this applying to the non-Treaty context of British Columbia, and it having an unlikely or immediate influence on Alberta due to the province's coverage by numbered treaties, there was definite concern on behalf of industry and government surrounding the successes of this First Nation, and others, at the Supreme Court. As noted by Participant A from the Consultants:

> [M]y advice to companies, and when I worked for one, they said 'well we got better lawyers than the Aboriginals', and I said 'you know what? You have a choice between going to court and going to work. They'll win … you don't stand a chance in the courts'. Literally, the evidence is almost overwhelmingly in favour of indigenous interests.

Understood in this context, the political consideration given to the idea of co-management can be viewed as a means by which government and industry are able to retain overarching decision-making power while simultaneously placating First Nations, redirecting them away from the court system and any judgments which would force a change in government behaviour. Indeed, to address many of the concerns surrounding cumulative environmental impacts, an effective co-management system would need to provide opportunity for the 'sterilisation', or non-development, of bitumen. The unlikelihood of such an approach is reflected in a comment made by Participant B from the LUS, in discussing the request by a First Nation for a 'buffer zone' around their village:

> We would have to go to those three or four companies and say to them 'here's 20 million dollars for the lease that you bought from us five years ago. Sorry, you're out of luck, we've sterilised the resource underneath the ground and we've sterilised the land'. That's a huge, huge policy decision. That's a huge decision for the government to have to make, right? To say, you know, to the lobby group 'oh, by the way, those four companies that were going to make a billion dollars out of a SAGD *(Steam Assisted Gravity Drainage)* operation, they're out of business because a First Nation pushed us to build an oasis for them'. That's a huge precedent, it's a huge decision.

Considering this, the primacy given to the oil deposits within the development of the LARP, and the reluctance attached to regulatory alterations which may inhibit industrial expansion and operation, none of the evidence suggests that government would pursue a co-management model for reasons other than to avoid further challenges and opposition to expansion, particularly through the courts.

Throughout the process of developing the LARP it is clear that First Nations have been heard but not listened to, consulted but not accommodated. Their input was omitted from the final inventory of conservation areas because of its incompatibility with the predetermined purpose of the plan, and any movement towards a more conciliatory approach suggested by those involved with its administration have been similarly sidelined by actors higher in the government hierarchy. Indeed, it would appear that only the coercive authority of the SCC can force change to the contrary, the threat of which has stimulated government reception to the more open-ended approach of resource co-management. That said, a number of participants were sceptical about how much power would be delegated if co-management were to become a reality. Indeed, the label encompasses a broad spectrum of approaches, each of which delegates a different range and proportion of powers to First Nations (see Doyle 2015). Considering the aversion even to regulatory modifications which may introduce time delays into the scheme of oil sands development, it is not unreasonable to imagine that if a government-advocated approach were to be introduced then it would be constrained along similar lines. Nevertheless, the space which has opened up as a result of First Nation successes at the Supreme Court appears to have created opportunities for change at this level, however slight, which were absent before. As such, recourse to the courts is clearly a site of vulnerability for government and, indirectly, industry.

The disregarding of First Nation voices at the strategic level of the LARP also brings to the fore a discrepancy with the extensive consultation purported to have occurred during its creation (see Chapter 3). With this representing the only characteristic associated with 'strong' ecological modernisation throughout policy and strategy, the 'weak' strain of the philosophy not only underpins the objectives for 'sustainable development' but also the consultation that occurred on the latest strategy for its acquisition. Ultimately, with the LARP sitting above the regulatory process, equipped to provide information on thresholds where necessary and inform direction of development on the landscape, the marginalisation underpinning its creation, and the manner in which its default position is one advocating industrial expansion, occurred not least because of the challenge indigenous participation would pose to the growth of extractive activities across the entire oil sands deposit.

The Marginalisation of First Nation Voices and Abstraction of Treaty Rights from Material Reality

As outlined in Chapter 2, the disposition of land leases is the first step within the 'approval' stage of the regulatory process. It is also the first point at which First Nations directed criticism at the regulatory process governing individual project approvals, with their key contention being that government agencies sell these leases before consulting on the possible consequences for Treaty rights (Participants A and B, FNIRD 1). Participant B from the LUS explained the rationale behind the Government of Alberta's approach:

> In some jurisdictions in Canada, at the issuance of a lease stage, there's actually consultation with a First Nation … because in their mind that's the watermark for when the land becomes taken up. We say no, we're not going to consult at the lease phase because the company might walk away from the lease, they might not actually do anything with the land; we're not sure it's taken up until the company proposes an activity.

This justification acknowledges that converting land 'parcels' into 'producing leases' is not guaranteed, and that their development largely depends on whether exploration is a success following purchase. This does, however, disregard the extent to which the process of land disposition encourages oil sands development from the outset (see Chapter 7).

Following the granting of land leases, First Nation criticism centred on the way in which the Government of Alberta passed initial consultation responsibilities to industrial proponents prior to project approval. Justifications for this delegation were based on the purported expertise held by companies themselves: 'A lot is delegated to industry because in order to mitigate impacts they're in the best position to do so' (Participant C, ACO). However, a tension arises at the point where this consultation mechanism meets indigenous concerns about cumulative environmental effects:

> First Nations cannot broach issues to do with cumulative effects at the point of consultation with industry, and government delegates all of that to industry. They can only do it, and deal with issues like project emissions, on a project-by-project basis.
>
> (Participant A, FNIRD 1)

In light of this, the initial point at which industrial proponents are required to consult with First Nations reveals a restricted capacity to address one of their key environmental concerns. This is exacerbated by a 'nuance' referred to by Participant B of the LUS – that First Nations are not only concerned about cumulative effects, but also the subsequent impact of these effects on the exercise of Treaty rights. It therefore follows that not only are individual companies unable to view even the first stage of harm, the cumulative environmental effects, but that they are also blind to the cultural loss which results from its materialisation. Speaking of those instances where concerns surrounding cumulative effects are raised with proponents, Participant A from Industry explained that, in business, '[a] lot of the time it's described as a provincial matter'. This was made in reference to the lack of both capacity and perceived responsibility for industry to address such concerns.

Even when consultation focuses on mitigating environmental impacts at the relatively limited project level, the amount delegated to individual proponents raises questions about consistency and depth. Broadly accepted across the spectrum of groups interviewed, the picture painted is one of an irregularity of quality, of an industry characterised by variation in the extent to which individual corporations conduct consultation to a level above the minimum standard advocated by the ACO. Considering that the industry contains over 30 companies directly engaged in extractive operations, this is a cause for concern. As Participant A from Industry described it, 'We can take our consultation process, we can slow it down, we can work with the people, but then there might be twenty other companies that are not.' This variability is reflected in the differences between individual companies in the region, mirroring similarly inconsistent adherence regulatory standards more generally:

> [T]here are companies that you have great respect for and you may not have to go and look at them frequently because they're really good. And there are others that you just, boy, they're, I use the word 'edge', they're 'edge companies'. They'll do exactly what they have to up to the law, but they won't go any further than that. And some of them are very big players; it's just their business philosophy.
>
> (Participant A, LUS)

Several participants noted that a drop in global oil prices would be likely to cause a rolling back of consultation practices which were willingly deployed over and above the standard required, linking such variability to the primacy of economics in corporate decision-making. As Participant A from the LUS explained,

> When you talk to CEO's and Vice Presidents and Presidents, you know, informally, and not putting stuff down in writing, a lot of them will say 'we're willing to do anything we can to get that social license … but the bottom line is still the dollar. We can't lose, we can't go out of business. I can't do everything and then all of a sudden I'm out of business because it's just too costly'.

Participant B from the Consultants concurred, noting that 'industry's not going to do stuff that typically government doesn't ask them to'. Taken together, participants broadly recognised that the quality of consultation was determined by the approaches adopted by individual corporations and the suitability of economic context, with the extent of the former fluctuating in accordance with variations in the latter.

Despite this reflecting the reality of oil sands development, where 'good players, bad players and those that fall in between' exist throughout the industry (Participant A, FNIRD 2), it should be recalled that the final decision pertaining to the adequacy of proponent consultation lies with the ACO. As such, this agency also drew criticism from First Nations who considered it to 'only work at industry's side': 'They basically see consultation as information, or giving information to First Nations and receiving some in return. Consultation is a minimal process' (Participant B, FNIRD 1). The source of this criticism focused on the inability of the ACO to request that companies account for cumulative effects during consultation. Members of the agency acknowledged this, noting that '[t]he problem is that the concerns dealt with by the ACO are specific to the process' and, as this is 'a narrow process', issues surrounding cumulative environmental effects 'are more appropriately addressed elsewhere' (Participant C, ACO). This 'elsewhere' is a reference to the LARP, the creation of which, as seen above, was characterised by the exclusion of indigenous input.

In light of this, the fundamental issue with regard to delegation is not only that industry lacks consistency in its approach, although this is certainly problematic, but that the basic standard of consultation expected by the ACO is considered inadequate by First Nations. Indeed, they characterised the ACO as being 'very administrative' (Participant A, FNIRD 2), facilitating a process that is blind to detrimental cumulative environmental and Treaty impacts outside of those caused by isolated projects:

> [I]t seems … to set out a process which is flawed, and which has systemic discrimination, where you can never actually demonstrate impact because the Alberta government is collecting information that's based on trying to understand impacts based on a site within a box, within where the activity is going to occur by the company. Nothing outside of that box … it seems to me that it's creating a system that … [is] very difficult to wade through and actually have a good discussion about what those impacts could be.
>
> (Participant A, FNIRD 2)

This criticism was tied to the provincial government's narrow interpretation of Treaty rights. Outlined in its 2005 and 2013 policies on consultation (see Government of Alberta 2005, 2013a), this interpretation underpins the ACO's minimum standard of consultation by setting out the content of said rights in light of SCC judgments. The basic divergence of these views was summarised by Participant C from the ACO, where 'First Nations believe Treaty rights is to a broad suite of things, whereas Alberta believes the right only extends to hunt, fish and trap for food'. Participant A from FNIRD 2 expanded on this with direct regard to oil sands developments, demonstrating not only the differences in interpretation but also the potential implications of such divergence:

> Alberta states that the Aboriginal and Treaty rights to fish, hunt and trap is not pegged to any site-specific location. So it's more about the right to hunt as opposed to the right to hunt on that little plot over there … or the plot across the river. Those are not protected, but it's about your ability and right to do it somewhere out on the landscape. And recently I got a letter from the Aboriginal Consultation Office that reaffirmed also that not only is it not site-specific, but your right to hunt is not species-specific. And so a good question would be, what does that mean? Because they've not actually said that in writing before. What that would mean to me is that Alberta is looking at protecting First Nations' rights to hunt, fish and trap on the landscape, but not guarantee any specific location, and not guaranteeing that there'll be a certain species or abundance of a certain

> quality in a certain area. So that, of course, is a direct opposite interpretation about how First Nations view it, because … our interpretation of Aboriginal Treaty rights are to all parts of the land…. So that interpretation is really at the opposite ends of the scale of how you look at what a [Treaty] right is.

In divorcing Treaty rights from the material quality and quantity of resources which underpin their execution, the Government of Alberta has adopted a relatively diluted interpretation of their content. This enables fewer environmental and Treaty impact factors to be taken into account during consultation, narrowing issues open to discussion and permitting decisions on adequacy of consultation to be determined at a point much earlier in the regulatory process than First Nations consider appropriate. As such, the ACO not only oversees a narrow consultation process governed by a project-by-project approach to understanding impacts, but deploys a distinctly abstracted interpretation of Treaty rights that further dilutes the breadth and depth of issues on which First Nations are consulted.

Although the ACO attracted considerable criticism, their approach is informed by the 2013 policy on consultation. Despite participants recognising the narrow interpretation of Treaty rights to be rooted in this policy, this was frequently accompanied by concurrent recognition that the policy was finalised without adequate integration of First Nation input. Indeed, engagement with First Nations on both the 2005 and 2013 policies bear similarity to the consultation process deployed in development of the LARP, in that they both excluded substantial proportions of indigenous input:

> So, we came out with our first policy in 2005, we came out with our next policy in 2013. The first one didn't work, wasn't supported by First Nations, so we kind of scratched our head; okay what did we get wrong? We asked them, let's talk about that. [They said] 'Well, you didn't engage us the way we wanted to be engaged'. So, in 2008 we went into a policy review that took years, and we engaged one to one with each community, but it was the same model. Go out and look for it, seek input, and then bring it back and see what you can come up with. We did that for this policy; still not supported.
>
> (Participant A, ACO)

This approach was not only recognised in specific relation to Alberta's consultation policy, but was viewed as characteristic of the province's approach to consulting with First Nations more generally – a feature which is dictated and justified by these underpinning policies on consultation:

> The push back … not just for First Nations but for Aboriginal Peoples in general, is government like to come out and say 'hey, this is what we're

> doing, tell us what you think', and then they go back and write out their policy and their paper and they've never included a single thing of what they've heard.'
>
> (Participant D, Energy Regulator)

> What we've traditionally done is we'll say 'okay, we're going to develop a policy around this and we'll go consult and we'll gather up this information input, from Aboriginal communities and other stakeholders, and we'll take it back, dissect it and analyse it, come up with something and then put it back out and say, you know, here's our policy, thanks for the input'. The reality is that it doesn't work in the Aboriginal context. I've never seen it work and I've been doing this work now for over a decade. It just doesn't work.
>
> (Participant A, ACO)

Although Participant C from the ACO attempted to explain this lack of progress by recourse to it 'only being 10 years' since the 2005 Mikisew decision, the situation experienced by First Nations, with regard to their input into both the 2005 and 2013 policies on consultation, is one characterised by repeated marginalisation. Over a decade may have passed since the duty to consult was enshrined in law, but the lack of progress made during this time only lends further support to a comment made by one of the First Nation participants: 'It's an attitudinal change that's required [–] the attitude of government to the duty to consult [and] Treaty rights. They pay lip service to consultation' (Participant B, FNIRD 1).

Throughout this initial phase of the regulatory process, encompassing the selling of land leases through to the decision confirming the adequacy of the duty to consult and accommodate, consultation is either non-existent, as with regard to the former, or narrow and unable to account for cumulative environmental effects, with regard to the latter. Set against a backdrop of a-then-incomplete land use plan that excluded substantial portions of indigenous input prior to its release, the subsequent consultation on individual projects is seen by First Nations as occurring too late in the process. Indeed, the land has already been divided up by the time consultation is required by the ACO. Even then, the depth of consultation carried out by individual project proponents varies according to the corporation in question, causing the issues around cumulative environmental effects to be omitted from discussion and redirected to the growth-orientated LARP.

Facilitated by a narrow interpretation of Treaty rights on behalf of the ACO, which abstracts hunting, fishing, and trapping rights from the material environmental dimensions which permit their exercise, the 2005 and 2013 policies on consultation underpinning these interpretations were developed with little integration of First Nation input. It would therefore appear that not only are First Nation voices excluded as part of each project-by-project consultation, but that this exclusion is premised on some previous higher level exclusion, be it on the LARP or the provincial policies on consultation. This forces First Nations to bear the brunt of concessions by eroding their ability to hunt, fish, and trap on the land. As such, the pattern of cultural loss identified in Chapter 1 can be seen to result, at least in part, from an operational process characterised by the continued and systemic marginalisation of First Nation input. The restricted participation of these groups goes beyond the LARP, extending to the applications for individual projects and the policies on consultation themselves. As such, the feature of 'strong' ecological modernisation identified throughout the policies and strategies, which suggested extensive consultation with First Nations had occurred, can be seen to be almost entirely without foundation. In reality, it is very much the 'weak' strain of the philosophy that is being operationalised in both consultation policy and practice.

Justifying Marginalisation: Paternalistic Provincialism and the Disinterested Stance of Government in Modifying Consultation

Decisions which resulted in the marginalisation of First Nation concerns at this 'planning' stage of the regulatory process were described not as occurring in a vacuum, or through maliciousness, but as part of a more fundamental justification for acting on behalf of the provincial majority. Indeed, many of the participants expressed frustration at the institutional arrangements serving to exclude First Nation concerns. Nevertheless, there was evidence to suggest the existence of an ideological, yet no less operational, institutional bias against the specific rights held by First Nations. This was communicated through the justifications made for regulatory decisions, taking the form of a conceptual coupling, where a perceived moral authority to act on behalf of an imagined majority was anchored to the assumption that resource development was in their common interest.

Several of the participants framed this marginalisation as a form of institutionalised bias, considering prejudice to enter consultation procedures through its governing agencies. This was described as having both individual and systemic elements, and as being realised in the present but having roots in Canada's colonial history:

> It's a white man constructed process. So there's very little in the way in which we go, typically, on an oil project of one sort or another, that we go into a consultative process that pays attention to any of the cultural realities or process wishes of First Nations. So we've already created a structure that is ours, not theirs, meaning whites not [Aboriginal] … it's not a collectively agreed upon structure.
>
> (Participant B, Consultants)

While this speaks to regulatory characteristics giving contemporary form to a historical bias, participants from FNIRD 1 described in greater detail the more micro-level conditions underpinning its manifestation. Participant A noted that the Government of Alberta 'treat us like any other stakeholder', considering the process to negate their specific rights. Such a reality has already been seen in the broad marginalisation of their input at the strategic level of land use planning, in consultation policy, and in their engagement in consultation on individual projects. Another participant similarly described how the pursuit of oil sands development comes into conflict with Treaty rights, but explained this tension as being associated with the province's broader reliance on the oil sands industry:

> It's about perceptions. Treaty and Aboriginal Rights get in the way, right? It [resource development] is for the greater good of society. Economic well-being drives attitudes, racial attitudes ... people have a problem with First Nations in Canada, and believe that they [First Nations] have special privileges.
>
> (Participant B, FNIRD 1)

During the course of the interviews this notion of indigenous rights serving to 'get in the way' of oil sands expansion was a recurring theme. While this was entwined with broader justifications surrounding what activities were in the best interests of the provincial majority, and has a number of related dimensions, the more direct 'racial attitudes' spoken about here were observed in one particular instance.

Although the findings overwhelmingly suggest that the Treaty rights of First Nations are being indirectly undermined by a more systemic, and somewhat structural, marginalisation of their concerns, via a consultation process which operates according to the pluralist assumption that expansive resource development is an unquestionable 'social good', another, more direct form of marginalisation was observed which has parity with First Nation comments on attitudinal prejudice. With the consultation process requiring agency recommendations to be ultimately decided on by government officials, the system has built within it a space in which the individual bias of those with power has the potential to influence outcomes. The risks associated with this were reflected in comments made by a participant from the Ministry of Environment and Sustainable Resource Development. Under any other scenario the singular origin of these comments would be disregarded as an outlier within the data, but the seniority of the participant's position, and associated role in departmental decision-making with regard to recommendations made during the regulatory process, gives greater significance to the content. Indeed, this participant was the most senior interviewed, being situated in the sphere of the provincial government. First, the specific constitutional rights held by Aboriginal peoples in relation to non-Aboriginals were viewed negatively, as though they conferred a degree of unwarranted privilege:

> If you've read the Constitution we're all equal, but Aboriginals are more equal than others.
>
> (Participant A, ESRD)

Such a comment embodied a derisory view on the source of antagonism between First Nations and the provincial government, where First Nation claims to being self-governing nations, which dates back to their status at the signing of the original numbered treaties, were treated disparagingly:

> The First Nations want government-to-government relations. What I would ask in response is, 'What country is on your passport?' Don't say that to them, though.
>
> (Participant A, ESRD)

The ideological imprint of colonialism is clearly visible in such comments, contributing a more targeted prejudicial agency to a process otherwise characterised by a relatively impersonal systemic marginalisation. They demonstrate how individual attitudes can penetrate a system of regulation which requires recommendations on consultation to be channelled through specific individuals for approval, also showing how public interest justifications may act as a vehicle for individual partiality, cloaking prejudice in the rhetoric of mutual benefit.

Although this individual bias is distinct, it must be understood as part of much more prevalent and indirect systemic and institutionalised bias, which the findings suggest operate through the more impersonal recourse to a notion of 'social good'. Confined to the interviews focusing on agencies involved with consultation, a very particular form of 'social good', manifest as provincialism, was invoked to justify the narrower, government interpretation of Treaty rights and concomitant consultation standards over those held by First Nations. Essentially, it was maintained that over-riding First Nation interpretations was justified because such marginalisation permitted oil sands expansion, which was understood to be for the good of the provincial majority. Indeed, the comments did not dispute the practice of over-riding First Nation interpretations, but juxtaposed, both implicitly and explicitly, First Nation rights against those interests assumed to be held by broader provincial society:

> Alberta's view is that revenue generated by resource development is … for the benefit of all Albertans.
>
> (Participant A, ACO)

> The development of the resources in the Province is to the benefit of all Albertans.
>
> (Participant B, ACO)

> We work on behalf of all Albertans, everybody, not just First Nations.
> (Participant C, ACO)

> At a practical level we've tried to balance industry with First Nations, where what we do has positive outcomes for all Albertans.
> (Participant A, ESRD)

Such language is mirrored in the overarching policies relevant to the ACO and the LUS. In the 2013 policy on consultation (Government of Alberta 2013a: 3), it is noted that the purpose of consultation by the Government of Alberta is to reconcile First Nation Treaty rights 'within its mandate to manage provincial Crown Lands and Resources for the benefit of all Albertans'. This is an echo of the 2005 policy on consultation, which was 'designed to create an approach to consultation that benefits all Albertans' (Government of Alberta 2005: 2). Similarly, the purpose of the 2008 LUF is to 'propose a path to the future that Albertans want' (Government of Alberta 2008b: 15). The 2009 Alberta Land Stewardship Act establishes the legal basis for land use plans, describing its purpose as 'providing a means to plan for the future, recognising the need to manage activity to meet the reasonably foreseeable needs of the current and future generations of Albertans, including aboriginal peoples' (Government of Alberta 2009c: 4). Finally, the LARP is intended to inform decision-makers about how to manage activities so that they 'meet the reasonably foreseeable needs of current and future generations of Albertans', also specifically including aboriginal peoples in this conception (Government of Alberta 2012a: 8). The language of 'all Albertans' is also visible in several of the policies governing oil sands development stretching back to 1999, where it is used in conjunction with bitumen extraction to frame industrialisation of the resource as a provincial 'social good'. In this sense, the individual justifications given for over-riding First Nation interpretations of Treaty rights borrow credibility from the language deployed in broader policies and strategies governing oil sands extraction.

While reflecting Alberta's constitutional mandate to 'make laws in relation to … development, conservation and management of non-renewable natural resources' (Government of Canada 2013: 29–30), the references made to a specific provincial 'social good' during the interviews acted to discursively undermine the more specific and unique rights and interests of First Nations. By invoking the imagined wishes of a similarly imagined provincial majority, and automatically aligning such interests with expansive resource development, the more environmental aspects of First Nation rights and interests were rendered problematic. This is because such a process situates First Nation interests in opposition to this perceived majority goal. In this sense it reflects the 'moral majority' justifications spoken of by Beyleveld and Brownsword (2007: 272) – a pattern of reasoning used by states to oppose indigenous campaigns attempting to enshrine standards of Free, Prior and Informed Consent (FPIC) into national laws (see also Doyle 2015).

This justification for acting on behalf of some provincial majority allowed for decisions to be made in opposition to First Nation interests, and potentially in breach of their Treaty rights, without challenging the perceived moral integrity of the process. However, there was also simultaneous recognition that these decisions may not be meeting the legal duty to consult and accommodate, and that the SCC was the only institution with the authority to decide whether this was indeed the case. This deference to a higher authority created a space characterised by ambivalence, in which government agencies could act with relative impunity, under the comforting rubric of a provincialism anchored to extractives operations, until some future form of litigation forced them to change by expanding on First Nation Treaty rights. This was described by a variety of participants:

> So we don't know, for sure, like I don't know if all this work we've been doing, all this consultation and engagement we've been doing would satisfy the Supreme Court. Let's just say it goes all the way up. Will the Supreme Court say 'Alberta, you've done your job on consultation?' Yes or no? I have absolutely no idea.
>
> (Participant A, LUS)

> We'll come out with a policy, and we'll operate in a certain way, we'll get challenged, the Supreme Court will decide at some point, and give us further guidance, and then we'll operate under that further guidance and it continues to evolve. So it's this weird system of always … it ends up the Supreme Court dictates for the most part how things happen. We as a government take a minimalist approach until the Supreme Court forces us to inch a little further along.
>
> (Participant B, LUS)

> Really, the conversation boils down to 'what does case law in Canada tell us that we need to do to govern ourselves accordingly and to comply with it, and how we need to consult?' Because that's ultimately the authority in Canada … our court system and what it's telling us we need to do and how we need to define ourselves and our processes.
>
> (Participant A, ACO)

Indicative of an absence of proactive government guidance with regard to the duty to consult and accommodate, the situation described was one in which the expectation of First Nation litigation had become normalised. Indeed, this is such an omnipresent possibility that it appeared to provide the dominant standard by which agencies expect to validate the legality of their own decisions and processes. In this sense, the Government of Alberta is not taking a positive approach to the recognition of First Nation rights and interests, choosing instead to adopt a distinctively negative and almost casual stance that not only invites but provokes conflict and tension. It is as Participant A from Industry observed: 'All the policy is coming from Supreme Court decisions ... it's not government leading and knowing.' Ultimately, the potential illegality of existing consultation policy and practice was acknowledged by regulatory personnel, but the lack of official recognition given to existing practice by the SCC only served to permit its continuation in accordance with the 'moral majority' justification. Put another way, consultation policy and practice, while subordinating First Nation interpretations of Treaty rights and being potentially illegal, was justifiable in the present because the authority of the SCC had not yet validated the criticisms.

A third justification was also visible in comments made by participants who maintained positions higher in the government hierarchy, or had done so in the past. This was demonstrably paternalistic, proceeding from the basis that government aversion to expanding on its minimalist interpretation of Treaty rights was justified because of the benefits seen to accrue to First Nations under existing arrangements. The narrow government interpretation was considered to be conducive to an expansive pattern of resource extraction. In turn, this was seen by these higher-level participants as the most appropriate means for addressing what Participant A from FNIRD 1 labelled 'very serious social and economic concerns'. These issues actually formed the basis for the labelling of the situation in Canada as a 'crisis' by the UN Special Rapporteur on the Rights of Indigenous Peoples, where reference was made to the living conditions and employment rates being much lower among the indigenous population, and their incarceration and suicide rates much higher, than found for its non-indigenous population (Anaya 2013; see also Kirmayer *et al.* 2007). However, despite recognising these issues only one option was available for their resolution. This has parity with the 'social good' assumptions of 'all Albertans', in that the answer lies with greater First Nation engagement with processes of oil sands industrialisation:

> We're trying to help them build businesses to make them sustainable. We believe what happened over the last 200 years is that a remove ghetto system has developed. The key is education and business development.
>
> (Participant A, ESRD)

> [T]he Courts keep creating these new process rights and a lot of the problems that we're having right now [in First Nation communities], the dysfunction, is around processes that can't really resolve the underlying issues. They create very, very high time and money cost structures associated with development.
>
> (Participant A, Research Organisation 1)

Viewed through this lens, the prosperity of First Nations can be achieved only if recognition of their specific rights does not interrupt the overarching plan of action determined to be in their best interests. Here, that plan of action is the expansion of the oil sands industry. It is therefore recognised that the government's interpretation of Treaty rights is opposed by First Nations, but also that this interpretation is justified because it is seen to be for their own good. Within this context, the possibility that First Nations may be able to determine their own, alternative path of development is not an option. By assuming that industrial expansion is for the benefit of 'all Albertans', *including* First Nations, the specific rights of the latter are negated by equating them with the expansionary interests assumed to be maintained by the former, meaning First Nation interests are never fully appreciated or accounted for. This undermines the consultation process from the outset because what is in the best interests of First Nations has already been decided, establishing a paternalistic pathway from which deviation is not possible. As Participant A from Research Organisation 1 noted with respect to developing the economic capacity of First Nations, '[S]ubstantive Treaty rights will get in the way and process rights will get in the way.' This culminated in perceived tension between the SCC and the provincial government: '[T]here's a really fundamental lack of interest on the parts of government to further develop the process rights base' (Participant A, Research Organisation 1). The precise reason for this is clear: because such rights risk interrupting growth of the oil sands industry.

Conclusion

As can be seen, First Nations face systemic marginalisation throughout the initial 'planning stage' of the regulatory process. The three key clusters of process-specific tension, surrounding consultation on the LARP, the level of consultation delegated to industry proponents, and the Crown's narrow interpretation of Treaty rights, are anchored to an underpinning paternalistic justification for subsuming the specific rights of First Nations into an overarching interest imagined to represent the province's population as a whole. As this perceived interest is aligned with the expansion of oil sands extraction, any consultation or modification to the regulatory process is weighed against the potential threat such actions would have on achieving this objective. This includes expanding on the narrow government interpretation of Treaty rights. Considering the limited accommodation of First Nation input throughout this stage of the process, and the similarly limited inclusion of their considerations into the LARP and policies governing consultation, the situation can only be described as one of widespread and perennial systemic marginalisation. With this occurring under the auspices of a pattern of industrial expansion perceived to be in the interests of a provincial majority, decisions resulting in the negation of First Nation rights and interests become justified despite knowledge of their harmful consequences.

Chapter 5

Issues with the 'Approval' Stage of the Regulatory Process

The previous chapter demonstrated that, at the 'planning' stage of the regulatory process, the input of First Nations has been roundly excluded from the creation of policy and strategy, with the marginalisation of their voices also extending to consultation that occurs on individual oil sands projects. While the former of these issues is characterised by consultation without accommodation, particularly when discussing responses to cumulative environmental effects, the latter exhibits an absence of both. This is because the procedural component is delegated to individual proponents who cannot see these overarching issues. With this project-level marginalisation being premised on the provincial government's diluted interpretation of Treaty rights, which effectively annexes the material conditions required for their exercise, and justified through the use of 'moral majority' reasonings, the 'planning' stage of the process operates to displace First Nation concerns into the future instead of addressing them in the present. As such, the marginalisation of their voices creates a space in which policy objectives can proceed uninhibited and unaltered by the duty to consult. The subsequent 'approval' stage therefore forms the final and most visible point at which First Nation concerns are subordinated to those pertaining to capital. The difference here, however, is that it occurs in a different forum and according to a different test.

As explained in Chapter 2, the hearings at the 'approval' stage of the regulatory process allow the energy regulator to make a decision on whether construction of an oil sands project is in the 'public interest'. Over the 12 public hearing documents analysed, the factors underpinning this consideration have been consistent with the legislation governing hearing Panel decision-making: through examination of the social, economic, and environmental impacts of each project. However, there is yet to be a single hearing in which an oil sands project has been rejected, ultimately because 'the public interest lies not in eliminating risk but by managing risks so that they are "acceptable"' (Low 2011: 38). As such, the means for mitigating the risks highlighted by First Nations in these hearings requires examination. Here, analysis of the 12 oil sands projects approved between 1997 and 2013 is presented, with a focus on how the hearing Panels address First Nation concerns in each. The 2013 project for expansion of the Shell Jackpine mine is the latest open-pit mine scheme to be approved, with a subsequent project awaiting a decision in 2019. Reflecting the organisational alterations outlined in Chapter 2, the term 'Panel' is here used to refer to both the 'Boards' and 'Panels' that have presided over the hearings since the mid-1990s. While their name has changed over time, the function of these regulatory bodies has not.

Presented according to the three periods in which Panel decisions on expansion were clustered, 1997–1999, 2004–2007, and 2011–2013, this chapter demonstrates that the process of determining the 'public interest' is founded on a particular pattern of reasoning. Through recourse to a future point in time, where anticipated techno-scientific advances are expected to mitigate the risks raised by First Nations in the present, the Panels repeatedly grant approvals despite lacking data on the possible impacts which could arise, or the effectiveness of possible mitigation measures. This is visible throughout each of the three sections analysed: water quantity, water quality, and the more general area of cumulative effects management, making repetition a defining characteristic of this chapter. Although this has been avoided elsewhere, it is here intentional and necessary as it serves to highlight a consistent aspect of the deliberation process – that the same techno-scientific risk-based approach to approving projects under the rubric of the 'public interest' has been utilised time and time again, over almost two decades and without deviation.

1997–1999: Absent Data and Unforeseen Consequences

Between 1997 and 1999, five approvals were issued under the public interest test, all of which are characterised by an uncertainty about uncertainty. Put another way, and with the benefit of hindsight, the Panels do not know what they do not know. This reflects the immaturity of the industry. During this time the Panels are only just beginning to appreciate the scale of oil sands operations, leading to an emerging recognition of the types of initiatives required to address the resulting regional effects. However, at no point does this appear to challenge a project application. It only results in greater recourse to a future point in time where expected technological advances will mitigate the risks raised by First Nations. As will be seen, this marks the beginning of an almost two-decade period in which such faith is deployed as a risk-mitigation strategy, allowing for projects to be approved under the rubric of the 'public interest' despite the widespread unavailability of data pertaining to both impacts and the most appropriate means for their redress.

1997–1999: Water Quantity and In-flow Needs

The reliability of data on water management, groundwater levels, and surface water quantity attracted criticism from First Nations throughout most of the approval documents. Here, the main area of concern is with establishing a minimum amount of water in the Athabasca River at a particular point in time. This level is generally referred to as the 'in-flow needs' (IFN). Absent from the concerns expressed by First Nations during the 1997 Steepbank (AEUB 1997a), 1997 Aurora (AEUB 1997b), 1999 Millennium (AEUB 1999a), and 1999 Muskeg River Project decisions (AEUB 1999b), the lack of consideration given during this period reflects the incipient nature of the industry and associated lack of awareness surrounding its potential impacts. Nevertheless, independent of this input, and despite its complete absence from the initial Steepbank and Aurora decisions, the Panel did consider the impact of water withdrawal at the project level in the subsequent Millennium and Muskeg River project decisions. In the former, the proponent's 'efforts to maximise water reuse and minimize water releases' (AEUB 1999a: 29) was noted, whereas in the latter, monitoring was advocated as a means of meeting the flow volume requirements established by government agencies (AEUB 1999b: 34). Crucially, however, such considerations did not extend to the sections on cumulative effects, meaning that these four approvals were granted without any substantive consideration of their collective impact on regional water levels.

It is not until the 1999 Mildred Lake decision that concerns about water quantity are raised by First Nations, exhibiting the delayed recognition associated with various forms of environmental victimisation (see Hall 2015). Sharing these concerns (see AEUB 1999c: 18), the Panel's response is not to suspend the project until empirical data can be gathered on the impact itself, or attain greater certainty on the means by which such risk could be mitigated. Instead, it invokes a faith in the future capacity of science and technology to lessen the risk following approval:

> The Board encourages Syncrude and other operators to place a priority on developing strategies and technologies to maximize water withdrawal, minimize water reuse, and decrease on-site water inventories. The Board will require Syncrude to report every year on its effort in this regard … [and for] Syncrude to actively participate in addressing the water management issues raised under the RSDS.
>
> (Ibid.: 18–19)

Although this continues to allude to project-specific mitigation, visible here is also the relatively brief suggestion that, in future, such risks need to be addressed at a regional level and in participation with others. It is around this point that regional multi-stakeholder initiatives are recognised as necessary to tackle cumulative environmental effects. Nevertheless, the implication of this particular response is that sufficient evidence does not yet exist to require a specific measure for mitigation, but that, at some point in the future, it will. This carries within it the associated notions that techno-scientific mitigation is materially possible, that the expected advances will work even if developed, and that the actors tasked with pursuing these solutions have the capacity to do so. Without questioning these assumptions, the suggested means of mitigation were considered an adequate response under the 'public interest' test and formed part of the justification for the Mildred Lake project approval.

1997–1999: Water Quality and Tailings Management

The impact of oil sands development on the quality of water in northern Alberta was another of the concerns expressed consistently throughout the decision documents. Although this is related to many different aspects of development, two of the key areas in which these arose relate to tailings management practices and end pit lake (EPL) technology. Consisting of the waste by-product of oil sands extraction processes, tailings are a mixture of water, sand, silt, clay, unrecovered hydrocarbons, and other contaminants (Timoney 2013). This liquid is stored in large open lakes, known as 'tailings ponds', where the mixture undergoes processing in an attempt to separate water from waste. The purpose of this is to solidify the latter so that the land can be eventually reclaimed. EPL technology is a variation on this method of storage, but instead of creating lakes above ground the mixture is stored in a post-mining pit and becomes a permanent feature of the final reclaimed landscape. Although the latter of these methods is the newest, the uncertainties associated with both tailings pond and EPL technology are present throughout Panel deliberations.

First recognised in the 1997 Steepbank decision, and echoed in the 1997 Aurora hearing, uncertainty about the efficacy of tailings pond technology, along with the concurrent expectation of further technological development to address this post-approval, was present from the beginning. As the Panel notes, '[T]ailings management by CT (consolidated tailings) technology is still under development … full scale trials of CT are required to understand this process' (AEUB 1997a: 8). By 1999, in the decision on the Shell Muskeg River mine, the ACFN were raising concerns about the impact of water quality on human health. In response to this, the Panel again deployed a future faith in science and technology to mitigate the risk associated with the uncertainty. Recognising that 'the experimental nature of CT technology … continues to be of some concern', it here approves the plan with the caveat that 'future amendments may be required should more suitable technologies or closure methods be developed within the operating life of the mine' (AEUB 1999b: 34). Adding a requirement for 'further research', the decision to approve the project under the rubric of the 'public interest' was made without a full understanding of the efficacy or environmental effects of tailings technology. This was in addition to the associated expectation that future techno-scientific advances would both address the knowledge gaps and, through subsequent application, mitigate the risks.

1997–1999: The Need for Cumulative Effects Monitoring

Although the more specific concerns of water quantity and quality have regional dimensions, the means for addressing cumulative environmental effects are generally considered separately within the hearings. The first three projects for which decision documents are available, the 1997 Suncor Steepbank, 1997 Syncrude Aurora, and 1999 Suncor Millennium mines, show that First Nations did not raise any concerns about cumulative environmental effects. This is not only consistent with the decision of First Nations to initially participate in industrial development, but also echoes the reality of the situation – that these projects mark the very beginning of rapid industrial development in the region. Concerns surrounding cumulative effects had not yet materialised. However, the Panel does consider the need to enhance 'the efficiency of individual application reviews' through 'a broadly accepted regional plan' as early as 1997, noting that such 'cooperative effort might reduce resource losses, enhance environmental protection, and reduce costs' (AEUB 1997b: 29). That said, the overriding concern here is with making the application process more efficient for industrial expansion. It is not until 1999, with the hearing for the Suncor Millennium project, that the Panel begins to recognise a pressing need for regional mechanisms to address the cumulative environmental effects of rapid industrial expansion:

> The Board believes that ... the combination of CEEM and RSDS provides a means to address regional issues. It is satisfied that all uncertainties associated with the cumulative impact predictions, including size of study area and the need for wildlife corridors can be managed through processes such as the RSDS.
>
> (AEUB 1999a: 37–38)

Visible here is the first instance in which the Panel attempts to mitigate the risk associated with approval by citing its confidence in the capacity of CEEM. This is the industry-led, multi-stakeholder initiative tasked with studying the 72 issues of research priority outlined in the province's 1999 RSDS. The CEEM would later transform into CEMA, as referenced throughout later decision documents.

This pattern of mitigating risk through a belief in the future capacity of, as yet partly established, multi-stakeholder initiatives continues in the 1999 Shell Muskeg River Mine, where the ACFN raise three concerns. Two of these reference regional aspects of project-specific effects and one is dedicated solely to methods for addressing regional cumulative issues. The Panel acknowledged their concerns, noting that the view originally outlined in the 1997 Aurora Mine hearing, of the need for a way to address regional cumulative effects, 'is still relevant' (AEUB 1999b: 39). However, this hearing is also the first point at which an associated and subsequently recurring theme emerges:

of the Panel acknowledging problems with the multi-stakeholder initiatives tasked with mitigating cumulative environmental effects, but using them to address participant concerns anyway:

> The Board believes an industry led multi-stakeholder approach could be effective in addressing the regional environmental issues.... The Cumulative Environmental Effects Management initiative ... is still, however, under design ... well over a year has transpired since the announcement of several new development projects, yet the CEEM initiative is just now beginning to address certain aspects of its structure and operating process. The Board is becoming increasingly concerned that these processes may not be moving forward at a speed sufficient to meet the Board's regulatory requirements to ensure that energy developments are carried out in an orderly and efficient manner that protects the public interest.
>
> (AEUB 1999b: 39)

Despite this recognition, the Panel goes on to note that it 'continues to believe that the two processes [of CEEM and the RSDS] ... will create an acceptable and effective framework within which regional cumulative effects can be assessed within the oil sands region' (ibid.). As such, the project was approved despite concerns with the mechanisms responsible for addressing cumulative environmental effects, progressing under the assumption that risk would be mitigated through the future output of these initiatives. An identical course of action is undertaken during the 1999 hearing on the Mildred Lake project, where the Panel 'recognizes the potentially significant impacts predicted to occur as a result of current and proposed industrial development in the Fort McMurray region' (AEUB 1999c: 20). Going on to note 'the high degree of uncertainty surrounding the science of predicting cumulative effects' (ibid.), the risks associated with such impacts are again allayed by recourse to project-specific mitigation measures and the additional participation of proponents in CEEM, the RSDS, and the more general framework of the Wood Buffalo Environment Association (WBEA) (ibid.).

Taken together, the approvals issued during this initial stage of oil sands development reflect the immaturity of the industry. Demonstrating a broad unknowing around not only the environmental effects that may arise from approvals, but also the specific means by which their associated risks can be addressed, Panel recourse to some future point in time where techno-scientific advances would provide a solution is repetitive. Importantly, because of this lack of data the proposed solutions are not specific; the faith in science and technology is deployed in abstract form, where little detail is presented on the most appropriate research to pursue or technology to develop. Indeed, during this period the Panels do not have the data to fully appreciate the scope of issues which will later arise, or to consider what the most effective means for mitigation will be. They instead rely on an optimistic belief that future advances, which at this point are removed from any of the more material or organisational barriers to success, will mitigate the risks post-approval, and to a sufficient extent to meet the apparent balance required to approve the project. There is also increasing recognition of the need for a regional mechanism through which these knowledge-based techno-scientific advances are to be achieved, becoming ever more pronounced as the approvals are made. It is therefore clear that, during this phase of development, the pace, eventual extent, and possible regional effects are unforeseen or, at the very least, underestimated by the Panels. This allows relatively broad recommendations for future scientific advances to satiate the 'public interest' test in the course of approving expansion of the oil sands industry.

2004–2007: Risk-based Mitigation, Faith in Future Technology and the Increasing Awareness of Flawed Cumulative Effects Management Initiatives

There is a gap of almost five years until the next hearing for the 2004 CNRL Horizon project. This delay is largely down to heavily publicised environmental concerns and political wrangling between the federal and provincial governments over energy policy in the intervening period (see Chastko 2007). Yet, the Panels continue to approve projects despite increased recognition of their potential impacts. Indeed, for the five approvals issued under the public interest test between 2004 and 2007, the quality and extent of data informing the hearing process noticeably increases. This is particularly apparent in the number of concerns raised by First Nations and the evidence base used in support. However, instead of providing greater certainty, this pattern only clarifies just how much is still unknown, not only in relation to the potential for environmental impacts but also the feasibility of measures proposed for their mitigation. The pattern of techno-scientific risk-based reasoning continues, but here there is greater reliance on the industry-led multi-stakeholder initiatives to deal with cumulative environmental effects. Those called upon are again CEMA, which emerged from CEEM in 2000, and RAMP, the Regional Aquatics Monitoring Program. Recourse to these initiatives coincides with the Panel becoming increasingly aware of their deficiencies, reaching a peak in the hearing on the 2007 Imperial Oil Kearl project where the number and significance of concerns raised are, by this point, unprecedented. As such, the repetition between areas of environmental concern and the periods under discussion illustrates the consistency of Panel justifications. Indeed, very little progress is made, in terms of reducing the uncertainty associated with the efficacy of mitigation measures, despite all of the projects in this period being approved as before.

2004–2007: Water Quantity and In-flow Needs

At the 2004 hearing on the CNRL Horizon project, First Nations raised concerns about the increasing number of water licenses issued, particularly in the context of climate change-induced alterations to the flow of the Athabasca River (AEUB 2004a: 37). Recognising the need to ensure a minimum level of flow in this river at any one time, maintaining the IFN is considered by the Panel to be 'critically important to mitigate against cumulative environmental effects of water withdrawal' (ibid.: 41). However, the Panel also openly acknowledges the lack of data on this impact, viewing the solution as stemming from the approval itself: '[T]he additional data collection and monitoring requirements that CNRL will be subject to under the conditions of its licenses will assist in addressing these concerns' (ibid.: 42–43).

Such a decision runs contrary to the alternative offered by the MCFN, which was more precautionary. Their request to 'delay … CNRL's approvals and licenses until an IFN had been established, or an interim IFN was declared based on scientific evidence' (ibid.: 38), was rejected, as was the second, more conciliatory suggestion of pursuing a temporary IFN. Instead, the Panel continues to deploy its belief in the capacity of future techno-scientific breakthroughs to provide solutions, despite the lack of data on the feasibility of such an outcome. However, in between the uncertainty and expected means for risk mitigation now sits an increased reliance on the CEMA. Crucial to the Panel's mitigation strategy, this is tasked with addressing the lack of progress on establishing the IFN, believing that 'CEMA's IFN subgroup is the most appropriate forum in which the scientific data can be gathered and all stakeholders' needs can be addressed' (ibid.: 41).

Coming into contrast here are two inter-related aspects of the Panel's recurrent faith in the mitigating power of techno-scientific advancement: its reliance on CEMA as the primary organisational enabler of this belief, and the simultaneous failure of the organisation to achieve the responsibilities asked of it. Even at this early point, the lack of confidence in CEMA is implied by the Panel's use of government agencies as a 'regulatory backstop', where responsibility for developing the IFN is accompanied by a caveat that such agencies 'establish an IFN in the event that CEMA is unable to do so by the end of 2005' (ibid.). This is similar to the subsequent 2004 Shell Jackpine decision, where government departments were required to complete the IFN framework by 31 December 2005, if CEMA failed to do so (AEUB 2004b: 30). In January 2006, in the absence of a fully developed framework, Alberta Environment (AENV) published an interim framework for public review and comment – a request first made by the MCFN back in 2004, during the CNRL Horizon project hearing (AEUB 2004a: 37), and again in the 2004 Jackpine decision (AEUB 2004b: 29). Further demonstrating its belief in mitigating risk by finding solutions post-approval, on both occasions the Panel gave CEMA the benefit of the doubt instead of adopting the more precautionary recommendations suggested by the First Nation. This theme continues in the Steepbank Extension and Voyageur hearing two years later, where CEMA is relied upon to a lesser extent and greater reference is made to regulatory backstops.

The subsequent hearing on the expansion of the Muskeg River Mine, later in 2006, demonstrates not only the failure of existing attempts to establish an IFN, but also the Panel's steadfast adherence to post-approval means of risk mitigation. At this hearing the First Nations criticise the IFN Water Management Framework on several grounds, not least because of its unsuitability for protecting the Athabasca River (AEUB 2006b: 68). Despite such clear significance, at this hearing the relevant government agencies 'have not yet released a finalized backstop IFN Water Management Framework' (ibid.: 72). Furthermore, despite providing assurances that the IFN would be released prior to the issuance of licenses, such guarantees mask the Panel's admission that 'overall project average daily water use within the total project area will increase' anyway (ibid.). This demonstrates the markedly limited capacity of an IFN to address First Nation concerns even in the event of its introduction. This also skirts around the uncertainty emerging from Phase I of the IFN Framework, along with that surrounding subsequent implementation of Phase II, which the Panel posits as the future solution to these very knowledge gaps (ibid.).

Bringing the total number of projects approved without an appropriate framework for managing regional water use up to nine, the faith invested by the Panel in the introduction of an IFN Framework has, at this point, yet to materialise. Despite this, the Panel considers that 'significant adverse environmental effects associated with water withdrawn from the Athabasca River for use in the project are unlikely' (ibid.: 72), continuing the overarching pattern of post-approval risk-mitigation. It is also important to note that attached to this is the Panel's recognition that the proponent 'is not requesting additional water allocations' (ibid.), a comment deployed as a means of further demonstrating the absence of risk. This may well be true, but it is only because the proponent had previously acquired water allocation licenses with a limit set beyond its existing capacity (ibid.: 67). This is problematic because its physical withdrawal of water would still increase and, in the absence of an IFN Framework, the threshold at which this increase could be accommodated by the surrounding ecosystem would remain unknown. As such, the Panel's decision is no more precautionary than any of those made previously.

By the 2007 hearing, on Imperial Oil's Kearl project, an IFN had still not been established. At this point the Athabasca Chipewyan, Mikisew Cree, Fort McKay, and Deninu K'ue First Nations all raise extensive concerns with the existing draft IFN and Framework. However, as before, precaution takes the form of risk-based mitigation expected to occur through future, post-approval advances, where the Panel expects government agencies and industry:

> [T]o dedicate the resources, staff and funding necessary to ensure that Phase II of the Water Management Framework … is completed in a

> comprehensive manner and according to the timelines established in the current Water Management Framework.
>
> (AEUB 2007: 73)

Going on to recommend that government agencies incorporate the, at that point conceptual, ecological base flow in the final Water Management Framework, the Panel goes on to note that 'Phase II *should* provide the needed information to support the inclusion of a measure that *could* provide long-term certainty to industry and other users of the Athabasca River' (ibid.: emphasis added). Going on to issue five recommendations to government agencies, to include in any conditions they subsequently issue to the proponent, the Panel later acknowledges that four of these recommendations 'would form part of Phase II of the framework development and could be completed as part of a multistakeholder process' (ibid.). Industry-led multi-stakeholder initiatives are broadly considered to have, by this point, failed. This is particularly true with regard to the delayed finalisation of Phase I of the Water Management Framework, and applies equally to its Phase II, the completion of which is not realised over the course of the entire collection of hearing documents analysed. Despite this, and a range of other calls for greater co-operation between government and industry to participate in research, the Panel concludes that 'significant adverse environmental effects associated with water withdrawal from the Athabasca River ... are unlikely' (ibid.: 74). As in previous hearings, their recourse to future scientific and technological advancements, facilitated by greater multi-stakeholder co-operation through industry-led initiatives, is enough to mitigate the risks raised and approve the project under the rubric of the 'public interest'.

2004–2007: Water Quality and Tailings Management

Returning to the 2004 hearing for CNRL's Horizon project, First Nations raised concerns about the data on surface water quality. The MCFN targeted criticism at the Environmental Impact Assessment for omitting data on the quality of proposed fish habitat, the type of mercury contamination focused on, and the unreliability of assessment models, noting in particular that the 'model predictions pertaining to water quality in EPLs ... are unverified' (AEUB 2004a: 44–45). The Panel's response is consistent with others aimed at water quantity issues during this period, recommending that government agencies 'condition any approvals' to 'develop and implement a comprehensive monitoring program' as part of its post-approval risk-based mitigation (ibid.: 47). The implied lack of existing mechanisms to deal with water quality concerns is echoed in its subsequent reasoning, where '[t]he Panel expects CNRL to support CEMA in its efforts to develop water quality objectives for the lower Athabasca River'. The concern with EPLs is ignored and the point about mercury contamination dismissed, although the latter of these contains the caveat that CNRL must monitor for mercury until no longer required by the regulator. Consistent with the justifications provided in other hearings, the risk is mitigated by recourse to expected future techno-scientific advances.

The water quality section in the CNRL Horizon hearing is also instructive because it illustrates that, even when faced with the relatively rare scientific certainty of an environmental threshold breach, the Panel will still deploy its faith in future technological developments as a solution:

> Although there are some predicted exceedances of water quality guidelines, the Panel believes that by implementing a comprehensive monitoring plan and adaptive management strategies to ensure adherence to the water quality guidelines, the project is unlikely to result in significant adverse environmental effects on water quality.
>
> (Ibid.)

This continued use of a faith in future techno-scientific advancement also characterised the Panel's response to First Nation concerns about the expansive reliance of industry on tailings ponds. Here the Panel explicitly recognised 'that NST (non-segregating tailings) is in the development stage', subsequently noting that 'ongoing development and additional research efforts will be required to advance the NST technology' (ibid.: 26). This contributed to the justification for project approval, allowing the Panel to conclude that 'close attention to design and operations supported by continued aggressive research by CNRL', coupled with continued monitoring by government agencies, 'will ensure that the proposed tailings management scheme is unlikely to have significant adverse environmental effects' (ibid.: 28). This is mirrored in the subsequent 2004 Shell Jackpine decision, where the Panel acknowledges that Shell's proposed tailings technology 'would not meet the objective of eliminating long-term storage of fluid fine tailings in the reclaimed landscape (AEUB 2004b: 25). Yet, despite this, it decides that 'close attention to design and operations supported by continued aggressive research by Shell' will ensure that tailings are 'unlikely to have significant adverse environmental effects' (ibid.). As with preceding hearings, the issues raised by First Nations in the present are mitigated through some supposed techno-scientific advances expected to occur in the future.

By 2006, at the hearing on the expansion of the original Steepbank mine, First Nation concerns surrounding tailings management come to the fore. Here the MCFN questioned whether the suggested CT (consolidated tailings) method produced a trafficable surface, requesting 'that until CT [is] proven successful, Suncor not be granted approval for expansions using CT technology' (AEUB 2006a: 30). Now more able to view industry progress on the previous conditions and recommendations made in other hearings, the Panel 'remains concerned that Suncor has not met proposed targets in the management of its tailings as stated in its [original] STP (Steepbank) and Millennium applications' (ibid.). The extent of this failure is revealed in the Panel's follow-up remarks, where it notes that 'Suncor's CT production was 19 percent of projected values' (ibid.). In response, the Panel requires the proponent to 'meet its predicted 76 percent CT efficiency on a quarterly basis', adding that '[u]ntil these targets are met Suncor shall not mine oil sands' because the additional material produced by such activity will 'impact Suncor's ability to meet its CT performance predictions' (ibid.). Although this appears to be a more precautionary approach to regulation, this condition was later modified by the ERCB in its acceptance of Suncor's updated tailings plan in 2010 (see ERCB 2010: 2–3). Here the requirement for 76 per cent CT efficiency was retained while the threat of production inhibition, in the event of non-compliance, was removed (ERCB 2009: Sec. 21). This left intact the faith in technological advancement while removing the threat to expansion in the event of failure. Alongside this, the Panel acknowledges that 'progress was slow' in the development of performance criteria for tailings management (AEUB 2006a: 31). In its final comment aimed at risk mitigation, the faith underpinning the techno-scientific reasoning of the Panel becomes visible in that it 'is aware of several industry and government initiatives that address tailings in various capacities and is *hopeful* that these initiatives will be successful' (ibid.: emphasis added). Exactly the same pattern of reasoning is used in response to First Nation concerns about tailings technology, which is also seen at the subsequent 2006 hearing for expansion of Albian's Muskeg River Mine (MRME). Here, in responding to First Nation concerns about water quality, the Panel notes that the 'EPL reclamation strategy remains an unproven and unapproved reclamation option' (AEUB 2006b: 64). Yet again, however, after requiring submission of an annual report that describes Albian's research and development efforts, the Panel concludes that 'it is unlikely that there will be significant adverse environmental effects' (ibid.: 65). Again, the referenced mitigation measures do not yet exist, and their eventual existence is heavily dependent on the results of future research.

At the 2007 hearing for Imperial Oil's Kearl mine the Athabasca Chipewyan and Deninu Kue First Nations raise concerns about water quality, eliciting Panel responses broadly consistent with earlier hearings. Implicitly acknowledging the validity of these concerns, which centre on the credibility and suitability of the water quality data submitted by Imperial Oil within its application, the Panel's response was almost entirely composed of recommendations for further research by industry-led multi-stakeholder organisations. CEMA is mentioned seven times in this single response, with recourse to future research by RAMP and the newly developed Canadian Oil Sands Network for Research and Development (CONRAD) having a lesser but still central role in the Panel's approach to mitigation (see AEUB 2007: 82–83). A similar theme is exhibited in its response to ACFN concerns about the environmental effects of EPLs:

> [T]he panel expects that the impacts of EPLs will be fully addressed in the studies that are already under way to prove the efficacy of EPLs.... The Joint Panel supports the use of Syncrude's Base Mine Lake as a test project beginning in 2009 ... [and] encourages Imperial Oil to continue to work with Syncrude and other oil sands industry members on developing this demonstration lake to ensure the viability of EPLs as a reclamation concept.
>
> (Ibid.: 45)

This recourse to expected technological advances is also mirrored in the Panel's response to First Nation concerns on tailings technology, specifically that 'the use of thickeners to produce CT has not been commercially demonstrated' (ibid.: 42). Here, in response, the Panel 'encourage Imperial Oil to demonstrate this technology in a pilot-scale project ... prior to start-up of CT production' (ibid.). Although this appears more precautionary when compared to some of the previous deliberations, the ensuing approval is still an example of risk being negated by recourse to expected techno-scientific developments realised post-approval. Indeed, this accompanied the Panel's final response to the concerns raised in the area of tailings technology, where its conclusion that 'the KOS (Kearl Oil Sands) Project is unlikely to result in significant adverse environmental effects' is contingent on Imperial Oil's implementation of the proposed tailings technology, along with its commitment to ongoing testing.

2004–2007: Concerns Surrounding Industry-led Cumulative Effects Initiatives

The delay of around four years between the 1999 Muskeg River and 2004 CNRL Horizon projects did little to alter Panel approaches to deliberating over cumulative effects. Indeed, the latter of these was approved despite the presence of uncertainties in the data on the potential cumulative impact. However, the difference here is that the concerns surrounding the capabilities of the multi-stakeholder initiatives to address cumulative effects begin to come to the fore. Indeed, the 2004 CNRL hearing is the first to dedicate an entire section of discussion to the efficacy of regional initiatives, prompted in response to First Nation concerns about their slow progress in achieving objectives. This issue is particularly problematic when considering their central role in the expected mitigation of risks associated with the more specific impacts on water quantity and quality. After hearing submissions on CEMA's problems with funding, ability to obtain expert consultants, and the ineffective participation by some of its members, the Panel express additional concerns that:

> CEMA's effectiveness may also be influenced by the volume and complexity of its work, multiple priorities of stakeholders, and funding mechanisms

> that may not keep pace with CEMA's increased workload from oil sands expansions....
>
> (AEUB 2004a: 77)

This culminates in the Panel having 'serious concerns about delays in the issuance of recommendations and the ability of CEMA to meet the proposed timelines' (ibid.). In order to mitigate such substantial criticism, the Panel recommends a host of remedial measures. Extensive in scope, these include, but are not limited to, a need for organisational restructuring, greater use of technical experts, a re-evaluation of its resourcing requirements, and greater staff accountability. Ultimately, this is the point at which the Panel's extensive apprehension with the organisation becomes fully visible (ibid.).

Although the Panel is clearly aware of CEMA's organisational flaws, demonstrated not least of all in its identification of restructuring as a 'first step' (ibid.), this does not detract from its reliance on the multi-stakeholder initiative to mitigate risk. Indeed, despite all of this, the Panel reaffirms that CEMA 'will assist the [A]EUB in meeting its regulatory mandate to ensure that energy developments are carried out in an orderly and efficient manner that protects the public interest' (ibid.: 76). As such, the Panel's means of addressing cumulative environmental concerns is consistent with its approach at other hearings, where risks identified in the present are addressed through technological advances expected to occur post-approval. However, the difference here is that this approach is taken following explicit recognition of the deficiencies inherent to the organisation primarily responsible for attaining such advances. During this hearing, First Nations also direct criticism at another primary multi-stakeholder initiative tasked with addressing cumulative environmental effects: the RAMP. Here the Panel's response differs to that used in support of CEMA, where it chooses instead to defer to the results of a peer review being conducted on RAMP at the time of the hearing, ultimately, 'expecting that improvements' emerging through this process 'be implemented in a timely manner' (ibid.: 78). This probably explains why RAMP is barely referred to throughout the Horizon hearing as a way of addressing First Nation concerns.

During the subsequent 2004 Jackpine hearing this peer review is still underway, partially explaining why the decision contained only two references to RAMP as a possible means for addressing First Nation concerns. Instead, CEMA is relied upon to a greater extent, despite similar concerns surfacing around its efficiency, lack of outputs, adequacy of funding, and creation of a water quality framework or Muskeg River basin management system (AEUB 2004b: 77–78). In its closing argument, the Fort McKay First Nation reiterated its 'significant reservations about CEMA's ability to fulfil its mandate' (ibid.: 75). The Panel's response is here almost identical to that issued in the previous CNRL Horizon project, where it recommends government agencies 'review the progress of CEMA', before going on to use exactly the same text in its comment, asserting that 'restructuring and reprioritization are the first steps in ensuring that CEMA meets its goals and the expectations others have of it' (ibid.: 78). Indeed, the majority of this section appears to have been lifted, with only slight adjustment, from the text of the Horizon hearing document, raising additional questions as to the extent to which attempts have here been made to address the specific concerns of First Nations. Those raised are, after all, qualitatively different from the concerns voiced in the previous 2004 hearing. The important role of CEMA in assisting the Panel to meet its public interest mandate is also repeated verbatim and, as before, the project is approved despite these concerns and uncertainties.

By 2006, at the hearing for the Suncor Steepbank expansion, little progress had been made on CEMA's organisational capacity. Here, the MCFN criticise the organisation in a wide range of respects, recommending that government agencies take responsibilities from CEMA to ensure effective mitigation is realised, including IFN reaches for the Athabasca River, water quality objectives, and reclamation standards for EPLs (AEUB 2006a: 66–67). Although dismissing the criticism levelled at the compliance-based nature of CEMA's decision-making, the Panel goes on to explicitly recognise the validity of the majority of these concerns. Tellingly, the Panel also subtly modifies its recognition of CEMA's role in its public interest deliberations, noting that CEMA 'may assist' it in meeting its mandate (ibid.: 68). This is a clear break from the 'will assist' language used in the previous 2004 CNRL and Jackpine hearings (AEUB 2004a: 77, 2004b: 75). However, its response is not to reject the application on the basis of these acknowledged areas of scientific uncertainty, or the implied lack of organisational capability to address the issues. Instead, it proposes that the Government of Alberta evaluates CEMA's purpose, review the 1999 RSDS, and make use of government-led 'regulatory backstops' in the event of continued underperformance. Again, despite such far-reaching concerns, these suggestions for improvement feed into another justification for project approval.

During the next hearing, for the 2006 expansion of the Muskeg River project, an entire section is dedicated to discussing the issues associated with CEMA. Examination of this is particularly important in this instance because, after hearing First Nation comments on eight areas of environmental concern, CEMA forms part of the recommended response in no fewer than six of them. Here, the Athabasca Chipewyan and Fort McKay First Nations criticise its lack of progress on addressing the issues identified in the RSDS, going on to note that, since its inception in 1999, only three management frameworks had been completed (AEUB 2006b: 75). The Panel's response is similar to that provided at the previous hearing, on the 2006 Steepbank expansion, where greater participation in CEMA, creation of more detailed timelines, and greater management of expectations by its participants are posited as remedies (ibid.: 75). There is, however, a difference here, in that the Panel recommends the creation of interim frameworks by CEMA sub-groups until their finalised versions are provided, going on to reinforce the role of the Government of Alberta in this CEMA-led task. Nevertheless, the concerns are still mitigated by recourse to the imagined future capacity of the organisation to develop adequate thresholds, contributing to the project approval.

By the 2007 hearing on the Imperial Oil Kearl project the concerns raised with CEMA are unprecedented. Here the ACFN confirm their withdrawal from the organisation, with the MCFN going on to note that it had begun to limit its participation due to 'frustrations over the slow progress' (AEUB 2007: 89). The criticisms levelled at the organisation are far-reaching, referring to the non-delivery of tangible results pertaining to the RSDS, a bias in favour of government and industry, and a funding format that determines priorities instead of environmental needs. In response, these concerns are once again acknowledged and validated by the Panel, but the recommendations made for improvement are now more extensive. Indeed, they include 'a need to develop specific timelines for priority projects' (ibid.: 93), for CEMA to meet established deadlines, and 'members in CEMA … to increase and improve their participation' (ibid.). The Panel suggests the need for a review to 'identify opportunities to streamline its operation' and 'improve communication among the various levels, … improve management support, and strengthen its strategic direction given to its committees and working groups' (ibid.: 93–94). It finishes by encouraging 'regulators to take a more direct leadership role in all aspects of CEMA' (ibid.: 94). In its concluding statement the Panel notes the absence of a 'satisfactory alternative' to CEMA, therefore considering its success 'critical' (ibid.). However, as with all of the hearings before it, these fundamental issues, with the primary organisation responsible for developing the management frameworks needed to address cumulative environmental effects, are nullified through recourse to some imagined future point in time where the project will be operationally effective. The Kearl project was therefore approved in the same manner as were its predecessors.

2011–2013: Absent Data, Foreseen Consequences and Requests for Greater Government Participation at the Level of Strategy

There is a gap of four years until the next hearing, for the 2011 Joslyn North project. During this time, the ERCB was created out of the dissolution of the AEUB, with the change coming into effect on 1 January 2008. A similar alteration was made on 17 June 2013, when the AER succeeded the ERCB. In keeping with this period of change, on 22 August 2012, a partially completed LARP was also introduced, mirroring other legislative alterations made during this time (see Chapter 2). Despite this, the mandate of the energy regulator, to balance social, economic, and environmental considerations in the process of making a decision on approval, did not substantively change.

This period does see the Panels forward stronger calls for greater government participation in environmental regulation, echoing the First Nation requests seen in earlier hearings. Culminating in the 2013 Jackpine decision, where the Panel issues an unprecedented number of recommendations to government to undertake such responsibility, this follows the criticisms previously levelled at the multi-stakeholder initiatives. Indeed, at this point the industry has matured and, although there are still many gaps in the understanding of both impacts and efficacy of measures for mitigation, the consequences of expansion are better understood. There is also a developing awareness of just how much is still unknown, as reflected in the decision document for the final, 2013 Jackpine decision:

> The Panel finds that the Project would likely have significant adverse environmental effects on wetlands, traditional plant potential areas, wetland-reliant species at risk, migratory birds that are wetland-reliant or species at risk, and biodiversity. There is also a lack of proposed mitigation measures that have been proven to be effective. The Panel also concludes that the Project, in combination with other existing, approved, and planned projects, would likely have significant adverse cumulative environmental effects on wetlands; traditional plant potential areas; old-growth forests; wetland-reliant species at risk and migratory birds; old-growth forest reliant species at risk and migratory birds; caribou; biodiversity; and Aboriginal traditional land use, rights, and culture. Further, there is a lack of proposed mitigation measures that have proven to be effective with respect to identified significant adverse cumulative environmental effects.
>
> (AER 2013b: 2–3)

This can therefore be seen as the period in which the explanation of industry immaturity loses credibility, bringing into view the economic dominance underpinning regulator decisions on expansion.

2011–2013: Water Quantity and In-flow Needs

Four years after the hearing for the 2007 Imperial Oil Kearl project, for the Joslyn North Mine Project of 2011, First Nation input was withdrawn prior to the hearing because of agreements reached with the proponent. However, concerns surrounding water quality were still submitted in the absence of any witnesses for cross-examination. As such, the ERCB still considered their content, providing insight into the reasoning used to support the eventual project approval. In response to concerns raised by the ACFN and Fort McKay First Nation regarding the water levels in the Athabasca River, and the issues with Phase II of the IFN Water Management Framework, the Panel continues to acknowledge their validity. The Panel also states that it 'understands that since the mid-1970s, the Athabasca River's average flow has been dropping' (ERCB 2011: 99). Its means of dealing with the issue is, however, consistent with previous hearings, in that it addresses existing information gaps by recourse to the presumed capability of future scientific and technological development. Here, it is a belief that the proposed Phase II Water Management Framework will commence in January 2011, be fully operational by January 2016, and ultimately address the concerns raised (ibid.). This allows the Panel to conclude that 'significant adverse cumulative environmental effects associated with water withdrawals from the Athabasca River during low flow periods are unlikely' (ibid.).

The final hearing record available for analysis is the 2013 decision on the expansion of the Shell Jackpine mine. Unprecedented in the extent of the evidence heard, the hearing document is 405 pages long. Considering that the original 1997 Steepbank decision document was 13 pages long, the progress made in terms of the scientific evidence available in support of the increasing variety of arguments is clearly visible. The recognition given to cumulative effects has also expanded significantly, now having dedicated consideration under many different sections and in addition to project-specific impacts. Indeed, here the levels of water withdrawal established under the finally completed Phase 1 Water Management Framework are referred to as one of Shell's post-approval commitments, with the Panel agreeing to a conceptual precautionary cut-off level which would equal the Ecological Base Flow requested by First Nations back in 2007, during the Imperial Oil Kearl project hearing (AEUB, 2007: 73; AER 2013b: 61). Although this demonstrates greater understanding of project-specific impacts and the most appropriate measures for their address, there are still knowledge gaps which continue to be mitigated by recourse to expected techno-scientific rectification post-approval. This is visible in the manner with which the Panel consider the credibility of monitoring data used by Shell, while concurrently recognising the deficiencies inherent to the agencies responsible for at least part of its production:

> The Panel believes that the data used by Shell was adequate based on what was available, including RAMP data. The Panel recognizes that RAMP will be wound down in due course and its monitoring activities will be assumed by an agency under government management. The Panel also recognizes that the Joint Canada-Alberta Implementation Plan for Oil Sands Monitoring [JOSM] proposes a more comprehensive monitoring program ... that will address concerns over deficiencies in current monitoring activities.
>
> (AER 2013b: 62)

Criticisms of the Regional Aquatic Monitoring Program (RAMP) were recognised almost a decade prior to this, in both the hearing for the 2004 CNRL project and peer review released the same year, but it would appear that the 'deficiencies in current monitoring activities' have persisted over this time (ibid.). In considering the data produced by RAMP to be valid anyway, and going on to use the expected future success of the Joint Canada-Alberta Implementation Plan for Oil Sands Monitoring (JOSM) as a method for mitigating the risk associated with doing so, the Panel's approach is still dependent on the imagined capability of initiatives to address issues post-approval. It is here worth noting that the JOSM was introduced in February 2012 as a response by the Governments of Alberta and Canada to the problems with existing monitoring mechanisms.

As a distinct but related issue in the area of water quality, the 2013 Jackpine hearing also saw First Nations express concerns with Shell's plan to divert 21 km, or 13 miles, of the upper reaches of the Muskeg River to gain access to the bitumen underneath. As expected, the significance of such a landscape modification, and the potential impact on the surrounding ecosystem, elicited a broad swath of concerns from the First Nations. These are worth quoting at length, even if from only one of the First Nations:

> … diverting the river would permanently affect water flows, water quality, and fishery resources. These impacts would in turn affect access to traditional lands, reducing the opportunities to use the resources in the area and significantly affecting spiritual values of the watershed.… The ACFN claimed that it was impossible for it to evaluate the impacts of the … Plan on the Muskeg River because Shell provided few quantitative details.… [The] ACFN considered that Shell's … Plan did not actually mitigate its concerns about disturbance.… [The ACFN] stated that the river has cultural and spiritual significance … [and] have used the Muskeg River basin for millennia and continue to use the river and to access the lands within the basin. ACFN's preferred option would be to not divert the river. ACFN stated that it believed the ore beneath the Muskeg River and its riparian zone should be sterilized and that full protection of the river be put in place. ACFN stated that should the Project be approved, it strongly urged the Panel to approve it only on the condition that the Muskeg River be left in a natural state and not be diverted.
>
> (Ibid.: 66)

The Panel's response to these concerns is consistent with the reasoning used in prior hearings. It explicitly 'recognizes that ACFN has significant unresolved concerns about the proposed diversion of the Muskeg River' (ibid.: 69). The Panel also recognises the absence of mechanisms capable of mitigating the cumulative environmental impacts likely to result:

> The Panel finds that although Shell has provided an acceptable degree of information at the Project level, the current Muskeg River Interim

> Management Framework for Water Quantity and Quality does not fully address cumulative effects on the Muskeg River from oil sands projects. The Panel finds that the province has not applied the precautionary approach in considering the Project's impacts on the Muskeg River.
>
> (Ibid.)

Appearing to disregard this important gap, the Panel immediately follows this with a statement that is not only inconsistent with the admissions surrounding the absence of measures for the mitigation of cumulative effects, but also demonstrates the degree of absolutism given to the economic dimension of decisions:

> The Panel has determined that diversion of the Muskeg River is in the public interest … there will be significant and unacceptable sterilization of oil sands resources if the diversion does not occur.
>
> (Ibid.)

In addition to the way in which the Panel elevates the economic value of this activity over all others, the subsequent reasoning is consistent with the pattern of decision-making during this period. Indeed, the Panel goes on to recommend the provincial government adopt a more leading role in developing the Muskeg River Water Management Plan, to negate the expected cumulative effects. As such, gaps in existing knowledge still persist and are recognised as such by the Panel, but the mitigation of risk is expected to be achieved at some future point in time, when the scientific and technological means to do so are supposed to manifest. While the 2007 Water Management Framework for the Lower Athabasca River was replaced in 2015 by the Lower Athabasca Region Surface Water Quantity Management Framework (Government of Alberta 2015a), as of October 2018 the completed Muskeg River Water Management Plan to which the Panel refers is yet to be published.

2011–2013: Water Quality and Tailings Management

At the hearing for the 2011 Joslyn North Project the First Nations again question the potential impact of approval on the water quality of the Athabasca River. These concerns centre on the absence of detailed monitoring mechanisms needed to assess its cumulative regional dimension. The means by which the Panel mitigates these concerns is, again, consistent with previous hearings, where risk is mitigated by recourse to some future techno-scientific development. In acknowledging that there are 'existing exceedances of water quality guidelines for several water quality criteria', recognising that '[t]he project … would likely add to some extent to these exceedances' and that, ultimately, 'there are uncertainties about the effects of industrial development on water quality in the lower Athabasca River', the Panel concludes that 'these *should* be resolved through better monitoring programs' (ERCB 2011: 102, emphasis added). In commending Environment Canada for its research progress towards this aim, the Panel notes that '[t]his research *might* help determine' the sources of contamination (ibid.: emphasis added). This is followed by other recommendations for future research before concluding there to be 'no reason to believe that these [cumulative] effects are significant' (ibid.) – a decision reached 'on the basis of the RAMP data' which, earlier in the hearing, the proponent had been criticised for using (ibid.: 58).

At the hearing on the expansion of the Shell Jackpine Mine, in 2013, First Nations did not raise any concerns within the section specifically dedicated to tailings technology. However, this is only because their concern with the increasing volume of tailings ponds is spread throughout the hearing. Indeed, the Panel is here still 'concerned about the viability of the Project's tailings management plan since Shell has not been able to demonstrate the success of its thickener technology at its Phase 1 operation' (AER 2013b: 37). The Panel's reservations with Shell's proposed technology are substantial, noting that the proposed technology has been unable to meet regulatory requirements up to this point (ibid.: 37–38). However, as before, the Panel responds to these concerns with a belief in the proponent's ability to make techno-scientific improvements of such capability, and within such a time frame, that they will mitigate the concerns raised and meet the regulatory standards. Despite requiring Shell to provide a tailings management plan prior to start-up, which should indicate compliance, its achievement is based on not only a faith in the possibility of its attainment, but also Shell's capacity to do so:

> The Panel concludes that Shell's Project tailings plan is overly optimistic and may not be achievable. However, the Panel recognizes that Shell has made improving the Phase 1 thickener performance a high priority. Shell intends to continue improving its understanding of fines in ore and will incorporate the knowledge gained from existing operations in the Project's thickener design. Shell will also continue to develop other technologies to improve its tailings management.
>
> (Ibid.: 38)

The uncertainty underpinning this proposed faith is further heightened by the acknowledged difficulty in deploying an alternative tailings management technology should the proposed technology be unsuccessful. In recognising this, the Panel raises a concern about the delay associated with such compliance 'because Shell indicated that it would take almost a decade to identify a technology and take it to full-scale commercial implementation' (ibid.). As such, significant uncertainty is associated with both the method proposed and any alternatives which may be pursued should it fail. Consistent with other hearings, such uncertainty does not pose a challenge to project approval because 'the Panel recognizes that Shell's commitment to have no fluid tailings at closure surpasses [regulatory] requirements in the long term' (ibid.). In the absence of evidence and in the presence of concerns, a commitment to future techno-scientific advances, irrespective of feasibility, facilitates the risk-based mitigation seen in previous hearings.

The concerns of First Nations surrounding the related area of Shell's proposed EPLs were heard in one dedicated section. Here the ACFN considered the 'littoral zone', the area at the edges of a lake able to support plant and animal populations, to be 'too small in current pit lake designs' (ibid.: 70). They also stated that 'Shell had not considered the cumulative effects of discharge from multiple EPLs into regional freshwater bodies', requesting that 'any approval or recommendation that the Project proceed be made conditional upon completion of an independent and scientifically rigorous assessment and verification of the accuracy of models used to predict the functioning of EPLs' (ibid.). As before, the Panel responds to the First Nations by acknowledging the validity of their concerns, following this with a reiteration of the need for further research as a means of mitigation (ibid.; 76–77):

> The Panel acknowledges interveners' concerns about the lack of evidence demonstrating that EPLs are technically and economically feasible and about Shell's reliance on adaptive management to address potential EPL did not perform as expected. The Panel recognizes that the work that industry and others have completed through CEMA to update the EPLGD (CEMA's 2012 End Pit Lake Guidance Document) is a positive step toward improving the design of EPLs. The Panel considers that this guidance document contains reliable research about EPL design, but that until more information becomes available (i.e. Syncrude BML [Base Mine Lake] test results), the Panel can only view the EPLGD as a guidance document and not as a regulatory tool. The Panel expects Shell to continue its participation in CEMA and other multi-stakeholder groups to research and refine assumptions about EPL development.

These recognised gaps in existing knowledge continue throughout the Panel's response. Indeed, it actively recommends that any approvals issued by government agencies include validating the models proposed, updating mitigation plans as more information becomes available, and developing a research schedule for testing EPL predictions and design features (ibid.: 75–76). The Panel also recognises that 'mineable oil sands operators will not be able to meet the expectation to demonstrate the efficacy of EPLs by 2018 that was established by previous joint review panels' (ibid.: 76). A wide variety of other recommendations and requirements for both government and proponent are subsequently issued, continuing the expectative nature of the risk-based mitigation deployed in other hearings. Taken together, this enables the Panel to conclude that 'it is unlikely that significant environmental effects would result', allowing for the project to be approved in the manner of those before (ibid.: 78).

2011–2013: Pursuit of Greater Government Involvement in Cumulative Effects Management

The hearing for the 2011 Joslyn North project did not contain a dedicated discussion of regional monitoring initiatives, but still made occasional reference to CEMA and RAMP in the course of mitigating the risks made visible by First Nation input. However, there is a qualitative shift here, in that the Panels no longer defer to these organisations, to the extent that they had done previously, in their responses. This is probably because December 2008 saw a significant shift in cumulative effects management, where the Government of Alberta announced the development of the LARP – the framework for managing cumulative issues beyond CEMA's existing remit. Concurrently establishing the LUF, which replaced the RSDS after its nine years in operation, the government also initiated a major review of CEMA's governance structure, the findings from which were highly critical (see Chapter 6). It therefore becomes clear as to why reliance on the organisation during the 2011 Joslyn North project is seen to diminish, and why the Panel increasingly defers to 'regulatory backstops' in the period prior to this. Indeed, these reports not only speak to CEMA's limitations as an organisation, but also retrospectively confirm the flaws underpinning the years of expectation-based, techno-scientific mitigation deployed as the rationale for approvals, particularly as realisation of these advances was largely contingent on the success of this very organisation.

By 2013, and the hearing on the expansion of the Shell Jackpine project, it is clear that the Panel is in a difficult situation with regard to making decisions on cumulative environmental effects. At this point, knowledge of the potential impacts has grown, but so too has the awareness of what is still unknown. Cumulative effects are taken into account to a far greater extent than in prior hearings, with both project-specific and regional impacts being given dedicated attention within most of the separate areas in which concerns have been raised. There is also a section dedicated to ten regional effects which 'may or may not be contributed to directly by the Project' (AER 2013b: 300). Of these, the Panel recognises the limits to existing mitigation measures in nine, suggesting use of the LARP as a possible means for future mitigation in five of these. Indeed, the criticisms levelled at existing measures for mitigation are numerous. Not only are the management plans in use prior to the LARP seen as 'of limited use' because they are 'at varying scales, out of date, and not reflective of the present state of development' (ibid.: 301), but 'there is still insufficient evidence to demonstrate that reclamation works or will work as intended' (ibid.: 302). The Panel considers there to have been a 'lack of mitigation that has been shown to be effective' with respect to losses of wetlands and old-growth forests (ibid.: 304), that Phase II of the Water Management Framework has yet to be developed as a means of mitigating risks to water quantity and quality (ibid.: 305), and that 'there is still uncertainty regarding cumulative effects on fish and fish habitat' (ibid.: 306). Finally, recognition is given to the lack of a regional monitoring initiative, with the panel noting that 'funding has not yet been finalized' for the proposed JOSM (ibid.). Yet, despite these quite clear acknowledgments of the insufficiency of existing knowledge, as before, the risks raised are mitigated by recourse to the expected future potential of the LARP, which is broadly recognised as incomplete at the time of the hearing, and recommendations for further scientific or technological advancements by government departments. This culminates in a now-familiar outcome for the latest and final oil sands project which went to hearing; approval in the name of the 'public interest'.

Public Hearing Decisions at the 'Approval' Stage: A Summary

Despite occurring over almost two decades, the pattern of reasoning used by the regulatory Panels to consider whether a project is in the 'public interest' exhibits several consistent characteristics. Although occasionally deviating from the particular order presented here, the deliberation process contains several features which have remained largely constant over this time. First, the concerns of First Nations, with regard to water quantity and quality, and broader cumulative effects, tend to be acknowledged, meaning that the presence of an issue is officially recognised. Second, the Panels may expand on this, either recognising that a current measure for mitigation is inadequate or, more commonly, that there is a gap in the existing understanding of the concern raised. Taken together these present a risk to the 'public interest', acting as a counterweight to the acceptability of the project because, if it was approved at this point, without the provision of solutions, the balance internal to the test would be compromised. As a means of mitigating this risk to approval, the Panel subsequently refers to some proposed techno-scientific means by which the issue might be addressed in the future. This response contains three implicit assumptions; that techno-scientific mitigation is materially possible, that the expected advances will work even if developed, and that the actors tasked with pursuing these solutions have the capacity to do so. As these characteristics are unchallenged throughout the hearings, the broad recourse to some future techno-scientific means of risk-based mitigation serves to discursively rebalance the drawbacks associated with the environmental dimension of the social, economic, and environmental trio. This allows for the procedural mitigation of First Nation concerns in the course of approving an oil sands project under the rubric of the 'public interest'.

As is visible throughout the hearings, it is the difficulty in realising future advances that has been a persistent issue for both the Panels and the First

Nations, the latter of which have seen little progress made in addressing their concerns. Indeed, it is here where the crux of the issue lies; the Panels have not significantly altered their approach to deliberation in almost two decades. They have granted approvals founded on an evidentially insufficient process of techno-scientific risk-based mitigation time and time again. Although a counter-argument could be made, that the conditions and recommendations come into effect prior to project construction, this ignores the central role of First Nation and public participation in the process of ensuring transparency and accountability. Following their approval at the hearings, projects move past the point at which they can be subjected to such scrutiny, meaning that the progress on the supposed advances, which are the very features relied upon to bring projects into accordance with the 'public interest', is more difficult to ascertain. This effectively shields them from further questioning. Indeed, the projects are effectively removed from the public realm after the hearings, with their progress on any expectations, recommendations, or conditions only resurfacing at a hearing in the future, where the same process of techno-scientific, risk-based mediation is then repeated, First Nation concerns nullified, and approvals issued. Taken together, Panel use of techno-scientific forms of risk-based mitigation exhibits a 'weak' form of precaution married to the 'weak' strand of eco-modernist philosophy (see Chapter 2). Furthermore, despite their supposed 'independence' from vested interests, the Panels appear able only to make choices about project modifications with the aim of mitigation, but not about the ultimate existence of a project. Data on the validity of this observation was gathered through interviews with regulatory personnel and is presented in the next section.

Issues Raised by Regulatory Personnel and the Influences on their Decision-Making

While analysing Panel decision documents provides important insight into the techno-scientific, risk-based means by which First Nation concerns have been mitigated at this 'approval' stage of the regulatory process, interviews were conducted with those within the energy regulator itself to understand where the impetus for this approach originates. From these interviews three primary issues can be seen to influence the decisions made. The first centres on the insufficient technical information available to inform regulator decision-making on cumulative environmental effects. The second focuses on the limited avenues available for public and First Nation discussion on the direction and pace of development at the level of strategy. Both of these points refer to deficiencies in the LARP, largely due to its purpose of informing regulatory decision-making at the point of the hearings. The third category is different, focusing on the regulator's preference for reaching a consensus with industry. This obscures the issues arising conflating economic growth with 'public interest', and exerts influence on the regulator's ability to reject a project application.

The Technical and Participatory Inadequacies of the Lower Athabasca Regional Plan

The unfinished status of the LARP was seen to exacerbate tensions around cumulative environmental effects by hindering the ability of regulatory personnel to make informed judgments on project approvals. Broadly supportive of the LARP as a concept, criticism was directed at the difference between what was being espoused in policy and what was occurring in practice. Indeed, participants noted that decisions were being made on expansion in the absence of complete or suitable scientific data:

> [T]he province … in my mind, hasn't been fast enough in developing these tools that would help to provide sufficient guidance to decision makers like ourselves. That's an area where there's still a gap. There's been lots of talk but there isn't enough action in the area. So that's certainly an area where our system could improve, because we now make decisions without having that kind of guidance, and you keep making these decisions and the problems from the stakeholder standpoint and the First Nations standpoint, just get more and more critical … so the level of anxiety and conflict rise[s]….
>
> (Participant A, Energy Regulator)

While there was never any suggestion that the lack of accurate data on environmental effects could lead to the rejection of an application, it was explained as imposing clear constraints on the ability of Panels to impose specific conditions on individual proponents.

In addition to criticising the technical dimension of the LARP, participants from the Energy Regulator noted that the absence of a forum for public discussion on the strategic direction and pace of development raised additional problems during the hearings. Indeed, it was the opinion of various participants from within the Energy Regulator that cumulative effects concerns were only raised during the hearings because there were no appropriate avenues for discussing the issue elsewhere. This observation encompasses the LARP because 'the [consultation] process leading to the development and affirmation of the Land Use Plan was intended to address and deal with, among other things, the issue of cumulative effects' (Participant E, Energy Regulator). Described as the 'crux of the matter' by Participant C, this position was shared by multiple participants:

> [W]e're the only game in town in terms of a place to bring those [cumulative effects] concerns, so it creates frustration for parties.
>
> (Participant A, Energy Regulator)

> [W]hen either a community or First Nations group come to a hearing they are concerned about cumulative effects, but … the ability of an

> individual proponent to assess regional cumulative effects is limited.... Because there doesn't seem to be a good forum for discussing and getting a resolution on these broad regional cumulative effects issues, people come to our hearings and want to talk about government policy ... and those are not things that we have any direct control over.
>
> (Participant C, Energy Regulator)

> If I could highlight a point of frustration that I think some people have, is that when it comes to things like cumulative effects, some of the more policy-oriented discussions about what's going on in the whole region; that becomes very difficult to manage because all of our tools are designed around making decisions around a single project.
>
> (Participant F, Energy Regulator)

The regulator's limited ability to deal effectively with concerns about cumulative environmental effects is here related to the lack of alternative avenues, including the LARP, through which they can be addressed. Noting the absence of First Nation input and information omitted from certain aspects of the LARP, regulator criticisms and related confidence in the land use plan were concisely summarised:

> The process [of finalising the LARP] is incomplete, inadequate and therefore can't be assumed to take care of all the things it's supposed to be taking care of.
>
> (Participant E, Energy Regulator)

Despite being under construction since 2008, the LARP was still – at this point, in 2015 – viewed with criticism by regulatory personnel. The legacy of approvals being made in the presence of deficient cumulative effects management initiatives therefore continues at this later point, echoing the technical and participatory flaws identified with CEMA and RAMP between 1999 and 2008. However, the issue for the Energy Regulator, particularly at the point of the hearings, is that this deficiency forces them to consider cumulative environmental effects within the mechanism designed for applications on single projects. If this were addressed at the level of strategy or during the 'planning' stage, encompassing the possibility for the relocation or even rejection of projects, then it was thought that fewer issues about cumulative effects would be raised at this point in the process.

Influences on the Regulator's Ability to Reject a Project Application

Although criticism of the overarching land use plan clearly constrains the ability of the regulator to make informed decisions on cumulative environmental effects, including making recommendations to government and proponents on how to mitigate their impacts, this does not explain why projects have been consistently approved despite these broadly recognised flaws. Indeed, when introduced in 2013, the AER was described as 'operat[ing] at arms-length from the Government of Alberta' (see Government of Alberta 2016b: 29), suggesting an independence which may permit the rejection of project applications. However, as explained by Participant C of the Energy Regulator, 'Whenever someone says they're arms-length, the first question you gotta ask is, "Well, how long is the arm?".' Answers to this question were provided during the interviews, particularly at those points where discussion turned to First Nation criticisms of the hearing process, and the reasons for the wholesale approval of oil sands applications over the past two decades. The reasons given were linked to the policy priorities of government:

> [P]eople sometimes think that, as a regulator, we can do whatever we want, right? We're independent, we can turn down projects? And while that's true, we can turn down projects, it has to be because they're not in compliance with government policy, there's some very significant adverse effect that we think the company can and should mitigate but isn't … those kinds of things.
>
> (Participant C, Energy Regulator)

Considering government policy has been distinctly pro-growth for almost two decades (see Chapter 3), the regulator's capacity to reject a project application is determined by the overarching direction outlined within these documents. The same participant clarified this further, using language which identifies both the origin of influence and the reasoning process through which it flows:

> As regulators … we're really implementers of government policy. So we have an eye for: this is the government's policy, these are the technical requirements that are in place, [and] how does the proponent do in terms of meeting those?
>
> (Participant C, Energy Regulator)

As seen within the hearing documents, this is an echo of the rather technical, administrative approach which allows for First Nation concerns to be addressed through future advances in science and technology. However, an additional feature of decision-making is here rendered manifest, and one which is not explicitly visible within the hearing documents: the limited options available to the regulator when deciding on an application.

Interview participants described government policy as having an influence throughout the 'approval' stage of the regulatory process, beginning from the point at which an application is submitted. Appearing as an omnipresent consideration, various policies and strategies were described as having an influence akin to 'steering', suggesting that the regulator can recommend modifications to a project as long as it does not threaten its existence or economic feasibility. For instance, the first 'Regional Outcome' for the LARP requires agencies to ensure '[t]he economic potential of the oil sands is optimized' (Government of Alberta 2012a: 37), and although this is only one of seven outcomes, two of which are more environment-orientated, the primary influence of this upon regulatory decision-making was made clear:

> [I]f an application comes along and it is squarely within an area that's been identified and established through an approved and adopted land use planning process as being a priority for oil sands development, then that's a clear policy signal to the decision maker that it's our intention, after going through all this process, through consultation, balancing, that that should be the primary activity.
>
> (Participant E, Energy Regulator)

As such, the framework established by government policy and strategy sets the limits within which the regulator can act, influencing the relative weightings required to strike a balance between the social, economic, and environmental concerns under the public interest test. This means that, within an area designated a priority for oil sands development, a decision to reject a project can only occur if concerns raised to the contrary of said priority are of such significance that they outweigh its position as the dominant consideration. With development of the oil sands being consistently framed as a source of provincial economic importance, the relatively localised concerns of the First Nations are not deemed substantial enough to provide the counterweight necessary for this outcome. However, as can be seen throughout the hearings, the space situated between these two considerations is occupied by recurrent Panel use of techno-scientific, risk-based mitigation. In the context of zero application rejections over two decades, and with the clear priority given to growth within the LARP, the purpose of this mitigation process is made clear. Faced with the environmental concerns of First Nations and other stakeholders, which mount a challenge to this priority, Panel recourse to a faith in science and technology serves to rebalance considerations in favour of approval, irrespective of whether evidence exists as to its past success or future viability.

A related feature alluded to throughout the interviews was an approach to regulation founded on co-operation and compromise. Bearing the hallmarks of what is known as the 'compliance school' of regulation (Tombs 2017: 77–78), where negotiation with the regulated is favoured over conflict, this was explained by one of the most senior participants in the agency:

> More and more we're trying to shift away from a traffic/policeman approach to regulation, where we're just writing black and white rules

> and writing tickets, and we're getting more into … a dialogue with companies about the relative spectrum of performance. So if all the companies are compliant, some of them are doing better than others, even though they're all compliant, so it's really interesting to be able to learn from the companies who are leading, and helping the companies who are just barely compliant to get better. So we're trying to get into that space for them.
>
> [O]ur role really is to work with companies to make sure that, as the policy is translated into regulatory detail, that we set up a framework where they can be successful, they have clarity about what's expected, they know what to expect from us, in terms of our oversight, and we know what to expect from them, in terms of reporting and information sharing.
>
> (Participant F, Energy Regulator)

The issue here is not the communicating of standards, which is clearly an important part of any regulatory system, but the stated regulatory purpose of ensuring corporate entities 'can be successful'. While there are many instances where such a statement is not in itself problematic, those occasions where such success is equivalent to industrial expansion – and expansion itself is the key issue with regard to cumulative environmental effects – the very aspect that becomes unquestionable is at the same time the immediate source of tension.

From this it would appear the influence of government policy on the regulator occurs within the 'approval' stage of the regulatory process, but at a point separate from the hearings themselves, which are supposed to be independent and quasi-judicial. However, such a perspective makes an artificially clear distinction between 'the regulator' and the hearing panels, suggesting that the latter are a separate, non-partisan group. In reality, this compliance approach spills over into the hearings – a characteristic rendered visible by the approvals granted through consistent recourse to unproven strategies for techno-scientific, risk-based mitigation, which have been largely delegated to industry-led multi-stakeholder organisations. At no point in any of the hearing documents did there appear to be a possibility that an application may be rejected. Supported by comments from a senior member of the energy regulator, the influence of this compliance-based approach on the hearing process was made clear:

> [I]f you have a major project, and it's going to hearing, and there's any possibility … any genuine possibility, at that point, that it might not be approved, then it shouldn't be in the hearing. The regulator should go back to the proponent and say "this may not fly, you need to do something different". And none of that … [is] actively transparent. It's not in the hearing room, we don't issue notices, we don't tell people this is going on. It just happens.
>
> (Participant B, Energy Regulator)

This explanation has several implications. First, that the ultimate result of a hearing is a predetermined outcome: approval. Second, that these ultimate decisions are being made without First Nation, or even broader public, input or scrutiny. And finally, that the compliance-based approach is a characteristic of the energy regulator and not just the hearing panels. As a senior member of the regulatory agency explained, 'We're a development regulator. We do want development to take place, we believe that's inherently in the public service' (Participant F, Energy Regulator). Despite the apparently non-coercive nature of this influence, these considerations do compromise the balancing of social, economic, and environmental concerns in the process of making a 'public interest' determination. It leads to the assumption that increasing production automatically equates with the 'public interest' – an unquestionable, default feature from which no concessions can be taken and against which all other considerations are weighed.

Conclusion

This chapter has demonstrated that First Nation concerns are dealt with in a very particular way by decisions on project approval, being absorbed into a broader process which operates in the supposed 'public interest'. Through recourse to an operationalised belief in the future efficacy of science and technology, the risks made visible by First Nations are mitigated in the process of balancing regional and comparatively localised environmental concerns against the provincial socio-economic benefits which accompany such large-scale developments. As such, the Panels have been able to discharge their duty by appearing to negate risk to such an extent that projects have been approved in the name of the 'public interest'. This is despite such risk mitigation being based on very little, if any, evidence pertaining to the efficacy of this mitigation. It is therefore a belief in the capacity of science and technology to address concerns and uncertainties, as opposed to any evidence for its capability to do so, that has underpinned the deliberative balancing of social, economic, and environmental interests in pursuit of the 'public interest' determinations for almost two decades.

The decision documents also demonstrate that the dominant Panel responses to First Nation concerns on various environmental effects have been consistent over this period, being pursued in a very specific manner. Faced with First Nation concerns targeted at both the expected environmental effects of a project and the credibility and adequacy of the methods available for their monitoring, risk-mitigation occurs through recourse to some expected future techno-scientific development. This is despite their broad failure to materialise over time; a feature that the Panels become increasingly aware of as the number of issued approvals grows. An associated feature of this is that a significant proportion of the responsibility for meeting these expectations has been delegated to industry-led, multi-stakeholder initiatives. Despite persistent recognition of their flawed capacity to provide the solutions to issues assigned to them, the Panels still defer to the imagined capacity of these initiatives to mitigate the increasingly numerous problems identified by First Nations. Even when recognition of their multiple failures becomes acute, around 2008, recourse to government agencies in their stead has little apparent influence on the adequacy of data or the availability of options for impact mitigation. The outcome of this pattern of reasoning is ultimately the same, permitting the approval of each project by appearing to balance social, economic, and environmental concerns in the process of meeting the 'public interest' test.

While the means by which this 'public interest' is achieved forms an important part in understanding how First Nation concerns have been marginalised within the hearings, information pertaining to what those within the energy regulator itself consider to be problematic elements of the process provides important insight into why this course of action has been pursued. Painting the hearings as a meeting point, where issues within each stage of the process become both concentrated and most visible, participants from the energy regulator criticised the lack of adequate public and First Nation participation in determining the strategic direction of development, along with problems stemming from the more technical shortcomings of the LARP. More significantly, however, they indicate that the hearing outcomes are more a consequence of the regulatory tendency to seek consensus with industry behind closed doors, prior to the dates on which hearings are opened to the public. As such, by the time project applications are heard in the public forum they have, in essence, already been approved.

Part III

The Catalyst for Harm and Inefficacy of Control

Chapter 6

The Catalyst for Harm

'Weak' Ecological Modernisation in Policy and Practice

The previous three chapters have demonstrated the extent to which each stage of the regulatory process governing oil sands expansion has internalised many of the characteristics central to the environmental philosophy of 'weak' ecological modernisation. Operating within a context defined by the Government of Alberta's policy objective of 'sustainable growth' for almost two decades, the regulatory process is orientated towards a preconceived idea of 'hegemonic progress' (Christoff 1996: 487), maintains a staunch reliance on techno-scientific means of mitigating environmental risk, employs an energy regulator with a perspective firmly rooted in the 'compliance school' of regulation, which ensures decisions are made in a highly technocratic manner (see Hajer 1995), and displays a systematic disregard for the input of First Nations in both policy and practice. Taken together, the entire process, from policy through 'planning' to 'approval', is tasked with pursuing the 'green growth' seen as central to 'weak' eco-modernist philosophy. Supported by a broader, unquestioned assumption that acceleration of oil sands production is a 'good' common to all provincial inhabitants, including First Nations, these dimensions operate in tandem, acting to enable the overarching objective of apparently 'sustainable' industrial growth.

This chapter examines these eco-modernist characteristics in more detail, providing an explanation for why the regulatory process operates according to these philosophical principles despite an increasing awareness that their application has facilitated environmentally harmful expansion for almost two decades. With the overarching policies and strategies, those involved in consultation at the 'planning' stage, and hearing panels and senior regulatory personnel at the 'approval' stage, all considering expansive resource extraction to be in the 'public interest', or a 'social good', the origins of this claim are subject to examination. This accounts for the influence exerted by broader political-economic context upon policy objectives, paying heed to Kovel's (2007) observation that neither technology nor the regulatory mechanisms through which it is deployed can exist independently from the system in which it is operating. As such, the credibility of this prevalent and largely unchallenged assumption is tied to a reality manufactured according to certain neoliberal political and economic precepts.

The first section of this chapter brings into focus the particular strain of 'modernisation' being 'greened' by the regulatory process, taking into account contextual political-economic pressures. The second section examines the way in which this overarching narrow and economistic form of 'modernisation', given form by the policy and strategy objectives, is idealised and prioritised by those within the more operational, 'approval' stage of the process. Acting to justify a compliance-based approach to regulation that serves to undermine the public hearings and, by extension, give primacy to state and corporate actors throughout the decision-making process, the broader political-economic context provides the foundation upon which operational decisions favouring expansion are given credibility. As such, the second section presents a detailed examination of the assumptions upon which the economistic, rational-elitist dimension of 'weak' ecological modernisation rests. The third and final section evaluates a mainstay of eco-modernist philosophy: the extent to which the faith placed by both policy and regulatory Panels in techno-scientific methods of risk mitigation is vindicated. This demonstrates that the means for achieving 'sustainability' have proven to be less effective, and indeed less aggressively sought after, than those for achieving industrial expansion. Considering that growth has been repeatedly permitted despite recognition of this, and through use of an idealised image of the 'public interest', the 'approval' stage of the process is conceived of as a procedure that, instead of prohibiting environmental harm, is demonstrably catalytic in its production and reproduction. Taken together, this chapter explains that the 'weak' ecological modernisation in policy is operationalised in an almost dogmatic fashion throughout the regulatory process, where little attention is paid to its continuing and increasingly apparent inability to 'green' the growth being sought.

The Manufactured Necessity of 'Weak' Eco-Modernisation Policy in the Context of Neoliberal Political Economy

As illustrated in Chapter 3, the primary objective towards which policy and strategy are directed is that of 'sustainable growth'. With technology and science acting as the dominant means by which the oil sands industry is to be made 'sustainable', expansion is positioned in and of itself as the *ultimate* objective. It is in this context that the 'weak' form of ecological modernisation becomes apparent, with policy reflecting its associated and foremost emphasis on economic growth to such an extent that it 'remains only superficially or weakly *ecological*' (Christoff 1996: 486, emphasis in original). Within the philosophy more generally, this objective is justified by recourse to the notion that, without economic growth, protection efforts would be compromised because market-based solutions would remain undeveloped by interests with the capital to do otherwise (see Dryzek 2013). However, in this context the justifications upon which the policy objective of 'sustainable growth' have been based are anchored to more traditional justifications for economic expansion, including provision of public services and, to a lesser extent, employment opportunities. This further reinforces the subordination of environmental and social interests to those more economic, with similar language being used by personnel at both the 'planning' and 'approval' stages of the process (see Chapters 4 and 5). While such prioritisation is not to be unexpected under the capitalist mode of production, it does have a contextual specificity that is important to account for if the source of its justificatory power is to be fully understood. This is also necessary if the limited opportunities available for 'strong' forms of eco-modernist, or even eco-socialist, environmental reforms are to be appreciated. As Tombs (2012: 180) notes:

> [I]n any capitalist state, private corporations are key sources of providing goods, services, taxation and employment.... But the forms of such dependence are dynamic and historically specific – constituted in different ways, at different times, with different intensities and thus having different impacts.

In Alberta this dependence on private sector revenues is particularly high and, by virtue of its natural resources, largely concentrated on those collected from the extractives industry. Since 1990, between 19 and 41 per cent of annual provincial revenues has been derived from the non-renewables industry, averaging almost a quarter of total government revenues across the period (Government of Alberta 2018b). By situating this data in the context of total government expenditure, the extent of Alberta's dependency is more immediately visible. Figure 6.1 shows that there would indeed be a substantial funding shortfall, each year, for public services provision in the absence of revenues from non-renewables. It is this that lends credibility to the justifications for 'sustainable growth' outlined in policy and strategy, appearing to demonstrate existence of a fundamental alignment between private extractive and provincial social interests, in the form of public services. However, such a conclusion is premature, apolitical and decontextualized, serving to discount the way in which this reality has been purposefully manufactured over time, and according to the ideological precepts of neoliberalism.

Although government expenditure on public services depends on the revenues derived from resource extraction, this condition must be understood as tied to decisions made in the overarching context of provincial political economy. In Alberta (Miller 2007; Taylor and Friedel, 2011), and Canada more generally (Slowey 2008), these decisions are characterised by their affinity with neoliberal ideology. Indeed, this has been the case since the early 1970s (Miller 2007; see also Hayden 2014), when the doctrine first gained traction in political circles (see Litonjua 2008; Centeno and Cohen, 2012).

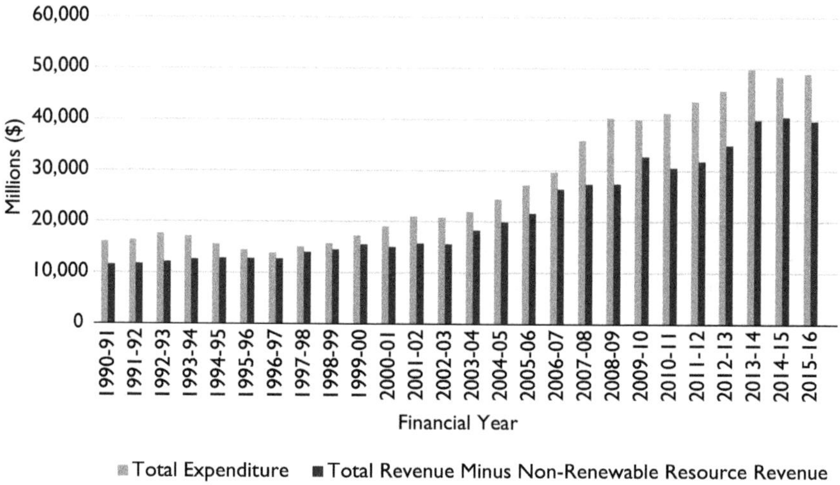

Figure 6.1 The Role of Non-Renewable Resource Revenue* in Meeting Provincial Expenditure, Nominal Data.

Source: Compiled from Government of Canada (2017: 33) and Government of Alberta (2018b).

Notes
* Includes oil sands and coal royalties, sale of leases, rentals, and fees.
** Figures taken from Government of Alberta 2017/18 End of Year Report.

While its particular forms are many and varied, according to Harvey (2005: 2) it can be generally recognised as a:

> theory of political economic practices proposing that human well-being can be best advanced by the maximisation of entrepreneurial freedoms within an institutional framework characterised by private property rights, individual liberty, unencumbered markets and free trade. The role of the state is to create and preserve an institutional framework appropriate to such practices.

The divided sovereignty of the Canadian state provided fertile ground for this ideology in advance of the free trade agreements established in the 1980s, such as the North American Free Trade Agreement, meaning that by the early 1990s 'neoliberalism had become a familiar framework in much of Western Canada – particularly in Alberta, Canada's most conservative, "free enterprise" province' (Carroll and Little 2001: 39). Such a transformation is also related to a broader shift towards the formation of an energy-based relationship with the USA, after the attacks of September the 11th, and the rise of Alberta's international political importance following the rapid growth of the oil sands in the mid-2000s (Stefanick 2015). However, there are several specific ways in which this ideology is manifested in provincial tax, royalty, and savings arrangements, all of which have increased provincial dependency on oil sands revenues over time. It is these factors that lend credibility to the public service justifications underpinning the pursuit of 'sustainable growth' in both policy and practice.

By virtue of its oil wealth, Alberta has led all other provinces in economic growth between 2005 and 2015, averaging an annual Gross Domestic Product (GDP) increase of 3.2 per cent year on year over this time, despite oil market volatility (Government of Alberta 2016c: 2). While global oil prices declined in 2015 and 2016, causing GDP to decrease for these two years, their recovery in 2017 caused provincial GDP to increase by 4.9 per cent for that year (Statistics Canada 2016a). It is to such data that past premiers and senior regulatory personnel speak when referring to the oil sands as the 'engine' of the provincial and national economies (Stelmach 2008; Prentice, cited in Fawcett 2015;). However, as Figure 6.2 demonstrates, the unparalleled increase in productivity has not been matched by a proportional growth in levels of provincial government expenditure, which has stood well below the average of the other nine provinces for almost three decades. The increase seen from 2015 onwards is attributed to the Government of Alberta responding to the provincial recession induced by the drop in global oil prices; while GDP decreased, the new, liberal provincial government borrowed instead of reducing expenditure.

This divergence, between GDP growth and provincial government expenditure, challenges the cogency of the relationship-based justifications

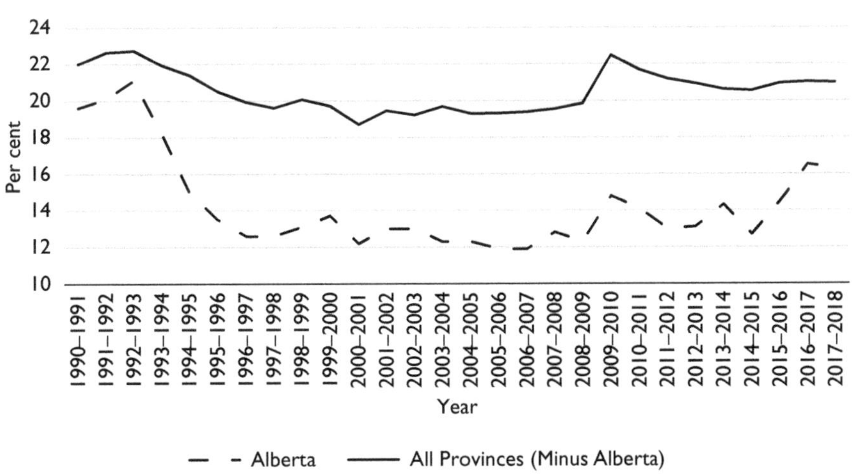

Figure 6.2 Provincial Government Expenditure Relative to GDP.

Source: Compiled from Royal Bank of Canada (2018: 9).

drawn throughout policy, where the economic need for 'sustainable growth' in oil sands production is premised on a more social need to provide public services. Indeed, examining some of the key destinations for the capital associated with this increase in GDP, including taxation rates, the primary provincial savings fund, and levels of corporate profit, illustrates that this need, although real to a certain extent, has been manufactured by application of broader policies associated with neoliberal political-economic doctrine for over 20 years. As such, the justifications for growth are not as infallible as they first appear, destabilising their credibility when considered in the context of the concomitant indigenous environmental victimisation and Treaty rights abuses that also result from its pursuit.

Gradual changes to provincial tax arrangements broadly mirror neoliberal justifications for limiting state intervention in markets (see Kotz 2002), with Alberta experiencing significant reductions in taxation for businesses and the investing class under the expectation that it will stimulate future economic growth. Beginning in 2000, Premier Klein introduced a single personal income tax rate of 10 per cent as a general means of stimulating the economy in response to a provincial deficit (Government of Alberta 2000d). Colloquially termed the 'flat tax', this was followed in 2006 by a reduction in the rate of corporate income tax, from a high of 15.5 per cent in 2000 to a level of 10 per cent (Government of Alberta 2006a: 2), being added to in 2009 with the elimination of all provincial healthcare insurance premiums payable by individuals and employers (Government of Alberta 2009d: 2). According to the budget documents, these changes were justified by recourse to their ability to stimulate a generalised economic growth, with increased revenues from expected expansion in non-renewable resource extraction intended to fill the gap. Alberta also has no provincial sales tax, although this is not a recent modification. Had such changes been avoided, the province would have collected an additional $5.7 billion revenue in 2009 alone (Lahey 2015: 21). For perspective, the deficit for 2015–2016, which resulted from the fall in world oil prices, was $6.4 billion, with those for the two years following standing at $10.8 and $8 billion, respectively (Government of Alberta 2016d: 4, 2017: 10, 2018c: 10). It is this situation that prompted Lahey (2015: 2) to conclude that:

> [B]udgetary reliance on ongoing sale of non-renewable resource assets to compensate for the lack of adequate provincial tax revenues has left crucial social programs underfunded and vulnerable to market swings in volatile oil prices.

It is worth noting that the individual tax savings resulting from these changes have been distributed inequitably across the province. In 2009, the 30 per cent of Alberta's population on the lowest income received only 6.9 per cent of this privatised revenue, compared with the 54.1 per cent received by the wealthiest 30 per cent (ibid.: 34). It is this that has contributed to an inequality gap described as a 'chasm' by Flanagan (2015b), who concludes that Alberta 'has the greatest inequality of income' in all of Canada, and that its tax system also produces 'the smallest improvement in levels of income equality' compared to other provinces. Considered in the context of the unprecedented wage increases which have appeared alongside the similarly unparalleled rise in homelessness and reductions in public service expenditure (see below), this is not controversial. In effect, these gradual changes to provincial tax arrangements have served to concentrate Alberta's dependence on revenue streams derived from non-renewable resources, with corporate income tax accounting for, on average, 10 per cent of government revenues between 2003 and 2014, compared to non-renewable resource revenues which stood at 29 per cent (Government of Alberta 2015b: 2). This has increased the sensitivity of provincial public service provision to market volatility, lending credibility to the idea forwarded in both policy and practice that industrial expansion in the oil sands is a provincial social necessity.

In addition to this lack of taxation, an imperative to continually permit oil sands growth also emerges from a marked government aversion to saving a proportion of oil-derived revenues over time. This would serve the dual purpose of providing a fund that could be used to smooth out the unavoidable volatility associated with future downturns in the oil market, while also ensuring that the economic wealth derived from natural resources could be shared with future generations (Roach *et al.* 2015). A mechanism introduced with this original intention does exist in the Alberta Heritage Fund (AHF), which was established in 1976 with the aim of saving as much as 30 per cent of annual revenues derived from non-renewable resource extraction (van den Bremer and van der Ploeg 2014). Instead of deducting from the amounts deposited into the fund, the interest resulting from its gradual accumulation could be spent as needed in the future. However, as the provincial government struggled with recession between 1984 and 1987, the proportion of non-renewable revenues moved into the account was revised to 15 per cent, with additional transfers frozen later that year and funds redirected into general revenue for spending (Tsalik 2003: 27). The issue with this is made clear by Murphy and Clemens (2013: 8):

> In strict economic theory, [non-renewable resource] revenues are not income in an accounting sense, but are a transformation of one type of capital asset (oil deposits in the ground, for example) into another type of asset – cash in the Treasury's bank account. Therefore, to treat these revenues as analogous to sales tax receipts and spend them on projects that provide a flow of present services, would be to engage in unwise capital consumption.… Intuitively, the present generation would be selfishly eating away at a finite stock pile of wealth, rather than acting as custodians of nature's gifts on behalf of future generations.

Despite this, the provincial government has since maintained the approach adopted in 1987, even in times of economic upturn. The period between 1992 and 2006 actually saw the value of the fund almost halved by inflation before it was finally protected from its influence (Gibson 2007a: 29; see also Murphy and Clemens 2013: 11). Some isolated deposits were made in the mid-2000 boom years but, ultimately, following the 40-year period in which the AHF has existed, the total directed into it stands at nearly $18 billion – less than 10 per cent of the $217,931 billion in non-renewable resource revenue collected between 1976 and 2014 (Roach *et al.* 2015: 18–21). Instead, Alberta has 'spent budgeted and "surprise" surpluses on a range of tax cuts, discretionary spending, and giveaways' (Thompson 2008: 3), with the latter of these referencing the tax-free amount of $400 given to every Alberta resident in 2005 as a result of a budgetary surplus (see also Milke and Palacios 2015). Controlling for population growth, this equates to a fund that was worth more than twice as much per member of the provincial population in 1983 than in 2017 (Figure 6.3). In essence, for the past four decades the provincial government has avoided prioritising saving-orientated measures that would reduce the impact of market volatility on future levels of public expenditure and employment security, simultaneously increasing the need to constantly expand the oil sands industry as it continues to operate as the dominant source of government revenue.

The reluctance demonstrated by the Government of Alberta to increase taxation rates or diversify revenue sources, tendency to adopt an apprehensive stance towards saving a portion of such revenues for some future point in time where state intervention may be socio-economically necessary, and its presiding over a substantially decreasing proportion of GDP expended on

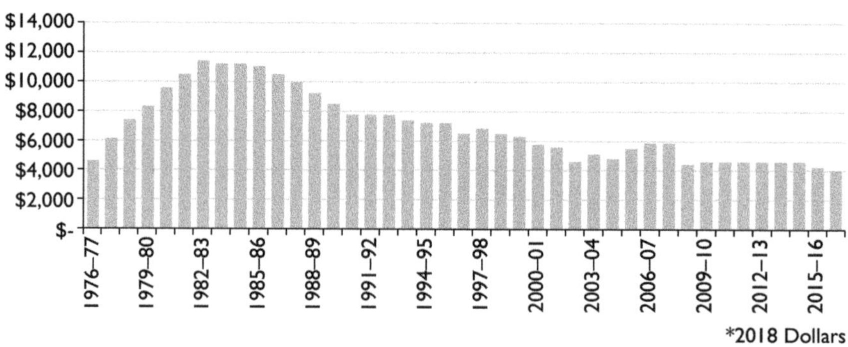

Figure 6.3 Inflation Adjusted Per Capita Market Value* of the Alberta Heritage Fund, 1976–2017.

Source: Alberta Treasury Board and Finance (2018: 12).

Note
* 2018 Dollars.

public services for much for the past three decades, are all hallmarks of the limited government role imagined under neoliberal political-economic theory (see Chang 2003; Centeno and Cohen 2012). Coupled with a continually low royalty rate that saw Alberta collect 23 per cent of oil sands industry profits in 2017 (Wilt 2018; see also Acuna 2016), it can be said that provincial dependence on extractive revenues is real, but that it is a reality constructed according to the key tenets of neoliberal doctrine. Lending credibility to the public service justifications underpinning the policy objective of 'sustainable growth', this highlights the constraints such a context exerts on the type of eco-modernist environmental reforms that can be achieved under a neoliberal political-economic regime. Indeed, Christoff (1996: 487) maintains that, in its 'strong' form, ecological modernisation may permit 'multiple possibilities' for 'modernisation', however defined, and not simply one dependent on 'Western science, technology and consumer culture'. However, what is presented throughout the policy documents is a fixed, 'hegemonic' (ibid.) notion of progress that is defined by a narrow, economistic emphasis on accelerating production, the 'greening' of which is to be facilitated not by recognising environmental limits, but by deploying science and technology to overcome them. With these being recognisable features of 'weak' eco-modernist philosophy (ibid.: 490), and pursuit of such characteristics rendered necessary, or at least justifiable, by the neoliberal political-economic context in which they are situated, then it is not unreasonable to invoke Ruggiero's (2013: 139) observation that '[n]eoliberalism does not observe and describe the economic reality, it creates that reality'. Indeed, the public service justifications offered throughout policy and strategy can be seen to 'legitimise economic conduct by conferring on it the character of inevitability, of a divine project aimed at the happiness of all' (ibid.: 137). In this sense, although fundamental questions about the 'modernisation' component of eco-modernist philosophy have yet to be answered by scholars, in the context of the oil sands it may be more accurate to speak of attempts at 'ecological neoliberalism', for this is the overarching system of production within which environmental modifications are pursued, and towards which attempts at 'sustainability' have been – and continue to be – directed.

Rational Elitism and the Justificatory Power of Idealised Consensus at the Level of Operations

While the manufactured imperative to continually expand the oil sands lends credibility to the public service justifications for 'sustainable growth' objectives at the level of policy and strategy, it also serves the same function at the more operational 'approval' stage of the regulatory process. However, at this level the assumed parity between public and private interests also extends to justifying a rational elitist approach to decision-making that further operationalises the 'weak' eco-modernist philosophy visible throughout the policy documents. Although the rationalist, 'technocratic' (see Christoff 1996: 490) aspect of this particular trait is mostly visible in the techno-scientific mitigation deployed within the hearings, its elitist element is more directly manifest in the stated process of ensuring oil sands projects are effectively approved at a point prior to the date on which public hearings are held. This undermining of the quasi-judicial process is inseparable from the more general regulatory preference for maintaining a dialogue with industry outside of the hearings to ensure its acquiescence. This alignment between regulator and regulated results in the prioritisation of 'techno-corporatist' measures (Hajer 1995), which are decided upon 'through corporatist relationships between government and industry' (Gibbs 1998: 12), ultimately 'serving to legitimise the continuing instrumental domination and destruction of the environment' through 'the promotion of less democratic forms of government' (Christoff 1996: 497). Put another way, buttressed by a provincial reliance on oil sands revenues rooted in a similarly provincial aversion to diversifying income streams, and supported by the imagined capacity of science and technology to mitigate environmental impacts, it is the perceived parity of purpose, between government and industry, that plays a substantial role in the sanctioning of oil sands project applications at the 'approval' stage of the regulatory process.

The influence of expansionary state-corporate interests upon the 'independent' energy regulator is manifest in two separate but ultimately related ways. This mirrors the duality identified by Ruggiero (2015: 34) in his analysis of relationships of authority, where harmful activities of the powerful are recognised as 'not based exclusively on coercion but also on some degree of consensus'. The first of these categories relates to the more direct influence exerted by government policy on regulatory behaviour, where operational decisions are made in accordance with overarching strategic parameters. Indeed, regulatory personnel frequently spoke of the need to act in accordance with policy priorities, such as the land use designations outlined in the LARP, describing the influence as stemming from the ordinary asymmetry of relations inherent to the vertical chain of command within the regulatory agency itself. In this sense, the consistent policy objective for 'sustainable growth' exerts direct influence on the activities of the energy regulator over time. This accords with Low's (2011: 38) analysis of public interest decisions made by hearing panels, where the legislative requirement to balance 'provincial public' interests against those of 'local publics' limits the ability of the regulator to stop or hinder project applications.

Coupled with this is the second relationship of authority spoken of by Ruggiero (2015: 34), that of 'consensus'. Depicting a more accordant relationship than the coercive variant identified above, regulatory personnel work alongside government and industry to ensure individual project applications are approved because of a perceived equalisation of interests. The most serious operational consequence of this is that oil sands projects are effectively approved at a point prior to the date on which public hearings are held, validating Hierlmeier's (2008: 4) observation that the 'public interest' decisions made at the hearings appear to be 'simply used to justify the decision that has been made'. In noting the preference for maintaining a dialogue with industry outside of the hearings, as a means of ensuring corporate acquiescence, regulatory personnel described their role as akin to 'consultants rather than the police' (Tombs and Whyte 2007: 154). With such strategies being founded on persuasion, bargaining and compromise between regulator and regulated (Tombs 2017), as opposed to the more prescriptive and state-directed 'command and control' varieties (Tombs 2002: 120), what is essentially being advocated is an approach affiliated with what is known as the 'compliance school' of regulation. The justification given by regulatory personnel for this echoed the content of justifications deployed in policy, and those given for approving projects under the rubric of the 'public interest' at the hearings, where public service provision is dependent on revenues collected from extractive activities:

> [W]ell, what kind of a society are we building? What's happening to the resource wealth that's being generated? If you track those dollars you can build a very compelling case that this is part of the engine of the Canadian economy and the dollars that are being generated are flowing back in for societal goods. If you look off into the horizon there, there's a new cancer centre, new hospitals, and … it's quite a wonderful country that we've built, and it's all been built on resource wealth. So, and I'm not saying that's a reason to set aside environmental concerns. You can have your cake and eat it. You can manage these things well. Create a healthy, wealthy society and, although the in-the-moment, when the mine is in active operation and looks ugly, it's something that you'd be willing to put up with for all these other good things that come along with it. So that story hasn't received nearly enough attention because it's a hard one to tell. A lot of it goes right back to the level of the average citizen's understanding of how the economy works, and it's not where it needs to be. Because people can isolate big bad development company over here, yet they walk down the street to their local playground and enjoy the amenities there, attend the public school and partake of all the benefits of the society that we've created, but they criticise the engine of the whole system.
>
> (Participant F, Energy Regulator)

As seen above, if taken at face value this linear, unidirectional relationship, between an expansive oil sands industry and the provision of public services, is not without foundation. Indeed, the substantial employment benefits created by the industry are undeniable, with over 228,000 direct and indirect jobs across Canada being linked to the oil sands industry as of 2017 (CAPP 2018a). However, focusing on these equivalences alone is highly selective and decontextualised, neglecting to account for the various detrimental province-wide social issues that have emerged alongside such benefits. This serves to privilege economic interests above all others in operationalising an idealised image of oil sands growth and ignores the societal tensions resulting from its singular pursuit.

At a fundamental level, a myriad of broader socio-economic problems emerges from tying government revenues so closely to the market for oil, not least because the former internalises the inherent volatility of the latter. As Figure 6.4 illustrates, provincial surpluses and deficits tend to correspond with respective increases and decreases in the share of revenue derived from natural resources. Not only does this expose Alberta's inhabitants to periodic disruptions in their socio-economic circumstances, as changes in the world price for oil influences the economic viability of bitumen products, but these spikes of rapid growth also generate a provincial scarcity in the labour and materials needed for expansion. Importantly, this precipitates an industry willingness to pay greater amounts for both (Lemphers and Woynillowicz 2012: 10). Contributing to a higher rate of inflation across the province (ibid.), which has been rising above the national average for the majority of the post-2002 period (Flanagan 2015a), this readiness to pay higher wages to attract and retain skilled labour has contributed to substantial levels of net inter-provincial migration into Alberta since at least 1995. Figure 6.5 illustrates the disproportionality of this

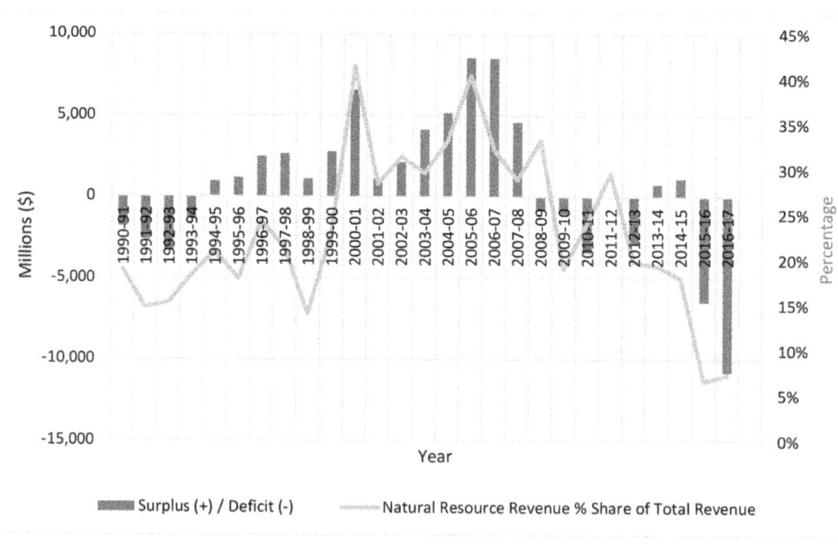

Figure 6.4 Alberta Provincial Government Surplus (+)/Deficits (–) and Natural Resource Revenue Shares (%), 1990/91–2016/17.

Source: Compiled from Government of Canada (2017: 33) and Government of Alberta (2018b).

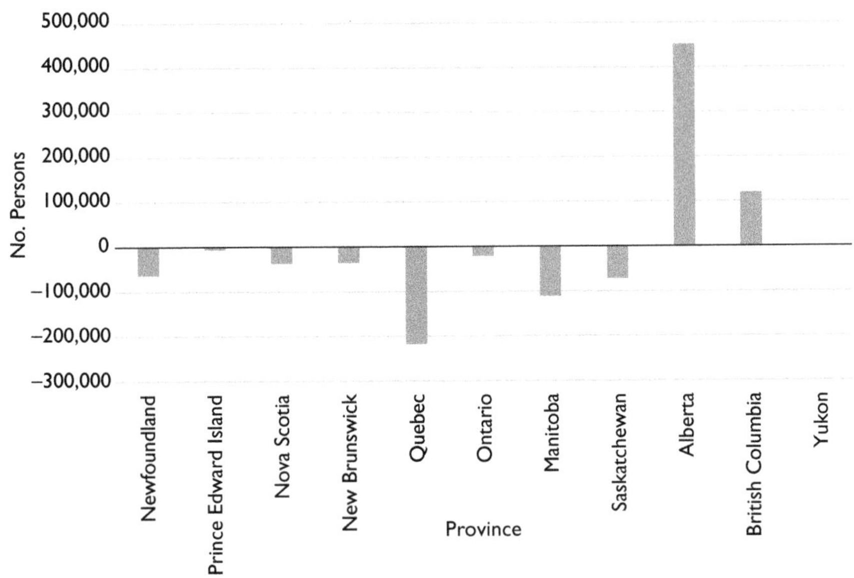

Figure 6.5 Net Inter-Provincial Migration, Q1, 1995 – Q1, 2018.
Source: Compiled from Statistics Canada (2018b).

movement in stark detail, showing British Columbia to be the only other province to have experienced a cumulative inflow of inter-provincial migrants over the same period of time. The only difference is that its figure of just over 100,000 comes a distant second to Alberta's sum of just over 450,000.

As of 2006, this rapid population growth had caused provincial infrastructure, transport, and support services to be 'stretched to the maximum' (Government of Alberta 2006b: i), even provoking opposition from organised labour, which is traditionally considered one of the major groups with a vested interest in accelerating production (Stretesky *et al.* 2013). As the Alberta Federation of Labour (AFL) (2007: 2) stated, provincial public projects have been 'priced out of reach as the energy sector soaks up the available labour and building materials'. This is a reference to the high demand on construction companies that occurred during the particularly rapid expansionary years of 2006–2008, which led to few or no tenders for public infrastructure projects. As a result of their deferral, and in the context of increasing inflation, this led to the steady escalation of costs to such an extent that public funding was spent on 'more-expensive infrastructure instead of more infrastructure' (Parkland Institute 2011). As of 2015, these consequences were still exerting influence, acting as a justificatory backdrop for investment by the incoming Notley administration:

> Alberta's continued population growth and an underinvestment in infrastructure has resulted in an infrastructure backlog, requiring significant reinvestment to 'catch-up' and meet the needs of Albertans, while also ensuring existing infrastructure is maintained in a sustainable manner.
>
> (Government of Alberta 2015c: 68)

In this sense, the assumed relationship between private extractive and provincial public service provision is not necessarily one of equivalence, as realisation of the former has had detrimental socio-economic consequences for the latter. The higher rate of inflation has also made public services proportionally more expensive in Alberta, all other factors constant, than any other jurisdiction in Canada (Flanagan 2015a). This has become particularly problematic in the aftermath of falling world oil prices after 2015, triggering calls for the provincial government to rapidly reduce public spending (Mason 2015; Lafleur, 2018). While these voices frame the issue of expenditure as one emerging from government over-spending on public services, leading to calls for austerity, it has already been demonstrated above that the problem is more closely related to a long-term over-reliance on the oil sands as a source of revenue.

Although the more direct consequences of such reductions would fall on the more vulnerable sections of the provincial population, particularly in the context of crisis-induced periods of unemployment (see, for example, Government of Alberta 2016e), other adverse effects of rapid inflation and cumulative inter-provincial migration are already visible. In noting that increased inflation translates into an erosion of household purchasing power, and a higher cost of living for provincial inhabitants on the whole, Gibson (2007b) argues that this has had a particularly detrimental effect on those with fixed incomes, seniors, and those dependent on minimum wage jobs or social assistance. Indeed, in the midst of resource development, Alberta 'has experienced some of the worst affordability problems and sharpest increases in homelessness in Canada' (Evans 2015: 313). Varying across the province, the significance of this was highlighted in a report on homelessness in Edmonton just prior to the 2015 recession, which records a 'strong link' between the increasing numbers of homeless and the rise in rent prices seen since 1999 (Homeward Trust Edmonton 2014: 11). In noting that 'an increase in income for the average person and an influx of workers from outside puts pressure on the housing market' (ibid.), it establishes the link between the more specific housing difficulties encountered by already-vulnerable groups and the socio-economic symptoms of oil sands expansion. With a near 260 per cent increase in homelessness witnessed in Edmonton since 1998 (ibid.), and an increase of 700 per cent recorded between 1992 and 2008 in Calgary (Calgary Homeless Foundation 2014: 4), it is to such figures that Campanella and Bower (2013: 1) speak when noting the 'rampant homelessness' associated with rapid growth of the industry.

Even those employed directly in the oil sands, or indirectly through one of the sectors supporting it, are not shielded from negative socio-economic consequences. While the average wages of those working in Alberta's oil and gas industry have been consistently higher than any other since at least 2005 (Government of Alberta 2018d), the employment created by the industry itself is largely temporary and precarious (Campanella and Bower 2013; Dobson *et al.* 2013). Not only has the industry relied on transitory forms of labour since its inception, with the population of both domestic and foreign workers housed in temporary trailer camps during the boom years increasing from 5,903 in 2000 to 9,178 in 2005, and up to 26,284 in 2008 (Ferguson 2011: 107), but provincial employment levels track closely to the spikes and drops in oil sands production. This generates labour conditions defined by an insecurity derived from oil market volatility. Indeed, the most recent downturn in world oil prices sparked a similarly rapid increase in unemployment, which rose from 4.6 per cent in January 2015 in a near-uninterrupted trajectory to almost 9 per cent two years later (Government of Alberta 2018e). As a result, relationships were drawn with the 30 per cent increase seen in provincial suicide rates compared to the pre-recession period (Mouallem 2015). Similar detrimental consequences were mirrored in data released by the Alberta Federation of Labour (AFL) (2012: 3), which noted that the number of workers in the four occupations with the highest rates of disabling injuries and fatalities, construction, mining, transportation, and manufacturing, increased by almost 50 per cent between 1991 and 2009. With this period being simultaneously marked by a decreasing spend on occupational health and safety measures per worker, the period of unprecedented oil sands expansion, between 2006 and 2008, also saw provincial workplace fatalities, per 100,000 workers, pushed beyond the national average (ibid.: 2).

More inter-generational consequences can be seen in the low graduation rates within the provincial education system. In 1999 the proportion of 18-year- olds graduating from Alberta's secondary schools stood at around 64 per cent, increasing to around 68 per cent by 2006 (Taylor-Vaisey 2008). The intervening decade has seen some improvement, with most recent statistics placing the figure at 74 per cent (see Figure 6.6). However, this is still more than 10 per cent below both the national and OECD averages. Each of these issues is seen to have resulted from the attraction of better-paid jobs in the oil sands region serving to pull people out of education early (Taylor-Vaisey 2008; Campanella and Bower 2013). While this funnelling of young people without a secondary education into the oil sands sector is not necessarily problematic in and of itself, issues arise when understood in the context of the industry's inherent volatility, which leads to peaks and troughs in employment rates, and the increasingly global attempt to move away from a reliance on the fossil fuel industry.

Considering these various socio-economic detriments, maintaining an unquestioned, blanket justification that equalises the continued expansion of

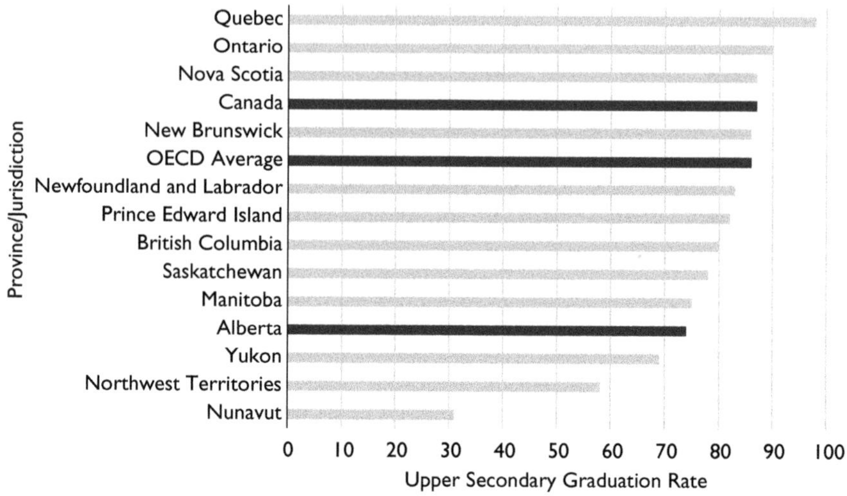

Figure 6.6 Upper Secondary School Graduation Rate by Province, 2015.
Source: Compiled from Statistics Canada (2018c).

the oil sands with some undifferentiated provincial public 'good' becomes not only untenable but, when used to facilitate the very expansion generating these consequences, harmful. Considered alongside the extensive environmental degradation occurring in the region, the approach taken to industry regulation belies an idealised consensus reminiscent of 'romantic pluralism'. Associated with the 'theory of balance' spoken of by Wright Mills (1956: 247), which 'rests upon the moral idea of a natural harmony of interests, in terms of which greed and ruthlessness are reconciled with justice and progress', the problem with this stance is that it overlooks concentrations of power (see Pearce and Tombs 1997; Tombs and Whyte, 2015). Echoing Schattschneider's (1960: 35) early contention, that '[t]he flaw in the pluralist heaven is that the heavenly chorus sings with a strong upperclass accent', this idealistic perception is operationalised by regulatory personnel in justification for the growth-enabling regulator–regulatee relationship. However, as claims forwarded under this 'social good' rubric 'are not likely to be credible on exclusively ideological grounds unless they are prepared to grant concessions ... to the powerless' (Ruggiero 2015: 40), then repeated reference to employment opportunities and public service provision enables this credibility to remain intact, despite the broader socio-economic and environmental consequences. In this sense, use of consensus-based reasoning by regulatory personnel demonstrates an internalisation and prioritisation of the narrow and idealised aspects of the structural, neoliberal state–industry relationship, generating 'mentalities' and 'sensibilities' conducive to producing, reinforcing, and reconstituting the social relations inherent to the political-economic realities in which they operate (Snider 2009: 4; see also Whyte 2012).

Whether the consensus-based approach adopted by the regulator is derived from a 'romantic pluralism' or coerced by the direction established in policy and strategy, each mode of influence, when taken to its logical conclusion, frames the expansion of natural resource extraction under the terms of an economistic and ultimately idealised 'public interest'. It is this that provides the justificatory foundation for the close relationship between state and corporate actors at the 'approval' stage of the process, permitting such extensive co-operation that individual oil sands projects are effectively approved at a point prior to the public hearings. This represents an operationalised form of rational elitism, where First Nations and other stakeholders may have token input into the types of environmental mitigation required, but the ultimate decision on expansion is a foregone conclusion. With the power of indigenous participants to decelerate or even relocate production almost completely diminished, it is left to the spheres of technology and science to 'green' the forthcoming industrialisation, mitigate its tensions with environmental limits, and achieve the overarching policy objective of 'sustainable growth'.

Flawed Techno-Scientific Precaution and the Fallacy of Dematerialisation

In order to 'green' the imperative to expand oil sands production, policies, strategies, and hearing panels made extensive reference to techno-scientific methods for addressing its environmental impact. Visible throughout their risk-assessment deliberations, where balance is sought between social, economic, and environmental issues in the process of making a 'public interest' decision, such methods were continually deployed as a form of precaution, appearing to negate the uncertainty and risks associated with project approvals. This is not especially unusual, as ecological modernisation was originally conceived as an operationalised form of precautionary principle (see Benn 2009). Indeed, while science was seen to 'detect possible dangers', the role of technological innovation was to 'develop alternative paths of development' (Andersen and Massa 2000: 338–339). In the oil sands these two aspects are broadly pursued by different parties, with ongoing environmental monitoring and data gathering being conducted by industry-led, multi-stakeholder initiatives, and technological innovation left to industry members themselves. It is to these two related spheres that the Panels defer in the process of mitigating environmental impacts, meaning that they are involved as separate but related aspects of precaution in the final determination of whether a project approval poses an 'acceptable' level of risk. As such, the extent to which these precautionary measures are successful holds the answer to the 'central question before ecological modernisation theory', which is 'whether the hare of institutional and technological transformation can outpace the tortoise of relentless growth' (York and Rosa 2003: 279).

With regard to the first of these spheres – science – the repeated requests for a greater degree of environmental monitoring and data collection, made by both Panels and First Nations throughout the hearings, mirror the emphasis placed in policy on the precautionary approach of adaptive management. With uncertainty acting as 'the unifying hallmark of environmental and natural resource regulation' (Doremus 2007: 548), the capacity of adaptive management to 'recognise the inherent uncertainties of dynamic and unpredictable ecosystems' and 'test these uncertainties [to] progressively improve' (Kingsford and Biggs 2012: 9), makes the approach itself appear well-suited to addressing the complex environmental issues identified in the oil sands. Indeed, the fundamental element underpinning this form of systematised improvement is learning-based modification of actions. Identified throughout the many and varied forms of adaptive management, such learning is viewed as a tool for responding to environmental complexity (Walters 1997; Allen *et al.* 2011), as a straightforward means of increasing knowledge about unpredictable ecosystems (Armitage *et al.* 2008), or as a method for recognising and managing the intricacies of socio-ecological relationships (Runge 2011). Whichever conception is used, value is placed on the process by which actions taken on objectives have their effects monitored and their results reflected on, leading to the iterative alteration of objectives to ensure social, economic, and environmental balance (Fabricius and Cundill 2014). However, one of the key issues in the oil sands is that the monitoring organisations have experienced recurrent and fundamental organisational deficiencies, undermining this very learning process and, by extension, the singular element upon which adaptive management is made achievable as a precautionary technique.

As illustrated throughout Chapter 5, two of the monitoring organisations repeatedly referred to by the Panels are the RAMP and CEMA. Although concerns were increasingly raised by First Nations over the period in which the hearings were held, culminating in calls for greater government leadership in environmental monitoring, the organisations were still referred to by the Panels as a means of negating risk in a substantial proportion of the hearings. This was despite widespread evidence demonstrating their fundamental flaws. With respect to the earliest concerns about the RAMP, the Panel convened to decide on the 2004 CNRL Horizon project being deferred to a scientific peer review of the organisation in response to First Nation concerns. However, upon publication it identified significant organisational deficiencies:

> In the current state, RAMP is not in a position to measure and assess development-related change locally or in a cumulative way. Reviewers reported serious problems related to scientific leadership and a lack of integration and consistency across components with respect to approach,

> design, implementation, and analysis. Reviewers also reported a lack of an overall regional plan, that clear questions were not been addressed in the monitoring and that there were sometimes significant shortfalls with respect to statistical design of the individual components.
>
> (Ayles *et al.* 2004: 59)

The Panels continued to defer to RAMP-derived data in the subsequent hearings, despite further evidence as to its organisational deficiencies being presented by First Nations. In a successive scientific review, Burn *et al.* (2011) considered the RAMP, since 2005, to have met only one of its ten organisational objectives. The reviewers concluded that the programme 'is not sufficient to detect changes [in the environment] if they occur, 'cannot sufficiently identify sources resulting in the change(s) if changes are detected', and that 'not all of the questions are being asked' or 'appropriate criteria being monitored to answer those questions' (ibid.: 2). This ultimately led the reviewers to conclude the RAMP, 13 years after its inception, to be 'incapable of detecting regional trends and cumulative effects' (ibid.: 3). This overarching criticism was also echoed by Kelly *et al.* (2010), with Dillon *et al.* (2011: iii) further noting that the RAMP 'has a very extensive monitoring design', but the systems being monitored are 'large, complex and variable, and their sampling frequencies are too low and the sampling locations are not adequate to account for this'. Dowdeswell *et al.* (2010: 33) added to this, describing the RAMP as 'not designed to be systemic, holistic or adaptive', lacking integration with other monitoring initiatives, and ultimately suffering from an absence of both scientific leadership and a peer-review process.

Similar deficiencies are also seen with the CEMA, which was referred to by Panels in the majority of the hearings as a means of mitigating environmental risk. Indeed, it was as early as 1999 when reference was first made to its precursor, CEEM. Although the Panels express concerns with the organisation in the subsequent Muskeg River hearing, and those for the 2004 CNRL and Jackpine projects, before reaching a head in the 2007 hearing for Imperial Oil's Kearl Mine, it is still used by the Panels to balance risk in the process of approving these projects. Despite this, the government-initiated review of the organisation in 2008 produced two reports that confirm the deficiencies spoken of by First Nations during the hearings. One of these considered CEMA to be ill-equipped to deal with the pace of oil sands expansion, that the lack of policy and planning in the region had blinded CEMA's participants to the implications of their recommendations, and that the absence of government direction made establishing regulatory backstops difficult (PricewaterhouseCoopers 2008). The other report was more explicit in its criticism:

> Traditional Ecological Knowledge has not been incorporated into CEMA Guidelines and Management Frameworks in a way that addresses the

> broader land management perspective of aboriginal people.... CEMA's immediate outcomes of having both resource developers and regulators apply cumulative effects-based environment management practices have not been successful over ... [its] nine year life.... A Regional Management System has not been achieved.... [CEMA] has not been successful in creating a forum for all interests to successfully work together ... [and] CEMA has not achieved a stakeholder driven process when considered in an aboriginal context....
>
> (Tumbleweed Consulting Ltd 2008: 53)

Expanding on its findings, the report also notes a 'lack of connection between CEMA's recommendations and government's implementation of these recommendations' (ibid.). It finishes by recognising that '[i]n addition to a lack of implementation by government, there has also been little evidence of implementation by corporate members and a resulting lack of participation by aboriginal groups' (ibid.). Although similarly critical, Kennett (2007) identifies the recursive relationship between Panel approvals and the difficulties encountered by CEMA. Recognising that since its inception the monitoring organisation has been 'perpetually playing catch up', he goes on to warn of the consequences associated with rapid industrial growth outstripping its effective monitoring, in that 'limits of acceptable ecological impacts may be crossed before they are even identified', and opportunities to 'direct development in ways that are less environmentally damaging may be missed' (ibid.: ix). Lott and Jones (2010: 36) take a broader view, noting that all of the monitoring programmes suffer from a lack of integration, where 'no one is pulling all of this data and information together to create an integrated, higher level monitoring report'. These findings are echoed by the subsequent Alberta Environment Monitoring Panel (2011), with Lott and Jones (2010) repeating some of the conclusions reached in the Radke Report from five years earlier (Radke 2006: 133–134). As of 1 April 2016, CEMA (2016) was closed down 'due to a shortage of funding'.

The final hearing document analysed, for the 2013 expansion of Shell Jackpine, shows the Panel referencing the JOSM. This plan was in existence until 2016, having the purpose of mitigating concerns surrounding water quantity, the acknowledged deficiencies in the RAMP, and the lack of integration between monitoring systems. However, the faith placed in the ability of these monitoring initiatives to address uncertainty and subsequently mitigate risks continued to be misplaced. In December 2014, the Auditor General of Alberta raised significant concerns with the first implementation report on the JOSM. Assessing whether the results in the report were complete and verifiable, he concluded that:

> Most projects we tested lacked project plans or had plans without key information such as clearly defined deliverables and timelines. Without

> clear deliverables, effective monitoring of progress is not possible. We found insufficient evidence that the department regularly monitored progress of most projects we tested. Evidence for the project status stated in the report was also insufficient. Despite committing to do so in the joint plan, neither government [of Alberta and Canada] monitored the projects the independent monitoring organizations were delivering to ensure they implemented them as required.
>
> (Office of the Auditor General of Alberta 2014: 25)

In another report, which analyses the technical adequacy of the JOSM and the extent to which its supporting institutional and legal structures can be considered sufficient to support its implementation, Olszynski (2014: 35) considers it 'unlikely to be an effective – let alone world class – monitoring program'. Although finding the technical component to offer some promise, this is hindered by a lack of institutional structures needed for its implementation. As such, over the near-20 years in which the oil sands industry has experienced rapid expansion, the initiatives and more recent plan, recourse to which has balanced the trio of factors underpinning the 'public interest test' at the hearings, have been consistently identified as unfit for purpose. Attempts at 'adapting' to the environmental changes resulting from oil sands expansion have therefore been fundamentally flawed for the entire period in which the industry has existed.

The monitoring and gathering of data forms only one side of the precautionary, eco-modernist duality of science and technology outlined by Andersen and Massa (2000). As Olszynski (2014: 25) recognises, 'even a "world class" monitoring system will not, in and of itself, prevent ecosystem decline', meaning that actions aimed at understanding ecological impacts must be followed by those able to modify material reality. In the context of 'sustainable growth', this role is largely undertaken by technological innovation. The faith in the idea that its advances will be able to mitigate the environmental harm associated with increases in production is an assumption consistently held by the Panels. However, available data indicates the presence of a challenge similar to that identified with respect to scientific monitoring, insofar as the expected gains have not materialised. This is not particularly unusual, as ecological modernisation is commonly recognised as a philosophy that 'endow[s] technology with heroic powers' (Bonds and Downey 2012: 168). Indeed, the characteristic is particularly visible in its 'weak' (Christoff 1996: 490), and 'techno-corporatist' forms (Hajer 1995). However, this is an over-simplification. In reality it is a very particular type of technological innovation that holds relevance for reducing environmental impacts. Differentiating between '[e]xplorative innovation', '[e]xtractive innovation', and 'end-use innovation', Czech (2013: 206) explains how the first allows producers to locate resources that were previously undetectable, whereas the second permits access to those previously inaccessible. As such, both are geared towards increasing the rate and extent of production. This can be seen in Figure 6.7, which illustrates the role played by new extractive technologies in increasing productive output in the oil sands.

In light of this, it is only forms of 'end-use innovation' that 'could conceivably reconcile economic growth with environmental protection' (Czech 2013: 207). This is because it is 'largely synonymous with increasing productive efficiency' (ibid.), which not only implies a proportional decrease in material input per unit of material output, suggesting fewer additions into and withdrawals from the surrounding ecosystem, but also a similarly proportional increase in value produced by a certain level of investment. 'End-use innovation' therefore holds the key to the 'green growth' valued by ecological modernisation, facilitating the production modifications needed for dematerialisation, or 'decoupling', to occur. However, it is this assumed potential of science and technology to mitigate environmental risks, and its sweeping presence throughout contemporary economics, that has led Foster *et al.* (2010: 112) to label it a 'transmutation myth'. This is because 'green techniques may reduce some forms of ecological risk, but they may also help to prop up, to sustain, an unsustaining social whole' (Davison 2004: 144). As seen in Chapter 5, the Panels increasingly begin to recognise this contradiction but ultimately echo the faith described in policy: that, at some point in the future, advances in science and technology will mitigate the environmental issues associated with expansion.

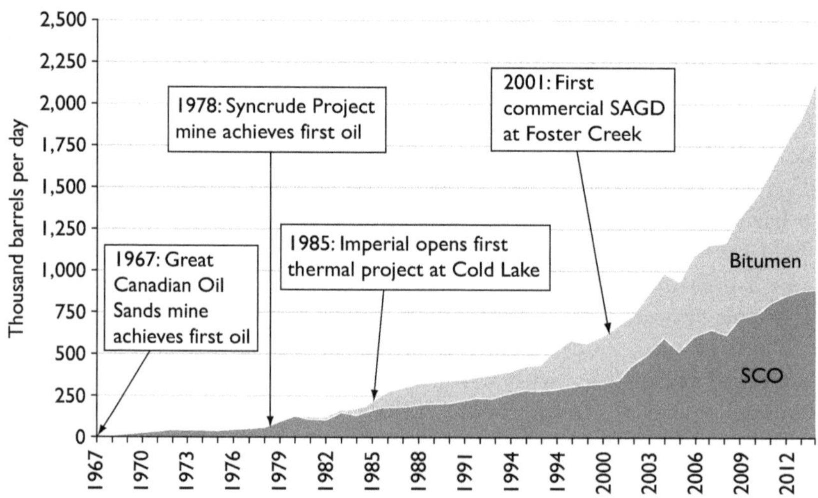

Figure 6.7 Technology and Oil Sands Production History, 1967–2014*.

Source: Birn and Meyer (2015: 8).

Note

* SCO – Synthetic Crude Oil (a product based on refined bitumen).

When examining the validity of eco-modernist claims of decoupling it is important to distinguish between its 'relative' and 'absolute' forms. Essentially, relative decoupling 'refers to a decline in the ecological intensity per unit of economic output' (Jackson 2009: 65), and is 'about doing more with less: more economic activity with less environmental damage' (ibid.: 68). In contrast, absolute decoupling occurs when environmental impacts decline in total, or absolutely, while total economic output increases. It is this latter situation that is 'essential if economic activity is to remain within ecological limits' (ibid.: 65). Against a backdrop of increasing production, freshwater intensity, which essentially refers to the number of barrels of fresh water used in the production of one barrel of bitumen, has fallen in relation to both mining and in-situ projects since at least 2005 and according to data from two separate sources (see Figure 6.8). Although certain corollaries must be attached, such as the difficulties in drawing trends from the highly variable mining data, it would appear that there has been a marked success in achieving the technological advances needed to decouple environmental impacts on water quantity from each barrel of bitumen produced.

However, these achievements, which ultimately demonstrate some progress with respect to relative decoupling, are not mirrored in the data on its absolute counterpart. As Figure 6.9 indicates, the total quantity of water withdrawn from the Athabasca River has increased alongside the total increase in production, meaning that the expected techno-scientific methods of risk mitigation have failed to materialise over the entire lifespan of the industry. The same situation can be seen in Figure 6.10, with respect to greenhouse gas

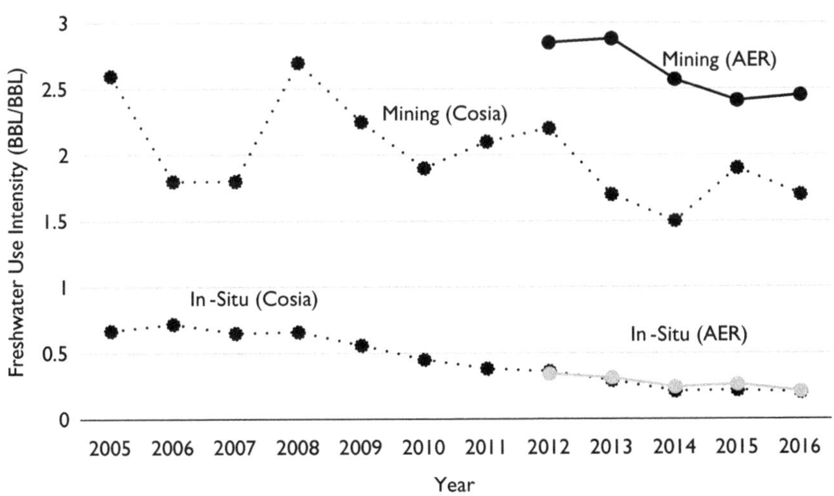

Figure 6.8 Fresh Water Use Intensity: In-Situ vs. Mining Operations.

Source: Compiled from Alberta Energy Regulator (2017a, 2017b) and COSIA (2017).

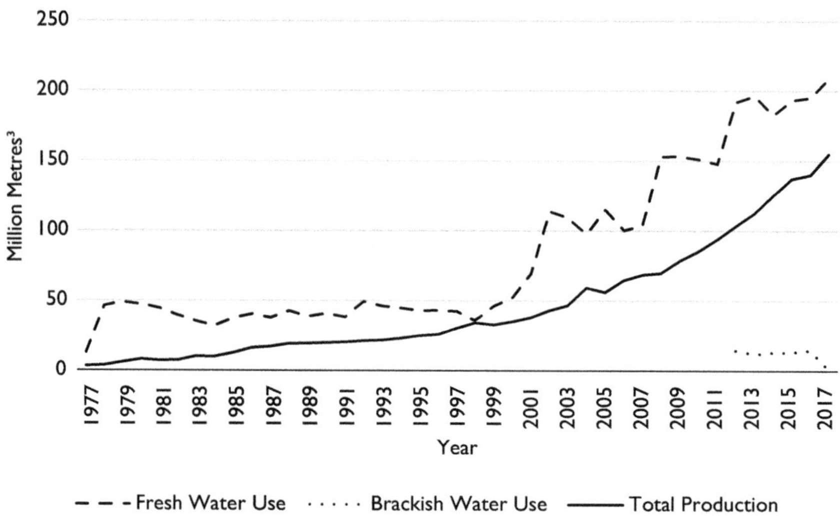

Figure 6.9 Total Industry Production* vs. Total Industry Water Use, 1977–2017.
Source: Compiled from AER (2018) and CAPP (2018b: Table 03-02).

Note
* Includes mines, in-situ, and upgrader production data.

emissions from oil sands projects post-1990, where since 1990 emissions and production have increased together. Put another way, the future arrival of some eco-modernist panacea, where the 'dirty and ugly caterpillar transforms into an ecological butterfly' (Huber 1985, cited in Spaargaren and Mol 1992: 34), has yet to emerge over two decades after the first contemporary project approval in 1997.

While comparably specific data pertaining to water quality is unavailable, other sources demonstrate the similar inadequacy of technologies referred to by the Panels in their pursuit of balance. Tailings technology is such an example, where the Panels repeatedly deploy a misplaced faith in its future development as a means of reducing the risks posed by tailings ponds to the quality of the surrounding water systems. Indeed, an Expert Panel, convened to evaluate the potential for new and emerging technologies to reduce the environmental impacts of oil sands development, highlight the continued lack of progress in this area. Noting that tailings 'remain a significant remediation challenge' (Council of Canadian Academies 2015: 170), it goes on to conclude that '[e]ven with complete adoption of the most promising technologies for tailings management and reduction, tailings volumes … are not expected to decline' (ibid.). This is problematic considering the extent to which efforts at decoupling bitumen production from tailings waste have consistently failed since the very inception of the industry (see Figure 6.11).

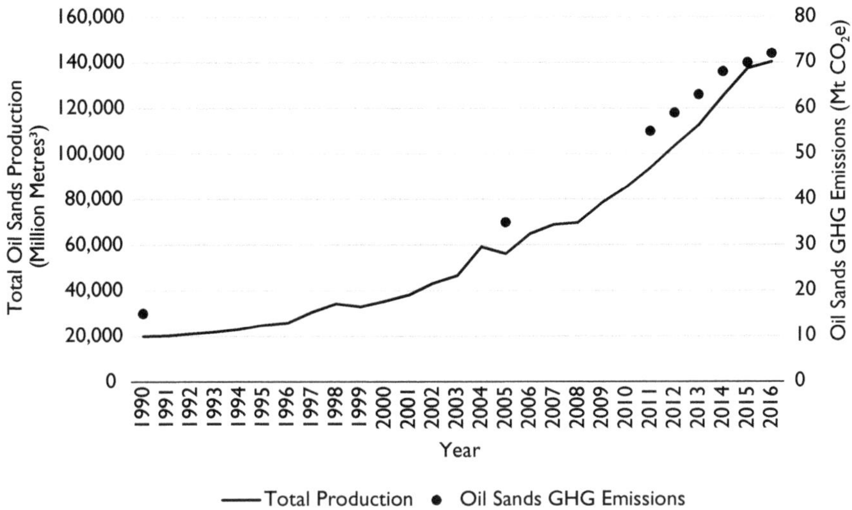

Figure 6.10 Oil Sands Production and GHG Emissions*, 1990–2016.

Source: Compiled from Government of Canada (2018) and CAPP (2018b: Table 03–02).

Note

* Includes mines, in-situ, and upgrader emissions data.

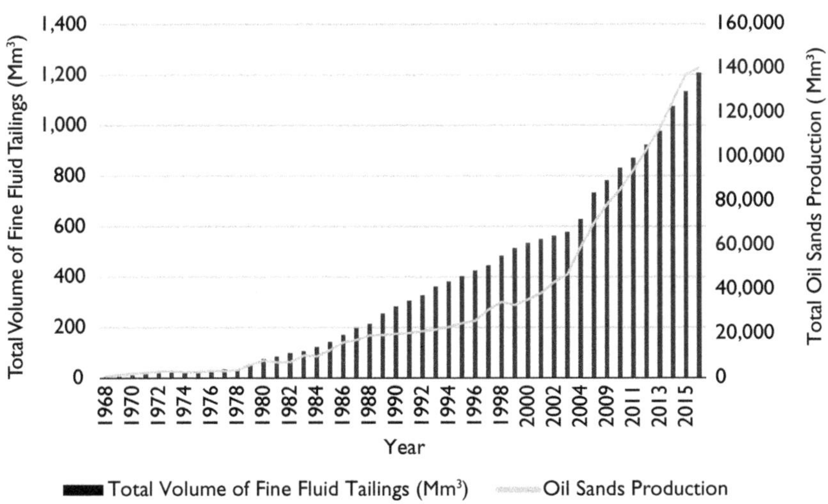

Figure 6.11 Fluid Tailings Pond Volume Growth, 1968–2016.

Source: Compiled from Government of Alberta (2015d) and Alberta Energy Regulator (2016b).

Yet, despite this, the AER continues to grant approvals for further tailings pond growth (Wilt 2018).

Even the faith placed by the hearing Panels in EPL technology, which was seen as a possible future alternative to tailings ponds, is misplaced, despite being referenced as a means of mitigating risk as early as 2004 (see Chapter 5). Indeed, the concerns forwarded by First Nations since this time, regarding the inadequacy of the technology, continue to hold relevance, being validated by the Expert Panel in its concluding remarks:

> Given known risks and lack of knowledge about their long-term viability, the Panel believes that much more research is needed before end-pit lakes become an accepted long-term solution to tailings pond management.
>
> (Council of Canadian Academies 2015: 168)

It is for these reasons that the EPLs are considered a 'problematic' and 'highly uncertain' 'grand experiment' (Millar 2012: 15), being labelled 'reckless' (Grant 2012) and found to risk large amounts of tailings material seeping into the surrounding environment (Kabwe *et al.* 2018). Even the demonstration site initially referred to by the regulatory Panels in 2006, as a means of improving scientific understanding of their efficacy and mitigating the risk associated with project approval, is still only in the 'planning' stages over a decade later (Canadian Oil Sands Innovation Alliance 2018). As the seminal report produced by CEMA (2012: 263) concluded, 'Planning, designing, constructing, monitoring, and certifying oil sands EPLs is expected to be a multi-decade process.' The ramifications of this become apparent in its subsequent clarification that 'it is not unreasonable to expect that perhaps 100 years will be required from initial planning of an oil sands mine to certification of an EPL at that mine' (ibid.). Despite this, 35 EPLs are still planned for the oil sands region (Brogly 2015).

Clearly, the faith placed in future techno-scientific innovation is fundamentally flawed, cannot be seen to fulfil the risk-mitigation role continually assigned to it by the Panels, and has ultimately been used to justify expansion of the very conditions which precipitate its own failure. The three implicit assumptions identified at the base of Panel approaches to mitigating risk – that techno-scientific mitigation is materially possible, that the expected advances will work even if developed, and that the actors tasked with pursuing these solutions have the capacity to do so – have yet to be empirically demonstrated. In this sense, the techno-scientific aspect of 'weak' ecological modernisation has been operationalised at the point of the hearings as a belief system, where the empirical evidence demonstrating the absence or failure of technology and science to mitigate ecological destruction and environmental harm lies beyond the boundaries of meaningful consideration. Appearing to deploy the eco-modernist vision where '[t]he only possible way *out* of the ecological crisis is by going further *into* the process of modernisation, toward ... hyper- or superindustrialisation' (Mol 1995: 42, emphasis in original), this approach rests on the assumption that the environmental degradation produced prior to this expected epochal shift can be returned to an original state via human means at some point in the future. This is particularly problematic if interests vested in expansive oil sands operations also govern this process of restoration, as is the case in the oil sands. As Participant B of the LUS commented:

> You can reclaim to a certain extent, but First Nations push us to change our reclamation standard. Their position, for the most part, is to say 'well, it was pristine boreal forest so ... we want it reclaimed to pristine boreal'. But our position is it just needs to be reclaimed to a usable state, so even, you know, non-native grasses; just plant a bunch of non-native grass and it's, you know, 'check' [motion of ticking], and it's vegetated.

Taken together, not only does the pattern of techno-scientific reasoning ignore the environmental harm that occurs prior to the point of supposed transformation, but it also neglects to account for the continued failure of technology, science, and the organisations tasked with their advance, to achieve the goals expected of them. Such a permissive attitude to industrial expansion, its concomitant and eventually foreseen risks, and dismissive attitude to the limits of technology, science, and multi-stakeholder initiatives, thus represent the operational deployment of a 'weak' ecological modernisation, the default position of which is not to challenge the growth imperative. In this sense, the Panel deliberations echo Christoff's (1996: 488) early warnings about the philosophy, where its repeated reliance on techno-scientific means of risk-mitigation can prove to be little more than 'a rhetorical device seeking to manage radical dissent', the purpose of which is to 'secure the legitimacy of existing policy while delivering limited, economically acceptable environmental improvements' (ibid.).

Conclusion

This chapter has demonstrated that the 'approval' phase of the regulatory process, along with its policy context, is characterised by the extensive operationalisation of 'weak' eco-modernist thought. Channelling the fixed, growth-orientated notion of 'hegemonic progress' visible in the language of 'sustainable growth' deployed throughout policy and strategy, which is granted credibility by broader, province-wide neoliberal reforms, those at the more operational level of the regulatory process echo this in justifying expansion by recourse to a narrow, provincial, economistic, and ultimately idealised interpretation of the 'public interest'. In accordance with the government–industry collaboration advocated by the philosophy, which effectively mirrors the 'win-win' approach of compliance-based regulation more broadly, these actors are given disproportionate influence in deciding on project approvals, elevating their interests above their public and First Nation counterparts. This effectively undermines the public hearings by ensuring projects are approved prior to the date on which they are held, transforming the regulatory process into one which facilitates and legitimates expansion irrespective of the risks posed to environmental integrity. Indeed, the final trait reflected at the 'approval' stage is the faith placed in the ability of science and technology to 'green' the extraction activities being permitted, which is repeated despite the almost total lack of evidence on its effectiveness. In light of these characteristics, the 'approval' stage of the regulatory process can be seen to be operationalising the 'weak' strain of eco-modernist philosophy forwarded in policy, acting as a catalyst for the production and reproduction of environmental harm in reality.

Chapter 7

The Inefficacy of Control

Systematic Infringement of Treaty Rights and the Justificatory Function of Compound Denial

This chapter forms the counterpart to Chapter 6, exploring how the depth of consultation conducted with First Nations throughout the regulatory process has permitted deployment of 'weak' eco-modernist philosophy at the 'approval' stage. Having a particular emphasis on the post-2005 legal duty to consult and accommodate First Nations on any activity that may affect their Treaty rights, along with the successive policies that emerged following the decision, this chapter provides an explanation as to how the expansionist eco-philosophy has been operationalised so broadly, and for so long, despite extensive evidence of environmental harm.

As Chapter 4 indicates, First Nation input at the 'planning' stage of the regulatory process is characterised by widespread and systemic marginalisation. This stems from a lack of accommodation on the LARP, the delegation of consultation to industry proponents who cannot address cumulative environmental issues, and an Aboriginal Consultation Office which makes premature decisions on the 'adequacy' of consultation by relying on a diluted interpretation of Treaty rights. As this stage interrupts the otherwise direct relationship between policy objectives and regulatory decisions at the 'approval' stage of the process, marginalisation at this point allows for the 'weak' eco-modernist philosophy advocated at the former level to proceed largely unimpeded into the latter. However, by virtue of the geographical-historical specificity of the oil sands, this limited participation is entwined with the way in which Treaty rights have been realised within the regulatory process. It is because of this that such actualisation is related to characteristics derived from the more structural dimensions of the settler-colonial state in which the oil sands are located.

This chapter demonstrates that the limited participation of First Nations at the 'planning' stage stems from the government's use of narrowly conceived Treaty rights. Deploying a diluted interpretation of their content, a distinct lack of accommodation on policies and strategies, and a delayed triggering of the duty to consult on individual oil sands projects, Treaty rights have been realised in a manner which allows for the broad subordination of First Nation interests to those of government and industry. The first half of the chapter illustrates this narrow realisation by demonstrating the disparity between such actualisation and the SCC judgments that have provided incremental guidance on their content. This is explored in terms of foundational interpretations, the trigger of the duty, the variable content of the duty once triggered, and the duty to accommodate. Building on this, the second half of the chapter identifies the influences exerted within the regulatory process to produce this disparity. Indeed, it is at this point where the justifications offered by regulatory personnel, for facilitating the diluted interpretation, are examined, describing the way in which more structural characteristics common to settler-colonial societies influence the continuation of this process. Visible here is the presence of a 'compound denial'. This underpins the 'planning' stage of the regulatory process, operating to ensure that First Nations do not meaningfully intervene in the ultimate provincial goal of industrial expansion. Taken together, these features quell dissenting voices and enable operationalisation of 'weak' ecological modernisation throughout the regulatory process, all under the rubric of 'sustainable development'.

Actualising a Diluted Duty to Consult and Accommodate

This section presents analysis on how the duty to consult and accommodate has been interpreted and deployed within the 'planning' stage of the regulatory process. As explained in Chapter 2, this more procedural dimension of First Nation Treaty rights is both the mechanism by which the substantive hunting, fishing, and trapping rights are protected, and the process through which policy objectives on oil sands expansion, and the eco-philosophies to which they are aligned, must pass in order to be operationalised. This permits the duty to consult to be interpreted as a mechanism for the control of harmful patterns of production. However, as confirmed in Chapter 4, regulatory attempts at meeting this duty are inadequate for such a purpose. Here, these shortcomings are analysed in the context of the two consultation policies published by the Government of Alberta in 2005 and 2013, and the SCC judgments of which they purport to follow. Demonstrating a widespread and systemic discrepancy between these overarching rulings and the operational practices conveyed by participants, this section examines the way in which a substantially diluted interpretation of the duty to consult and accommodate has been actualised at the 'planning' stage of the regulatory process.

Substantive Treaty Rights

As illustrated in Chapter 4, the Government of Alberta narrowly interprets the Treaty right to hunt, fish, and trap as only for food, also isolating it from geographic location and species quantity and quality. As such, it can be read as an extension of the 'colonial trick' mentioned by Huseman and Short (2012: 223). Taking the first of these as the point of departure, conceiving of Treaty rights as restricted to food is a conception outlined in the 2013 consultation policy (see Government of Alberta 2013a: 1). According to Laidlaw and Passelac-Ross (2014), this interpretation stems from the minority decision in paragraphs 2 and 7 of *R.* v. *Badger [1996] 1 SCR 771* (hereafter *Badger*), which considered Treaty 8 to have merged with the Natural Resources Transfer Agreement (NRTA) of 1930. This legislation states that Aboriginal peoples shall have the right 'of hunting, trapping and fishing game and fish *for food* at all seasons of the year on all unoccupied Crown lands and on any other lands to which the said Indians may have right of access' (Government of Alberta 1930: 2, emphasis added). However, the majority in the *Badger* (para 47) decision opposed the merger interpretation, maintaining that '[u]nless there is a direct conflict between the NRTA and a treaty, the NRTA will not have modified the treaty rights'. There is therefore a discrepancy between the case law and the approach adopted by the ACO; a feature that becomes particularly clear when considered in the context of other SCC judgments.

As noted in *Badger* (para 52), the words in a Treaty must be interpreted not in their strict technical sense, but rather in the manner they would have been understood by Aboriginal peoples and the Crown at the time of signing. The content of the Treaties was considered by the SCC in *R.* v. *Horseman [1990] 1 SCR 901* (hereafter *Horseman*), which considered the right to hunt, fish, and trap to include doing so for commercial purposes. Building on the examination conducted in *Frank* v. *The Queen [1977] 1 SCR 95* (hereafter *Frank*), into the differences between hunting rights in Treaty 6 and those in the NRTA, which concluded that 'under the former the hunting rights were at large while under the latter the right is limited to hunting for food', *Horseman* (para 47) concluded the following:

> An examination of the historical background leading to the negotiations for Treaty No. 8 and the other numbered treaties leads inevitably to the conclusion that the hunting rights reserved by the Treaty included hunting for commercial purposes. The Indians wished to protect the hunting rights which they possessed before the Treaty came into effect and the Federal Government wished to protect the native economy which was based upon those hunting rights. It can be seen that the Indians ceded title to the Treaty 8 lands on the condition that they could reserve exclusively to themselves 'their usual vocations of hunting, trapping and fishing throughout the tracts surrendered'.

Although this emphasises the commercial dimension to First Nation Treaty rights, the interpretation must not be restricted to a simplistic subsistence–commercial duality. Indeed, a wider, and arguably more accurate, reading is established in *Mikisew* (para 29, emphasis added), which states that the clause governing hunting, fishing, and trapping 'cannot be isolated from the Treaty as a whole, but must be read in the context of its *underlying purpose*, as intended by both the Crown and the First Nations peoples'. With this 'underlying purpose' referencing the assurance that 'the same means of earning a *livelihood* would continue after the treaty as existed before it' (ibid.: para 30, emphasis added), and considering that 'a large element of the Treaty 8 negotiations were the assurances of *continuity* in traditional patterns of economic activity … and occupation' (*Mikisew* para 47, emphasis added), reading Treaty rights as guarantees of a continuation of this 'livelihood' permits a broader interpretation. In arguing this, Laidlaw and Passelac-Ross (2014: 25) go on to note that '[t]his is the proper interpretation of Alberta's numbered Treaties', where 'livelihood was and remains interwoven in the distinctive cultures of Alberta First Nations'. Treaty rights should therefore be taken to encompass the right to harvest and gather for fuel, medicinal plants, and food; the right to exercise traditional governance, ceremonial, spiritual, and educational practices; and the right to the inter-generational transmission of language and culture (ibid.). As such, the interpretation communicated by regulatory personnel in Chapter 4, where the Treaty right to hunt, fish, and trap is seen as limited only to food, is not only narrow in and of itself but also inconsistent with SCC rulings.

The additional annexing of Treaty rights from geographic locations and species quantity and quality can be read as a further narrowing of this interpretation. On the surface this appears accordant with the text of Treaty 8, as the commitments made during its original negotiations were neither location- nor species-specific. The Crown only 'solemnly assure[d]' the Aboriginal peoples that 'they would be as free to hunt and fish after the treaty as they would be if they never entered into it' (*Badger* para 39). However, the *Badger* (para 52) decision also noted that, to account for their interpretation at the time of signature, Treaties relating to Aboriginal peoples should be 'liberally construed and any uncertainties, ambiguities or doubtful expressions should be resolved in favour of the Indians'. As such, the actual assurances given during the original negotiations recognised in *Mikisew* (para 47, emphasis added), for the 'continuity in *patterns* of economic activity' and respect for 'traditional *patterns* of activity and occupation', should be interpreted in terms of the location, and species quantity and quality relied upon for their exercise (Laidlaw and Passelac-Ross 2014).

This is the position taken in *West Moberly First Nations* v. *British Columbia (Chief Inspector of Mines) 2011 BCCA 247* (hereafter *West Moberly*) at the Court of Appeal for British Columbia, which upheld an Order of the BC Supreme Court stating that the Crown was in breach of its duty to consult and accommodate the West Moberly First Nations when granting permits to the First Coal Corporation. With regard to the question of whether Treaty rights are both species-specific and location-specific, it describes the *Mikisew* case as 'instructive on this point' (*West Moberly* para 138). While the *Mikisew* case itself involved construction of a winter road through an MCFN Reserve, the federal and provincial Crowns argued that only a small proportion of traditional territory would be taken up, suggesting that it fails the infringement threshold in *Badger* (para 18). This is set to 'where the Crown has taken up land in bad faith or has taken up so much land that no meaningful right to hunt remains' (*Mikisew* para 44), thus failing to trigger the duty to consult. However, in the *Mikisew* case Justice Binnie rejected this argument on the grounds that it implied the dismissal of First Nation procedural rights, that the proposal itself would reduce the territory over which the MCFN could carry out Treaty rights, that 'apart from everything else, there would be no hunting at all within the 200-meter road corridor' (ibid.), and that 'the road would injuriously affect the exercise of these rights in the surrounding bush' (ibid.). It is in his follow-up justification that the species- and site-specific nature of Treaty rights is visible:

> The Draft Environmental Assessment Report acknowledged the road could potentially result in a diminution in quantity of the Mikisew harvest of wildlife, as fewer furbearers (including fisher, muskrat, marten, wolverine and lynx) will be caught in their traps. Second, in qualitative terms, the more lucrative or rare species of furbearers may decline in population. Other potential impacts include fragmentation of wildlife habitat, disruption of migration patterns, loss of vegetations, increased poaching because of easier motor vehicle access to the area and increased wildlife mortality due to motor vehicle collisions.
>
> (Ibid.)

This ruling can be read as establishing a need to account for indirect and cumulative impacts on Aboriginal rights and traditional livelihoods, particularly when considering factors that risk triggering the duty to consult. Following this line of reasoning, Treaty rights should not be divorced from the specific material reality upon which their practice depends, irrespective of whether the impact is direct or cumulative. While in and of itself this narrow interpretation should be addressed by the Government of Alberta within its consultation policy, and as part of a concerted effort to make such clandestine modifications to its own conception more public, its existence has several detrimental consequences for subsequent stages of consultation.

The Trigger of the Duty to Consult

As explained in Chapter 4, consultation does not occur at the point at which land leases are granted to companies, which is the earliest stage in the regulatory process. Participants justified this by stating that a company in possession of a lease may not go on to conduct operations on the land, and that it is only when they eventually do so that it is deemed to be 'taken up'. This is a reference to the 'lands taken up provision' in Treaty 8, which describes the transferring of lands from a category in which First Nations retain the rights to hunt, fish, and trap and into one in which they do not (see *Mikisew* para 33). Existing practice places the trigger point for consultation at the exploratory drilling or seismic testing stages, which follows land lease disposition. This emphasises the requirement for there to be an observable alteration of the material landscape for an area to be considered 'taken up'; a definition given in the *Badger* (para 54) ruling, which described the process as 'being based upon a concept of visible, incompatible land use'. This is deemed consistent with interpretations of the original promises made. Thus evident is the systematised assumption that land is not to be considered 'taken up' until visible activity has transformed it into a state incompatible with the exercise of Treaty rights. This means that, under the present regime, consultation is not triggered unless this change of category occurs, hence the lack of consultation at the point of lease disposition.

Such an interpretation does not correspond to the decisions handed down by the Supreme Court. While the *Haida* (para 35) and *Rio Tinto Alcan Inc* v. *Carrier Sekani Tribal Council [2010] SCC 43* (hereafter *Rio Tinto*) (para 31) judgments suggest that the duty to consult is triggered by evidence pertaining to the *risk* of such an adverse effect on Treaty rights, the *Mikisew* judgment contains no such requirement for proof of a potential consequence. Indeed, it simply states that the Crown's right to take up lands under Treaty 'is subject to its duty to consult and, if appropriate, accommodate First Nations' interests before reducing the area over which their members may continue to pursue their hunting, fishing, and trapping rights' (ibid.: para 56). As such, while the granting of a lease does not in itself constitute a process by which land is rendered 'visibly incompatible' with Treaty rights, it can be read as the beginning of the process by which the category of land is altered in this manner. Therefore, in accordance with the text of the *Mikisew* judgment, consultation should arguably be triggered at the point of lease disposition.

Even if adhering to the stricter *Haida* (para 35, emphasis added) judgment, where consultation is only triggered 'when the Crown has knowledge, real or constructive, of the potential existence of the Aboriginal right or title and contemplates conduct that *might* adversely affect it', or *Rio Tinto* (para 79, emphasis added), where consultation begins when recognising the '*potential* that the contemplated conduct may adversely affect the Aboriginal claim or right', then the trigger is not an actual impact on the substantive component of Treaty rights, but a *possible* impact. Consultation should therefore still occur at the point of disposition because regulations governing the process are weighted in favour of activities clearly posing such a risk. For instance, Section 4 of the Oil Sands Tenure Regulation recognises an 'oil sands agreement' to 'convey the exclusive right to drill for, win, work, recover and remove oil sands that are the property of the Crown' (Government of Alberta

2010: 11), meaning there is little question as to the intent of the lease mechanism. Erring on the side of non-development of a land lease, as the regulatory interpretation of the trigger to consult does, also ignores the requirement for purchased parcels to meet the Minimum Level of Evaluation outlined in Section 2 of the Oil Sands Tenure Regulation. This requires 'the drilling of at least one evaluation well' prior to seismic testing (Government of Alberta 2010: 7–9). The lease disposition mechanism itself therefore contains within it a high likelihood that lands will be visibly altered in some fashion, from one category of use to another, particularly if compared to the reduced likelihood of conversion prior to disposition. Again, even if following this more stringent line of reasoning, consultation should be triggered at the point of lease disposition.

This position is supported by the *Haida* decision, where the SCC differentiated between the granting and renewal of Tree Farm Licenses, which gives companies exclusive rights to harvest timber within a designated area (para 73), and the implementation of these licenses through cutting permits and forest plans (para 76). While the provincial government argued that consultation at the former level was unnecessary, because the granting of licenses does not impact the substantive element of Treaty rights, this defence was rejected by the Chief Justice:

> Consultation at the operational level … has little effect on the quantity of the annual allowable cut, which in turn determines cutting permit terms. If consultation is to be meaningful, it must take place at the stage of granting or renewing Tree Farm Licenses.
>
> (*Haida* para 76)

Put another way, initiating consultation after the disposition of land leases cannot be considered meaningful because the questions asked at this later point are not 'whether' a proposal should go ahead and in what form, but 'how' it should be carried out (Passelac-Ross and Potes 2007: 6–7). Indeed, the *Mikisew* (para 44) judgment designated a *potential* impact upon the broader material conditions underpinning First Nation hunting, fishing, and trapping practices as an infringement adequate enough to trigger the duty to consult. Considering also that '[t]he flexibility lies not in the trigger ["might adversely affect it"] but in the variable content of the duty once triggered' (*Mikisew* para 34), the practice of delaying consultation with First Nations until the exploratory drilling or seismic testing stages appears to be in breach of the procedural component to First Nation Treaty rights.

The Duty to Consult

A large part of the frustration communicated throughout the interviews with First Nations centred on the lack of attention given to broader and cumulative effects during consultation on individual projects. This concurs with the findings of Lambrecht (2015: 119), who notes that 'Aboriginal concerns which are not atomistically project specific will be shunted to later dialogue' within the LARP. This caused First Nations to label the decisions made by the ACO, on the adequacy of said consultation, to be premature (see Chapter 4). Such a criticism refers to the variable scope and content of the duty to consult, the associated duty to accommodate, and the requirements used by the ACO to determine 'adequacy' in this regard. As noted in Chapter 2, the scope and depth of any consultation and accommodation is related to the strength of the claim to Aboriginal title or rights, the importance of said title or rights, and the degree to which their exercise would be impacted upon by the proposed activity (*Haida* para 39). Considering that, in a Treaty context, the Crown will always have knowledge of its content (*Mikisew* para 34), the question turns to the promises made within the specific Treaty and the degree of impact upon the Treaty rights conferred (ibid.: para 63). This essentially means that the depth of consultation required corresponds to the strength and seriousness of these criteria. However, as Passelac-Ross and Potes (2007: 15) note, 'While the location along the spectrum is important, what matters most are probably the obligations that each location entails.' The *Mikisew* (para 64) case demonstrates just how much is required even at the 'lower end of the spectrum':

> [G]iven that the Crown is proposing to build a fairly minor winter road on surrendered lands where the Mikisew treaty rights are expressly subject to the 'taking up' limitation, the content of the Crown's duty of consultation in this case lies at the lower end of the spectrum. The Crown is required to provide notice to the Mikisew and to engage directly with them. This engagement should include the provision of information about the project, addressing what the Crown knew to be the Mikisew's interests and what the Crown anticipated might be the potential adverse impact on those interests. The Crown must also solicit and listen carefully to the Mikisew's concerns, and attempt to minimize adverse impacts on its treaty rights.

Following this, Justice Binnie considers what is entailed by 'adequate consultation', drawing from the decision in *Halfway River First Nation* v. *British Columbia (Minister of Forests) [1999] BCCA 470* (hereafter *Halfway*) to highlight that the duty to consult has both 'informational' and 'response' components (ibid.). With regard to the former, the Crown has a positive obligation to ensure that Aboriginal peoples 'are provided with all necessary information in a timely way so that they have an opportunity to express their interests and concerns' (ibid.). With respect to the latter, it must also ensure that the representations of Aboriginal peoples 'are seriously considered and, wherever possible, demonstrably integrated into the proposed plan of action' (ibid.). It is this latter component which leads into the duty to accommodate. While the original consultation policy produced by the Government of Alberta neglected to specify the variable content along this spectrum, the 2014 guidance issued for the second policy provided a framework of assessment for such a purpose (Government of Alberta 2014b: 14).

The framework provided appears to mirror the spectrum and content requirements of SCC judgments, particularly as large oil sands mines automatically entail 'extensive' consultation in light of them being deemed to have a 'high impact' (ibid.: A3). At this level there is the requirement for '[p]reparation of a consultation plan, notification with opportunity for First Nation to respond, and required follow-up by proponent' (ibid.: 14). However, the heading of '[s]ensitivity of the location [based on Treaty rights and traditional uses]' references the assumption-based boundaries within which this 'extensive consultation', and subsequent accommodation, is to occur. Indeed, in its guidance to the ACO, and the determination of consultation requirements for particular categories of project, the policy establishes that '[t]he scope of consultation is related to 1) the nature of the project and 2) its potential impacts on *Treaty rights and traditional uses at that location*' (Government of Alberta 2014b: 13, emphasis added). As such, not only does the 'at that location' specification directly limit the geographical scope of any consultation, but this is further narrowed by the need to account for 'Treaty rights and traditional uses', directly operationalising the diluted interpretation of the substantive rights to hunt, fish, and trap illustrated above. Thus imposed are a number of pre-set constraints on the scope of consultation and accommodation even before the process has been initiated, not least of which is the annexing of considerations pertaining to the impact of environmental effects on wider geographical locations that may hold cultural significance to the First Nations. It is for this reason that the ACO considers consultation conducted by individual project proponents to be 'adequate' while overlooking issues surrounding cumulative impacts, vindicating the description of the ACO as 'very administrative' by FNIRD participants (see Chapter 4).

The Duty to Accommodate

Official attempts were made to gather First Nation concerns on cumulative effects in 2008, when consultation began on the LARP (see Government of Alberta, 2013b). Consultation on its content occurred with 21 First Nations and nine Metis organisations between December 2008 and September 2009, encompassing 107 meetings and a number of written follow-up responses by the First Nations themselves (ibid.: 3–4). Indeed, this degree of consultation was portrayed as increasingly informing the policies and strategies governing oil sands expansion, giving the appearance of a broad integration of First Nation input, particularly from 2008 onwards, thereby projecting a trait more closely associated with 'strong' ecological modernisation. However, as noted in

Chapter 4, despite this consultation First Nations still reported an almost complete lack of accommodation of their input into the LARP, which was finally published in 2012, particularly with regard to its designated conservation areas. Further evidence of this is provided by a 2015 report produced by the LARP Review Panel (2015). In considering whether First Nations had been directly and adversely affected by the provisions of the strategy, the report demonstrates a lack of progress made on the primary issues raised by First Nations during the initial period of consultation, between 2008 and 2009 (see Government of Alberta 2013b). This report was considered so 'damning' of the accommodation that occurred that the Government of Alberta delayed its publication until 2016 (Weber 2016). Indeed, fundamental concerns around land use planning and access, respect for constitutionally protected Treaty rights, traditional patterns of land use, and consultation standards have continued over the interim period, with all but one of the 20 issues raised by First Nations being confirmed by the panel presiding over the inquiry (LARP Review Panel 2015). Ultimately, when taking this evidence together, the accommodation of First Nation input at the level of strategy, and on the LARP in particular, has been both unsubstantial and inadequate for the purpose of protecting their Treaty rights.

When questioned about this lack of accommodation, the most senior participant interviewed provided justification by referencing its parity with SCC judgments, stating that the '*Mikisew* decision talked about plain language, used a bunch of "reasonable" wordings, and "reasonable" is a lower level test in law when compared to an "absolute" standard' (Participant A, ESRD). While this is largely accurate, it is actually the *Haida* case in which this language is used to discuss the standard by which the process of accommodation should be judged:

> The [consultation] process itself would likely fall to be examined on a standard of reasonableness. Perfect satisfaction is not required; the question is whether the regulatory scheme or government action 'viewed as a whole, accommodates the collective aboriginal right in question': Gladstone, supra, at para. 170. What is required is not perfection, but reasonableness. As stated in Nikal, supra, at para. 110, 'in … information and consultation the concept of reasonableness must come into play.… So long as every reasonable effort is made to inform and to consult, such efforts would suffice.' The government is required to make reasonable efforts to inform and consult. This suffices to discharge the duty.
>
> Should the government misconceive the seriousness of the claim or impact of the infringement, this question of law would likely be judged by correctness. Where the government is correct on these matters and acts on the appropriate standard, the decision will be set aside only if the government's process is unreasonable. The focus, as discussed above, is not on the outcome, but on the process of consultation and accommodation.
>
> (*Haida* paras 62–63)

The concept of 'reasonableness' represents the Court's deference to the Crown's judgment in relation to this duty, indicating that it 'require[s] political, as opposed to judicial competencies' (Craik 2016: 13). As Sossin (2009) makes clear, when coupled with the *Taku River Tlingit First Nation* v. *British Columbia (Project Assessment Director) [2004] 3 SCR 550* (hereafter *Taku River*) decision, this amounts to a consultation process that does not require a *particular* substantive outcome. However, while '[t]here is no duty to reach agreement' (*Haida* para 10), at the very least '[c]onsultation must be meaningful' (ibid.), and 'consultation that excludes from the outset any form of accommodation would be meaningless' (*Mikisew* para 54). As such, whenever the duty to consult is triggered, the default expectation should be that there is a duty to accommodate.

Taking this as the point of departure, while the substantive outcome corresponding to a particular level of consultation remains ill-defined by the SCC (Sossin 2009), guidance does exist on its content. In noting that 'consultation must be in good faith, and with the intention of substantially addressing the concerns' of Aboriginal peoples, the decision in *Delgamuukw* v. *British Columbia [1997] 3 SCR 1010* (hereafter *Delgamuukw*) (para 168) goes on to note that '[i]n most cases, it will be significantly deeper than mere consultation. Some cases may even require the full consent of an aboriginal nation'. *Haida* (para 48) clarifies this by differentiating between a Treaty and a non-Treaty context, stating that this consent 'is appropriate only in cases of established rights, and then by no means in every case. Rather, what is required is a process of balancing of interests, of give and take'. This is instructive because it demonstrates that the accommodation requirement shifts depending on the strength of the claim, much like the duty to consult, and that there must be compromise between parties. In this sense, *Haida* (para 44) provides guidance for situations involving pre-proof consultation, suggesting that accommodation in such a context should seek 'compromise in an attempt to harmonize conflicting interests and move further down the path of reconciliation'. Even in cases where 'a strong *prima-facie case* exists for the claim', and government action threatens to adversely affect it in some way, accommodation 'may require taking steps to avoid irreparable harm or to minimize the effects of infringement' (ibid.: para 47, emphasis added). As such, even in pre-proof situations, where treaties have not been established, the duty to accommodate requires that plans be adjusted to minimise their adverse effect on First Nations.

This holds significance because, if such measures correspond to situations where rights have not yet been established, then the type of accommodation expected in the context of established rights, such as those conferred by the historic treaties, 'requires more than a simple balancing of competing societal interests' (Laidlaw and Passelac-Ross 2014: 8). Such an argument is buttressed by the more general protection owed to constitutional rights and the limits they exert on state power, which informs the duty to accommodate. These arguments are supported by the *Sparrow* judgment, which notes that Section 35 of the Constitution of Canada dictates that Aboriginal interests should 'be given priority over the interests of other user groups', the objective of which is 'to guarantee that plans treat aboriginal peoples in a way ensuring that their rights are taken seriously' (*Sparrow*: 1079). Laidlaw and Passelac-Ross (2014: 8) thus conclude:

> The Crown's obligation to protect established Treaty rights leads to an expansion of the universe of accommodating measures including causing the least infringement possible, giving priority to Treaty rights, avoiding irreparable damage, compensation, recognizing the Aboriginal preferred means of exercising their rights, and recognizing that only demonstrably compelling and substantial objectives can trump Treaty rights.

In light of this case law, the accommodation of First Nation input on the LARP cannot be considered adequate. As described by participants from the ACO, government agencies consult with First Nations but fail to include any substantive aspects of the input. Ultimately, the consultation and accommodation that occurred on the LARP exemplifies Justice Binnie's description of an inadequate, 'meaningless' consultation process (*Mikisew* para 54), characterised as a situation in which First Nations are provided only with 'an opportunity to blow off steam before the Minister proceeds to do what she intended to do all along'.

Paternalistic Provincialism as a Form of Compound Denial

With the previous section illustrating 'how' the diluted interpretation of Treaty rights deployed within the regulatory process limits the extent to which First Nations can displace or decelerate production, this latter section examines the influences exerted within the process itself to facilitate this approach. As described in Chapter 4, questions focused on drawing out the justifications for regulatory subordination of First Nation interpretations of Treaty rights were met with three primary answers: that doing so is in the interests of 'all Albertans', that the SCC has not told them to act otherwise, and that such subordination is actually in the interests of First Nations because it permits their engagement with the oil sands industry. Such responses can be conceived not as straightforward 'explanations', which are statements 'where untoward action is not an issue and does not have critical implications for a relationship' (Scott and Lyman 1968: 47), but as 'accounts'. These are 'statement[s] made by … social actor[s] to explain unanticipated or untoward behaviour' (ibid.: 46). The specific sub-type of 'account' demonstrated here can be categorised as 'justifications', where 'one accepts responsibility for the act in question, but denies the pejorative quality associated with it' (ibid.: 47).

These serve to neutralise an act or its consequences when either of them is subject to a value-based inquiry: 'to justify an act is to assert its positive value in the face of a claim to the contrary' (ibid.: 51).

While the techniques of neutralisation developed by Sykes and Matza (1957) hold relevance here, providing a typology of justifications for relatively orthodox deviant activities, Cohen's (2001) work on denial can also be drawn from as it adapts this original conception for application to government agencies and actors. Each of the three justifications offered in Chapter 4 will be taken in turn, revealing their position as conduits through which more contextual, structural influences associated with settler-colonial societies are actively operationalised within the regulatory process, acting to justify the diluted interpretation of Treaty rights explored in the previous section. While presented separately, it should be clear that the boundaries between each specific form of denial are not clearly delineated and that, even within each separate manifestation, there exist multiple assumptions and disavowals that are built into one other. Representing an untidier arrangement than that presented by Whyte (2016: 179), who speaks of 'first order' and 'second order' justifications and brings attention to the role of 'common sense' in supporting neutralisations, visible here is a 'compound denial'. This can be defined as a justification offered for deviant organisational activity as expressed through various individual surface neutralisations, which are successful because they simultaneously draw upon a pool of broadly accepted background assumptions and deeper, societal disavowals.

Appeal to Higher Loyalties

In all instances, the act of overriding First Nation interpretations of Treaty rights was not refuted by regulatory personnel, but only the valuative category to which it has been assigned. As such, the justifications offered can be recognised as a form of 'implicatory denial' (Cohen 2001: 8), where '[t]here is no attempt to deny the facts or their conventional interpretation.... What are denied or minimised are the ... implications that conventionally follow'. Contrary to the technique of denying responsibility, which is typically considered the 'master account' within neutralisation theory (ibid.: 61), denial here is primarily manifest via an 'appeal to higher loyalties' (ibid.: 98), where the act is justified by recourse to some provincial 'social good'. As Chapter 4 illustrates, this was consistent among those involved with consultation at the 'planning' stage of the regulatory process, where the prioritisation of the government's interpretation of Treaty rights over that maintained by First Nations was considered acceptable because of the resulting benefit seen to accrue to 'all Albertans'. This bears similarity to the provincialised 'public interest' explanations offered by regulatory personnel at the 'approval' stage of the process, along with those pertaining to public service provision, which is not to be unexpected because '[m]uch of what is true about accounts will hold for explanations' (Scott and Lyman 1968: 47). However, it does demonstrate the consistency of penetration and acceptance of the 'strategic myths … crafted about [an] organisation's high morality' (Cohen 2001: 67). This is particularly so in the context of the narrow, idealistic, and ultimately fallible basis of these 'social good' claims (see Chapter 6).

The over-riding of First Nation interpretations of Treaty rights, by appealing to the perceived 'higher loyalties' associated with it being in the interests of 'all Albertans', implicates two separate but related characteristics. The first is the assumed legitimacy of majority rule inherent to liberal democracy and the second is the situated identity of such a claim, both of which are coloured by the status of Alberta as a settler-colonial province. This technique of neutralisation is not only derived from the language deployed in the consultation policies providing organisational guidance, but also wider and historical political, economic, and cultural characteristics of the provincial territory. This is entirely in accordance with Sykes and Matza's (1957: 669) original formulation, where neutralisations are conceived of as 'extensions of patterns of thought prevalent in society rather than something created de novo', and is echoed by Scott and Lyman (1968: 54), who recognise that '[o]rganisations systematically provide accounts for their members in a variety of situations … which "work" because of a set of background expectations'. Put another way, instead of being a private state of mind, denial is 'embedded in popular culture, banal language codes and state-encouraged legitimations' (Cohen 2001: 76), largely because these broadly established characteristics equip denials with a normativity that renders them acceptable to both user and recipient. Ultimately, it is this that allows neutralisations to be accepted by an audience instead of being dismissed.

The first feature inherent to the appeal to higher loyalties is the assumed legitimacy of majority rule, being operationalised via the notion that personnel within regulatory agencies are legitimately acting on behalf of 'all Albertans'. This is most clearly visible in the allusion to the government agencies of which the regulatory personnel are part. Indicative of the consensus-based 'unanimity illusion', and bearing similarity to the neutralisation technique labelled 'denial of personal responsibility' (see Cohen 2001: 88), when coupled with the mention of 'all Albertans' what is essentially being referred to is the legitimacy of decisions made by agencies operating under control of a democratically elected government. On the surface this is not without credibility: Alberta's Progressive Conservative party maintained power for the 44 years between 1971 and 2015. While voter turnout had been substantially lower than the provincial average during this period (Siaroff and Wesley 2015: 151), the consequences of this have already been discussed elsewhere (see Harrison 2015), and it is not the fundamental issue here. Instead, the central point of contention is the assumed legitimacy of a process where moral majority justifications are used to override the specific rights held by minority indigenous groups.

The mode of governance deployed in Alberta is broadly recognised as that of a 'liberal democracy' (Shrivistava and Stefanick 2015), despite both 'liberalism' and 'democracy' referencing a multiplicity of different and historically contingent theoretical positions (see Parekh 1992). This consists of the institutionalisation of two broadly consistent aspects of 'liberalism', which includes the primacy of individual agents and their moral equivalency, along with two elements of 'democracy' under liberalism, which include the equality of individual rights and the legitimacy conferred by majority rule (Short 2005: 271). The concept of legitimacy can here be defined as the equivalence 'between a given system of power and the beliefs, values, and expectations' which allow it to operate (Beetham 1991: 11). Resulting in a negotiated compromise between the collectivism of the latter and the individualism of the former, a system of government operating according to these tenets can be generally characterised by 'civil liberties, more than one political party competing for election, separation of power, the rule of law, and a representative government based on majority rule with protection for minority rights' (Shrivistava and Stefanick 2015: 8). The reference made by regulatory personnel to this latter, majoritarian feature is particularly problematic for minority First Nations because, according to liberal democratic theory, they are treated as little more than groups of 'outvoted citizens' (Freeman 2002: 116). Resulting in a situation where collectives are '*persistently* unrepresented' (Short 2005: 18, emphasis in original), First Nations are rendered structurally 'vulnerable to injustice at the hands of majorities' (Freeman 2002: 117). This is particularly pertinent in the context of a province where the majority has repeatedly elected governments that advocate expansion of the oil sands industry.

While the liberal democratic assumptions upon which Alberta's mode of governance operates provides the set of 'background expectations' from which the moral majority justification is drawn, this in itself belies a deeper aspect of denial that is tied to the province's position within a settler-colonial state. By drawing upon the presumed legitimacy of settler-government sovereignty, the denial implicitly relegates the alternative status of First Nation sovereignty to a secondary position. As such, while the appeal to higher loyalties is demonstrably ahistorical in its content, because it fails to differentiate between minority stakeholder groups on the one hand and the specific rights held by First Nations as 'colonised peoples' on the other (Freeman 2002: 121), its existence as a form of denial is actually historically contingent. The reason for this is straightforward:

> Settler societies were (are) premised on the elimination of native societies. The split tensing reflects a determinate feature of settler colonisation. The colonisers come to stay – invasion is a structure not an event.
>
> (Wolfe 1999: 2)

As such, settler-colonial societies are not only characterised by a 'logic of elimination' (Wolfe 2006: 390), which 'the native repressed continues to structure' (ibid.), but also a fundamental need to disavow their status as such (Veracini 2015). In this sense, denial is intrinsic; settler-colonial societies are 'by definition premised on the traumatic, that is *violent* replacement and/or displacement of indigenous others' (Veracini 2010: 364, emphasis in original).

This original founding violence intersects with subsequent troubling experiences, such as the residential schools used to break down indigenous autonomy (Miller 1996), dispossession of First Nation women's right to land and community membership under the sexist provisions of the Indian Act (Cannon 2007), and the theft of Aboriginal children under racist child welfare policies (Walmsley 2005), to produce 'traumatised societies *par excellence*' (Veracini 2010: 76, emphasis in original). As Rifkin (2014: 2) notes in his referencing of Apess's description of invader descendants:

> The shame borne by these "children" lies in their relation to those Indigenous peoples whose decimation and dispossession cleared the space for their occupancy and, by implication, that of all subjects of the state....

The point being made is that unconscious denial is an inherent and enduring feature of settler societies, not something resigned to history. Indeed, even contemporary attempts at reconciliation, where societies confront past injustices in order to 'establish a legitimate political order from the ashes of an illegitimate prior regime' (Short 2005: 269), are symptomatic of this very interpretation because their focus on overcoming some perceived 'legacy' of harm 'leav[es] the *present* structure of colonial rule largely unscathed' (Coulthard 2014: 22, emphasis added). As such, the presumed legitimacy of the liberal democratic mode of governance, upon which the credibility of the moral majority appeals rests, can be recognised as based on a deeper, historically derived background assumption regarding the legitimacy of settler-colonial sovereignty. By necessity, this is dependent upon a concurrent, conscious and unconscious disavowal of its indigenous counterpart (see Rifkin 2014), disregarding the struggle of First Nations for similar recognition by ignoring its continuation in the present.

The second assumption underpinning the appeal to higher loyalties is the situated identity of the province as an oil producer. The provincial identity assigned to the democratic majority is intertwined with the geographically fixed oil sands resource being exploited. In this sense, the justification draws upon the similar pool of assumptions underpinning the 'public interest' deliberations made by regulatory personnel at the level of approvals (see Chapter 6), where oil sands expansion is justified because it is seen to result in some 'public good' common to 'all Albertans'. However, the less specific way in which the denials were presented by personnel at the 'planning' stage raises a parallel and more informal source of 'background expectations' from which the credibility of the higher loyalties is derived. This is indicative of the way in which the contemporary cultural identity of the province has been built around the oil sands, acting to subtly establish a broadly acceptable image of symbiosis between the two.

The relatively recent success of the oil sands industry means that its concomitant cultural entrenchment is a relatively recent phenomenon. However, the oil and gas industry more generally has a long history in Alberta, of which the oil sands are a contemporary manifestation. In describing its direct and pervasive impact since the 1950s, Wall (2015: 338–341) explains how oil capital has been used to fund key cultural institutions, including museums, art exhibitions, college-based arts programmes, and individual indigenous artists, as a means of 'provid[ing] oil companies with social legitimacy, symbolic capital, and established audiences' (ibid.: 338). The result of this has been a transformation of provincial identity '[a]ssociated at various times with images of wilderness scenery, agricultural abundance, and the Wild West', to one where 'the notion of "being Albertan" resonates today with the oil and gas industry' (ibid.: 344). Indeed, Davidson and Gismondi (2011) explain how the giant bucket wheels used for bitumen extraction have been placed on postage stamps alongside hockey icons, animals, and provincial politicians. Trescott (2006) describes how a monster truck used in the bitumen mines was installed as a centre piece for a mall-based exhibition 'dedicated to the culture of Alberta'. This is mimicked at a more local level, and to a greater degree, with Fort McMurray boasting the Suncor Community Leisure Centre, which contains the Syncrude Aquatics Centre, Canadian Natural Resource Ltd Arena, and Nexen Energy Field House. This complex is situated next to Shell Place, which is a stadium built for recreation, sports, and conferencing, and also houses the China National Offshore Oil Corporation (CNOOC)-Nexen stage. Even the province's most successful ice hockey team, when judged according to the number of Stanley Cup wins, is named the 'Edmonton Oilers', indicative of the long history of oil and gas extraction operating in the province. Taken together, these features represent the contemporary consequences of the almost 70 years of influence exerted by both oil industry and government on the collective provincial identity.

The implications of this are visible in a response given by Taylor (2002: 33) to his own request to '[c]onsider what we mean by identity'. In answering '[i]t is who we are, where we're coming from', he brings to attention the relationship between the construction of Alberta's oil sands image and forms of nationalism common to settler-colonial societies. In this case, the specific area of overlap between the two is the projection of situatedness. Emerging from the same source as the disavowal of aboriginal sovereignty, where the historical perpetuation of trauma against original populations, including their displacement, 'lead[s] to stubborn and lingering anxieties over settler legitimacy *and belonging*' (Veracini 2010: 77, emphasis added), the label given to this particular strategy of identity creation is 'indigenisation' (ibid.: 21). Conceived of as the process by which settler societies attempt to reconcile their contemporary status as both indigenous and exogenous, its purpose is the 'settler acquisition of entitlement as *indigenous* ... [it] was and is about the replacement of one socio-political collective with another' (Veracini 2015: 61, emphasis in original). The necessity of this imagery, and the conflict with settler-colonial legitimacy it invokes, is made clear by Moran (2002: 1029):

> To the extent that indigenous peoples distinguish themselves as a community or communities from the settler nation, their connection with land – a powerful competing claim – becomes a problem and a source of tension for settler nationalists. This potential dilemma has been there for settlers from the beginning: the ideological function served by the creation of national space has been to enact 'legitimate' possession, through knowledge and sacrifice, of the land. Aboriginal knowledge of the land, its flora and fauna, and its spiritual meaning, has always been a source of potential illegitimacy for settler claims on land.

While the anchoring of provincial, territorial identity to the oil sands can be read alone, Wall's (2015) examination illustrates its position as a continuation of settler-colonial attempts at responding to this by rooting itself in space and, by extension, time. The vacillating images of wilderness, agriculture, and the Wild West, which maintained a dominant position within Alberta's early collective identity (ibid.), and indeed continue to do so, have given way to the geographical fixity of crude oil, gas, the oil sands, and the industrial 'frontier' that it represents. In this sense, the appeal to higher loyalties is drawing upon a contemporary extension of geographically and historically specific 'mythical reference[s]' which signify 'settler investment in place and landscape' (Veracini 2010: 21).

When taken together, the assumed legitimacy of majority rule, and its associated, provincialised territoriality, substantiate the appeal to higher loyalties, lending them a credibility which renders them operationally acceptable. However, these both rest upon a more fundamental assumption about the primacy of settler-colonial sovereignty, which itself is premised on the concurrent disavowal of its indigenous counterpart. The provincialism around which the more immediately perceptible denials are framed can therefore be seen as built on a deeper structure of disavowals specific to settler-colonial societies, invoking Orwell's (1945: 1) concerns about 'nationalism' and 'its inseperab[ility] from the desire for power'. Cohen (2001: 64) makes clear the specific relevance of this:

> Vocabularies of denial derive from the fact that social rules are negotiable, flexible, conditional and relative. The more tolerant, pluralistic and 'multi-cultural' the society, the richer and more varied will be its motivational accounting system. This may sound benign enough. But accounts that are embedded in coherent world views – drawing their legitimacy from appeals to God, the state, the revolution or the volk – become

> malignant in exactly the ways that Orwell warned about. By 'nationalism', he meant not just nationalism in the narrow sense, but all ideologies that maintain themselves by denial of other realities.

In the case of the oil sands, the provincialised 'coherent world view' from which the 'background expectations' and 'state-encouraged legitimations' derive their credibility has its basis in the historical subversion of indigenous sovereignty and its associated 'realities'. As such, instead of being premised on recognition of this history, the denials are anchored to a deeper societal disavowal that cloaks such an uncomfortable truth. This is a necessary component in preserving the perception of legitimacy with regard to settler-colonial sovereignty, the common compulsion of which Rifkin (2014: 2) illustrates in his assertion that the very 'everydayness of settler domestic life occurs in places whose availability for such inhabitance depends on the suspension of Native "rights"'. Indeed, the justificatory appeals to higher, provincial loyalties can be seen to channel historically situated, necessary, and deeply held assumptions, transforming them from passive and contextual expectations into active, operational components. Their purpose, of continuing to overrule indigenous interpretations of Treaty rights within deliberative processes, remains constant, thus conforming to Wolfe's (2006: 402, emphasis added) observation on invasion that '*its history does not stop* – or, more to the point, become relatively trivial – when it moves on from the era of frontier homicide'. Put another way, justifying the marginalisation of indigenous interpretations of Treaty rights by appealing to higher loyalties follows an iterative and self-referential pathway, borrowing 'background assumptions' from a provincial settler-colonial liberal democracy whose very sovereignty depends on the continued disavowal of that of its First Nation counterpart.

Denial of Responsibility

In addition to appealing to the assumed 'higher loyalties' of the provincial majority, regulatory personnel also consistently noted that, while the government interpretation of Treaty rights might subordinate that of the First Nations, this was because government consultation practice had not yet been rendered unlawful by the SCC (see Chapter 4). Leaving aside the assumed equivalence of existing consultation practice with SCC judgments, which is disputed above, such a position implies that it is the responsibility of this latter institution to modify the behaviour of the former. This represents a particular form of Cohen's (2001: 88) 'denial of responsibility' – a category which refers to various denials of agency, intent, autonomy, and choice for more ordinary crimes, and, for more political crimes, instructions issued by a superior authority, conformity with a group, or necessity (ibid.). In the case of justifications given by regulatory personnel for subordinating First Nation interpretations of Treaty rights, the clearest affiliation is with the denial sub-category 'obedience to authority' (ibid.), where the authority perceived as higher than the Government of Alberta is the SCC. While deference to SCC case law is the most immediately visible aspect of the justifications given, also invoked is the simultaneous recognition that the SCC, at some point in the future, may deem this existing practice to be illegal. As such, obedience stems not just from the perceived 'commands' rooted in policy and emerging from case law, but also from the absence of instructions telling personnel to behave otherwise by the 'ultimate' authority of the SCC. This results in the claimed 'minimalist approach' to consultation described as adopted by the Government of Alberta (see Chapter 4), where regulatory personnel are simply obeying instructions handed down by the SCC, or the lack thereof.

Another feature of this denial is also visible, in that it is less than absolute. Accompanying the deference to SCC case law were expressions of uncertainty around the legality of existing practice, meaning that regulatory personnel also expected the SCC to retroactively deem present consultation processes to be inadequate. Thus maintained in the same moment are two apparently contradictory positions. This is because, at the micro-level, agency personnel looking upwards see two competing sources of authority in tension: the Government of Alberta and the SCC. It is this lack of a monopoly on authority that generates ambivalence towards the legality of existing consultation practice, if 'ambivalence' is understood in the traditional sense of there being a co-existence of contradictory emotions or attitudes. This holds relevance in the context of Bauman's (1989) discussion on obedience to authority:

> The readiness to act against one's own better judgment, and against the voice of one's conscience, is not just the function of authoritative command, but the result of exposure to a single-minded, unequivocal and monopolistic source of authority.

As such, the maintenance of two apparently contradictory positions, on the legality and potential illegality of existing consultation practice, results from the ever-present possibility that the SCC will force the Government of Alberta to modify its approach to consultation at some future point in time. Informed by its historical tendency to do so, the omnipresent risk posed by this source disrupts the Government of Alberta's monopoly on authority, destabilising assumptions about the legality of consultation policy inside the very institutions tasked with its implementation. As such, the 'free-floating' (Bauman 1989: 161), or 'unanchored' (Cohen 2001: 88), responsibility seen to result from many individuals denying responsibility within a single bureaucratic organisation is here less than absolute. The disruption does not, however, result in organisational paralysis because the influences exerted by the two sources of authority are not equal. The perceived lawfulness of consultation policy is an immediate reality mediated by the organisational command structure inherent to the government agencies, whereas the risk of its rebuttal by the SCC is only a future possibility. This permits both the denial of responsibility and the production of obedience in the same space and time, albeit in a qualified form, facilitating the implementation of overarching consultation policy by personnel who have fundamental doubts about its legality.

The Metaphor of the Ledger

The paternalistic dimension to the provincialism visible in the preceding two sections becomes apparent in the justifications given by those regulatory personnel who were, or had been, in senior government positions. Differing slightly from those offered by more operational personnel, these denials function at a higher level, justifying government aversion to expanding its minimalist stance to Treaty rights by referencing the socio-economic benefits seen to accrue to First Nations under existing arrangements. As these did not refute the injustice of such a position, or frame the denial in terms which allow for such an approach to be interpreted otherwise, these justifications are not examples of 'literal denial' or 'interpretive denial' (Cohen 2001: 7), but, again, 'implicatory denial' (ibid.: 8), where the adverse consequences of an act are denied as opposed to the act itself. The particular way in which this form of denial was deployed references two related sub-categories of denial. The first is the 'metaphor of the ledger' (Minor 1981: 298), which rests upon the 'image of good and evil counterbalancing one another' (ibid.), and 'denial of injury' (Cohen 2001: 95). These are manifest jointly, where the balance inherent to the former frames the 'injury' as something less than absolute, thus tempering the status of the latter. Put another way, the injuriousness of marginalisation is perceived as qualified because some benefit is seen to also accrue to First Nations. If such 'injury' was seen to be unqualified then it would be deemed too serious to entertain the possibility of a positive outcome. Although not primarily relevant, it is worth noting that a third form of denial, 'denial of the victim' (Cohen 2001: 96), is present by association, because non-recognition of 'injury' also tends to deny a group victim status (see Maruna and Copes 2005).

Much like the denials outlined above, the acceptability of these justifications relies upon a set of 'background expectations' common to settler-colonial societies. The most prominent of these is visible in the references made to the 'remote ghetto system' and 'dysfunction' seen to have developed on First Nation reserves over the past 200 years (see Chapter 4). Although derogatory in form, these descriptions speak to the rates of illness, suicide, and poverty on First Nation reserves that are several times higher than for the rest of Canada (Anaya 2013), meaning they signal some aspects of reality. First Nations do have significant issues that have resulted from over two centuries of colonial oppression, and they 'bear the scars of that history' (ibid.). The issue here, however, is that the positioning of oil sands expansion, education, and business development as solutions to this reality annexes such socio-economic difficulties from historical context. It disregards the way in which this predetermined and paternalistic approach represents a continuation in the present of the very mechanisms which operated to deny indigenous peoples their self-determination in the past.

Reference to predetermined, fixed, and ultimately blanket solutions requires an equally homogeneous target upon which they can be applied. This brings into view the undifferentiated conception of First Nations upon which this assumption rests, where their 'needs' are uniform, irrespective of individual characteristics, location, degree of educational attainment, or existing engagement with business development. Indeed, the ACFN Business Group, which was re-branded ACDEN in 2013, comprises 17 businesses and joint ventures specialising in oil and gas services (Slowey and Stefanick 2015: 200), together generating a reported $250 million in annual revenue (Sterritt 2014). Similarly, the Mikisew Group of Companies oversees ten businesses under its banner, drawing a reported $100 million in revenue per year (O'Meara 2014), with the Fort McKay Group (2016) reporting a similar annual amount of $150 million. These characteristics go unregistered within this form of denial, belying the fundamental presence in its exercise of the historic image of First Nations as 'the Indian'. Acting as 'an entity that would stand for the whole' (King 2012: 83), this label originally served to collapse the myriad of individual characteristics held by each indigenous nation into one stereotype, discursively homogenising their individuality by 'giving this snarl of cultures a definitive and manageable form' (ibid.). The contemporary manifestation of this, when coupled with the socio-economic issues derived from their historical subjugation, is a perspective common to settler-colonial societies. The contemporary characteristics of this are described by King (ibid.: 124–125):

> Native people can't look after ourselves. We don't have the capacity to manage our own affairs; we don't know what's good for us. We haven't the level of sophistication to understand the workings of the contemporary world and to participate in the modern economy.

It is thus not simply that First Nations are depicted *en masse* as needing 'education and business development' across a 'remote ghetto system', but that this blanket assumption operates as one of the 'background expectations' which make it acceptable for decisions to be made on their behalf. It is as Rifkin (2014: 19) observes: '[T]he coding of Native people(s) as Indian allows for the articulation of propositional statements about them – including expressions of ambivalence, support, sympathy and guilt.' This permits their more efficient management by bureaucratic state machinery and closes avenues for more open-ended dialogue with individual First Nations, stymying opportunities for deeper and more meaningful consultation by presuming to know both the issues at hand and the most appropriate means for their resolution. Indeed, as the solution to First Nation socio-economic difficulties is being associated with further growth of the oil sands industry, the 'social good' status conferred on this process expands to encompass First Nations as well as 'all Albertans'. This assimilates the interests of the former into the broader, settler-colonial body politic of the latter, justifying the marginalisation of First Nation voices in decisions pertaining to the abuse of Treaty rights.

Conclusion

This chapter has illustrated that the 'planning' stage of the regulatory process is characterised by the systematic actualisation of a diluted duty to consult and accommodate. It demonstrates the various degrees of disparity between practice, policy, and SCC judgments, in terms of the foundational interpretation of Treaty rights, which is evacuated of material content, the trigger of the duty, which is set too late in the process, the depth of consultation, which is defined by a shallowness born of the foundational interpretation, and evidence of accommodation, which has essentially been absent from the LARP since consultation on its detail began in 2008. As illustrated throughout, such features are variously present in policy and practice, meaning there is a recognisable discrepancy between SCC judgments on Treaty rights and the way in which the Government of Alberta is attempting to honour them. Indeed, it is this gap that has allowed for the broad marginalisation of First Nation input at the levels of both policy and practice, destabilising their ability to alter or decelerate production. This has allowed the 'weak' ecological modernisation advocated in policy and realised in practice to be operationalised at the level of 'approvals'.

The second half of this chapter presented an analysis of the justifications given by regulatory personnel for actualising this conception over that of the First Nations. Taking the form of a 'compound denial', where a variety of individualised, surface justifications draw upon a pool of broadly accepted background assumptions and deeper, societal disavowals, the three key, overlapping justifications serving to subordinate First Nation interpretations include an appeal to higher loyalties, denial of responsibility, and the metaphor of the ledger. The first of these justifies over-riding First Nation interpretations of Treaty rights by recourse to it being in the interests of 'all Albertans', a justification also present in the policies on consultation. Relying on 'background expectations' rooted in settler-colonial anxiety, the legitimacy of settler-colonial liberal democracy, and, by extension, the non-recognition of First Nation sovereignty, this is the 'master account' (Cohen 2001: 61), borrowing from the language and legitimations also found in the 'social good' justifications for oil sands expansion.

The second denial, 'denial of responsibility', justifies the subordination of First Nation interpretations of Treaty rights via the notion that the SCC has yet to label it unlawful, while the final denial deployed is that of the 'metaphor of the ledger', where the socio-economic benefits seen to result from the government's minimalist approach to consultation is deemed to outweigh its detriments. It is here that the paternalistic dimension is most visible, wherein the Government of Alberta is assumed to know what is best for First Nations despite opposition. Taken together, this variety of denials has underpinned regulatory attempts at removing any opportunity for First Nations to effectively participate in the regulation of oil sands production. Indeed, it has channelled broader, and more structural, expectations and disavowals inherent to Alberta as a settler-colonial state into the regulatory process, transforming them from passive, contextual assumptions and into active components of influence. As such, the 'weak' ecological modernisation visible at the level of policy and strategy proceeds uninhibited through the control stage of 'planning', where systemic marginalisation of First Nation input ensures very little effective opposition, permitting its operationalisation at the 'approval' stage. This allows for the uninhibited expansion of the industry and, ultimately, the production and reproduction of environmental harm, all under the rubric of 'sustainable development'.

Chapter 8

'Sustainable Development' as Environmental Harm

The Lessons of the Canadian Oil Sands

Based on analyses of almost two decades of government policy and strategy documents, regulatory approval records for large oil sands projects issued since 1997, and transcripts from interviews with government agency, industry, and First Nation Industry Relations personnel, this book has demonstrated that the policy objective of 'sustainable development' has been operationalised at the level of regulation through the philosophical lens of eco-modernism since the mid-1990s. It is this that has enabled the consistent prioritisation of economic production over the land-based cultural interests of First Nations. Advocating widespread use of techno-scientific techniques for environmental mitigation, limited meaningful opportunities for First Nation participation in decision-making processes, and a regulatory approach that avoids problematising the tendency of production under neoliberal capitalism to accelerate, the operationalisation of ecological modernisation has acted as the 'catalyst' for indigenous environmental victimisation for the duration in which the contemporary oil sands industry has existed.

The influence of eco-modernist philosophy is particularly visible at the 'approval' stage of the regulatory process. Here, the regulatory panels overseeing the quasi-judicial public hearings have repeatedly sanctioned oil sands projects by referencing the future ability of science and technology to address their expected environmental impacts. Such measures are considered sufficient to mitigate these effects, constructing an equivalence between social, economic, and environmental issues which permits the issuance of an approval under the rubric of the 'public interest'. This is despite an absence of evidence pertaining to the viability of such mitigation, or even recognition of the effects for which mitigation is being sought. All open-pit oil sands projects have been sanctioned using this broadly recognisable pattern of reasoning. A distinct but related issue stems from this eco-modernist tendency to ignore not only the fundamental contradiction between economic growth and environmental protection, but also its positioning of the latter as contingent on the former. Giving rise to a 'consensus-based' approach to regulation, where a close relationship between an industry and its regulator develops to such an extent that co-operation between the two is more common than antagonism (see Tombs 2017), in Alberta this ensures oil sands projects are effectively approved at a point prior to the date on which the quasi-judicial hearings are opened to the public.

This predisposition to expansion is also underpinned by a perspective that frames oil sands growth as a 'social good', a position lent credibility by wider neoliberal reforms which have, over time, anchored government social expenditure to the natural resources industry. In this sense, operationalisation of eco-modernist philosophy is buttressed by the active internalisation, within the regulatory process itself, of an idealised image of the neoliberal, state–industry relationship. Under this conception, the role of the state and its regulatory apparatus is to facilitate industrial expansion in ways which enable environmental thresholds to be overcome, and not restrict it in accordance with such limits. It is at this juncture where the inability to mitigate the environmental impact of accelerating oil sands production comes to the fore, echoing the observation of Foster *et al.* (2010: 179) that a 'dematerialisation fallacy' lies at the heart of many claims to 'green growth'.

Importantly, the philosophy of ecological modernisation also extends to the 'planning' stage of the regulatory process, where First Nations are consulted on any action that may adversely affect their Treaty rights. This is reflected in the tendency to prioritise the input of political and economic actors over that of the First Nations, also evidencing the inefficacy of the consultative, participatory mechanism which should act to 'control' patterns of environmental harm. However, this process is deeply coloured by Alberta's status as a settler-colonial province and the position of First Nations within that context. The input of First Nations, in decisions pertaining to oil sands expansion, has been roundly marginalised at the levels of policy and practice since the inception of the contemporary industry in the mid-1990s. Facilitated by a diluted interpretation of Treaty rights that has been systematised through successive government policies on consultation, such marginalisation appears to contravene several high-profile judgments issued by the SCC. Importantly, the interviews also indicate how regulatory personnel justify this diluted interpretation at the level of operations. Based on what is here labelled a 'compound denial', which refers to a justification offered for deviant organisational activity as expressed through various individual surface neutralisations, all while simultaneously drawing upon a pool of broadly accepted background assumptions and deeper, societal disavowals, the operational marginalisation of First Nation interpretations of Treaty rights is seen to be in the best interests of the provincial majority. This is because such marginalisation facilitates expansion of the oil sands industry, demonstrating the operational internalisation of characteristics common to the entwined contexts of neoliberal political economy and settler colonialism.

Implications

This research has several potential implications, which can be broadly categorised as theoretical or policy-orientated. The first category, referring to the theoretical implications, is taken as the point of departure. These relate to attempts to explain environmental harm in the oil sands more specifically, and to the body of green criminological scholarship more generally. The second category of implications, referring to those relevant to policy and practice, highlights several potential areas on which First Nations and aligned interest groups may focus their efforts to pursue beneficial change.

Theoretical Implications

As explained in Chapter 1, existing explanations for environmental harm in the oil sands tend to focus on national and international influences at the macro level of analysis. Disguising the fundamental role of the provincial energy regulator in sanctioning industrial expansion, this has prevented regulation from being viewed, and thus analysed, as a mechanism for placating social conflict between broadly incompatible interests. By illuminating the largely unexplored convergence of these social relationships within the regulatory process, the most straightforward implication of this study is that it provides previously unavailable detail on how environmental harm in the region has been produced and reproduced over time through official regulatory processes. More specifically, it highlights how the macro-level features of neoliberal political economy, expansionist government strategies, and settler-colonial anxieties exert influence upon, within, and through the provincial regulatory apparatus. This demonstrates, in turn, how these influences serve to legitimise and normalise the notion of 'green growth' while rendering acceptable its concomitant indigenous and environmental impacts. As such, the findings illustrate how macro-level influences are invested in the very processes responsible for regulating industrial growth and its environmental consequences.

By investigating the internal workings of the more operational level of oil sands regulation, the findings have also added to the literature in several more specific ways. Provincial government efforts at rendering such development 'sustainable' through the regulatory process, have tended to be overlooked in the criminological literature (see Chapter 1). However, it has here been demonstrated that, in addition to it being 'a synonym for the oxymoronic "sustainable growth"' (Daly 1993: 267), the language of 'sustainable development' deployed in policy and strategy exerts influence at the level of operational regulation. Giving the appearance of balance between social, economic, and environmental interests, it allows for environmental risks to be discursively mitigated in the present by relying on the expected achievements of science and technology in the future. This is largely due to the environmental philosophy being operationalised under the rubric of 'sustainable development', which in this case is a specifically 'weak' form of ecological modernisation. As such, the 'effective deregulation' of the oil sands industry mentioned by Smandych and Kueneman (2010: 91), and the acceleration of production discussed by Lynch *et al.* (2016), are not being disputed. Instead, this research adds to, supports, and expands on their specific explanations by providing detail on the operational processes by which the characteristics they speak come to fruition.

While providing support and contributions to existing literature, this study also levels two substantive challenges against it. The first is targeted at the passive role envisaged for First Nations in many of the existing explanations (see Chapter 1; see also Woolford 2013). The role of indigenous peoples as active participants within the regulatory process governing industrial expansion marks such an approach as misplaced, generating incomplete explanations and accounts which inadvertently contribute to the subversion of their voices. With the recent development of criminologies sensitive to the global south (Carrington *et al.* 2015, 2018), a broader re-orientation is currently underway. Indeed, green criminology has also started to account for indigenous voices (see Goyes 2016; Goyes and South 2015, 2017), spurring a hybrid sub-field of 'southern green criminology' (Goyes 2018: 338). These are incipient developments, but it is an emerging movement to which this study contributes. The second challenge to existing literature is targeted at the dominant theoretical frameworks currently in use in green criminology, one of which is the treadmill of crime. Modification of its four-group structure could be attempted, to account for the place of indigenous peoples in the regulation of the oil sands industry, but the findings suggest that a more permanent expansion of its relatively rigid focus on 'environmental enforcement organisations' may be necessary, at least in settler-colonial contexts (Stretesky *et al.* 2013: 132). A similar adjustment could be made to the 'institutional' level of Kramer and Michalowski's (2006: 25) state-corporate analytical model, to introduce more flexibility and allow for its more straightforward application to situations involving indigenous peoples.

Policy Implications

While this study has several implications for provincial government objectives surrounding the 'sustainability' of oil sands extraction, they also highlight the need for modification of broader government policy. This is particularly so if the operation of industry within environmental thresholds is to be achieved over the long term. As highlighted in Chapter 6, provincial policies advocating 'sustainable growth' of the oil sands industry are justified by recourse to Alberta's dependency on its revenues for the provision of public services. This largely singular reliance has been exacerbated by extensive neoliberal reforms since the mid-1990s, where low corporate taxation, high corporate profits, and minimal diversion of oil sands revenues into provincial savings funds have been prioritised over economic diversification away from natural resources. As it is this neoliberal context that grants credibility to 'sustainable growth' objectives, its disruption via political, legal, or activist-orientated means is necessary to destabilise their justificatory basis. Doing so would provide the political and economic space in which regulatory techniques common to 'strong' forms of eco-modernist thought could be pursued.

Although an exhaustive examination of the measures needed to encourage such a transition is beyond the scope of this book, several more normative short- and long-term strategies can be suggested. Over the short term, measures to disrupt the relationship between government revenues and oil sands royalties may include increases to royalty rates and corporate taxation, and a diversion of greater proportions of oil sands revenues into a provincial savings fund. Such techniques could also be coupled with increases in personal and sales tax, although this may be particularly difficult, politically, in such a conservative province like Alberta. Taken together, these measures would begin the process of weaning the provincial government away from the oil sands industry by allowing for the collection of revenues from other sources. This would also decrease the risks associated with oil market volatility and provide a smoother transition away from such single-sector reliance.

Longer-term solutions would have to encompass some form of province-wide diversification away from oil sands extraction. One more politically manageable way of achieving this might be to avoid granting new approvals until previous projects have reached the end of their operating cycle. While this would not address the issues associated with the industry as it currently exists, it would provide somewhat of a cap on its physical footprint. This would also contribute to the gradual deceleration of expansion, notwithstanding the techno-scientific efficiencies that would probably be applied to existing operations as a means of increasing production. Such diversification, away from natural resource use, was advocated in the Government of Alberta's 2011 report, Shaping Alberta's Energy Future. Pointing to multiple scenarios which pose a risk to the energy industry, including global economic slowdown, markets being flooded with alternative supplies or lower-cost and lower-emission oil, environmental backlash, or 'growing regulation that drives up the cost of oil sands production' (Government of Alberta 2011b: 41), the report recommends provincial diversification into industries already established in the province. Expansion of the agriculture and forestry, medical, and biotechnology sectors is therefore advocated (ibid.: 45–47). While these have their own ecological problems, such diversification would go some way towards tackling the environmental harm at issue in the oil sands.

The second body of policy implications can be made in more direct relation to the agencies of the Government of Alberta, namely the LUS, the AER, and the ACO. Taking these in turn, the LUS should prioritise requests for buffer zones around First Nation reserves. Considering that such a decision was made in relation to the LARP, being based on the notion of economic interests having priority over the more environmental interests of First Nations (ibid.), and that the *Sparrow* decision affirms that Aboriginal interests should be given priority over others in accordance with Section 35 of the constitution (see Chapter 7), then continued government reluctance to introduce these buffer zones appears at odds with SCC judgments. This discrepancy should be rectified by replacing the prioritisation of oil sands extraction in the LARP with activities pertaining to the exercise of First Nation Treaty rights.

The book also suggests that the LUS could simultaneously reduce conflict and alleviate a degree of indigenous environmental victimisation by integrating principles of co-management into the LARP. While government opposition to this approach is buoyed by the contextual need to minimise obstacles to oil sands expansion, such a stance would be less defensible and necessary if the methods aimed at reducing oil sands dependency were pursued. Furthermore, First Nations support the existence of the extractives industry in some form, as they rely on it to participate in the market for wage labour. As such, co-management would not necessarily elicit the level of opposition feared. That said, the model adopted should give First Nations veto power over any future applications for projects on their lands, or at least the ability to relocate proposed oil sands projects. Indeed, efforts at decoupling have roundly failed. The relatively production-averse techniques associated with 'strong' forms of eco-modernisation should now be pursued, instead of recycling the evidentially misplaced faith in the future potential of science and technology to mitigate the detrimental effects of ever-accelerating production. Furthermore, in accordance with SCC judgments on the need to consult on any activity which may impact on First Nation Treaty rights, the final model of co-management should be decided upon only after full and meaningful consultation with the First Nations themselves.

Moving onto the AER, its 'compliance-based' approach to regulating the oil sands industry is problematic. Its effective approval of projects prior to the point at which hearings are opened to the public is both compromising its ability to reject a project application and undermining its legitimacy as an 'independent' authority. The weakening of this connection could be achieved, at least in part, by requiring transparency of communications between the regulator and the specific industrial actor in question prior to a hearing. While this would introduce elements of delay and even uncertainty into the regulatory process, such criticisms tend to be offered from the standpoint of 'consensus', where no contradictions are perceived between expansive oil sands capital and environmental integrity. As Chapter 6 has demonstrated, such a stance is illusory, particularly if the fallacy of materialisation is taken into account. Considering also that hearing panel personnel are influenced by the land uses designated in the LARP, removing the prioritisation of extractive operations from the strategy should provide regulatory personnel with the space needed to act contrary to such interests. Broader provincial diversification away from oil sands revenue should also destabilise the 'public interest' justifications repeatedly used in the approvals. Furthermore, as the projects are, in effect, approved in private, prior to the public hearings, the extent to which this also amounts to the issuance of an approval prior to a determination of consultation adequacy is unclear. Such a reality would be in clear contravention of the requirement under *Mikisew* (para 54) for consultation to be 'meaningful', as some of the core options for accommodation will have, by this point, already been annexed. Improving the transparency of regulator-regulatee communication may therefore prevent this from happening, or at least illuminate instances in which it is occurring, providing subsequent opportunities for legal challenge.

The book also has several implications for both the Government of Alberta's First Nation consultation policy and the ACO as the agency responsible for its implementation. First, the narrow interpretation of Treaty rights, as only for hunting, fishing, and trapping for food, needs to be addressed, as does the interpretation which isolates them from geographic location and species quantity and quality. As illustrated in Chapter 7, both interpretations appear to contravene SCC judgments. Second, consultation should be triggered earlier in the regulatory process, at the point of land lease disposition, and not at the stage of seismic or exploratory drilling. As it stands, this is another instance in which consultation practice appears to breach of SCC judgments.

Finally, the ability of the ACO to decide on the adequacy of its own consultation compromises the credibility of the process. Prior to the creation of the AER under the REDA, the decision on whether consultation had been adequate fell under the jurisdiction of the LUS and ERCB. This provided some degree of independence. While the REDA removes this power from the AER, Laidlaw (2016) suggests it is retained by the requirement for government agencies to act constitutionally. He therefore posits a return to the previous system as a means of restoring independence of judgement. However, such parity exists between justifications for oil sands expansion at the 'approval' stage and those given for marginalising First Nation interests at the 'planning' stage that Laidlaw's solution may simply continue the status quo. In other words, the compound denial visible within the regulatory process risks being too easily transferable between agencies. As such, it is recommended that a separate agency, operating at the federal level, be created to determine the adequacy of consultation, sitting outside not only the regulatory process itself but also the province. There are still issues with this: consultation policy is provincial and the federal government is settler-colonial and still maintains a heavy reliance on oil sands revenues. Indeed, this is particularly visible in its enthusiasm for pipeline expansion (see Chapter 1). However, this may provide enough distance from the province itself to permit decisions that accord more with SCC judgments.

So far, the suggested implications have been relatively apolitical in nature. Recommending changes to government agencies, policy, and process, there has been little mention of how such modifications would be made by a state apparatus with vested interests in maintaining the status quo. Following Williams' (2012) recommendation that implications should include proposals for policy and action aimed at entities with the capacity to implement them, it is important to consider the ways in which the suggested modifications could be pursued and enacted. First, advocating co-management as a strategy for the amelioration of indigenous environmental victimisation is not an unrealistic goal. The possibility for its introduction in some form has expanded since the interviews were conducted in January and February of 2015. Under Justin Trudeau's Liberal Party, which was elected later in 2015, the Government of Canada pledged early on to implement the United Nations Declaration on the Rights of Indigenous Peoples (UNDRIP) (Delacourt 2015; Smith 2015). Confirming this, the federal ministers of Indigenous and Northern Affairs and Justice stated that Canada would 'fully adopt and work to implement' the terms of the UNDRIP, making the announcement to the United Nations in May 2016 (Hill 2016). The provincial New Democratic Party, which took power in May 2015, also adopted this position, with the now-Premier, Rachel Notley (2015: 1), stating that the UNDRIP will be 'implemented in a way that is consistent with our constitution and with Alberta law'. While evidence of this pledge to 'work to implement' has yet, at the time of writing, to materialise at either level, it demonstrates the potential for co-management to act as the mechanism by which the consent requirement in the UNDRIP could be operationalised by these governments.

With the context apparently conducive for not only movement towards a co-management system, but one which embodies the right to free, prior, and informed consent outlined in the UNDRIP, there are several avenues available to those wishing to encourage its introduction. The first option, and that which elicits the least conflict over the short term, is to wait for the Governments of Alberta or Canada to consult on possible systems and subsequently decide on the one to implement. The issue here, however, is that consultation processes tend not to accommodate First Nation input on any meaningful level (see Chapter 7). Furthermore, as suggested in Chapter 4, governments have greater flexibility in reversing a decision they have made policy provision for, as opposed to one forced upon them by the SCC. As such, while First Nations and their allies should attempt to reach an agreement with respect to a co-management system, they should also consider their options at the SCC, particularly as this was identified as a site of vulnerability for the provincial government.

Conclusion

Looking to the future, whatever actions are pursued in relation to the oil sands resource, by federal, provincial, First Nation, public actors, or others, it is clear that the primary consequence of its 'sustainable development' has been environmental harm. The mercurial quality of the concept lends it a malleability which allows for co-option by dominant interests for demonstrably unsustainable ends. Indeed, questions over use of the term are not confined to the realm of conceptual abstraction. For two decades the Government of Alberta has operationalised the concept through the prism of ecological modernisation, transforming it into 'sustainable growth' and imbibing it with a faith that science and technology will mitigate its ills, both now and in the future. Injected into the regulatory process governing oil sands expansion through legislation, 'sustainable development' has not only been used to facilitate accelerating levels of extraction, but to pursue this goal despite an awareness of incremental degrees of environmental harm and Treaty abuse. Exposing it as a vessel into which growth-orientated interests pertaining to political economy and settler colonialism can find form, criminologists need to be both sensitive to and critical of its use. As the age of climate disruption proceeds, the apparently risk-mitigating cloak of 'sustainable development' is likely to become an increasingly attractive proposition for those seeking to maintain the status quo. It is incumbent on future scholarship to guard against this, for doing otherwise risks producing and reproducing environmental harm under its comforting rhetoric right at the very moment such a position becomes untenable.

References

Acuna, R. (2016) *The Good, the Bad and the Ugly of Alberta's New Royalty Framework*. Available at: www.parklandinstitute.ca/the_good_the_bad_and_the_ugly [Accessed 29.11.2018].

Alberta Energy and Utilities Board (1997a) Application by Suncor Inc. Oil Sands Group for Amendment of Approval No. 7632 for Proposed Steepbank Mine Amendment. Decision No. 97–1. Calgary, Alberta.

Alberta Energy and Utilities Board (1997b) Application by Syncrude for the Aurora Mine. Decision No. 97–13. Calgary, Alberta.

Alberta Energy and Utilities Board (1999a) Application by Suncor Energy Inc. for Amendment of Approval No. 8101 for the Proposed Project Millennium Development. Decision No. 99–7. Calgary, Alberta.

Alberta Energy and Utilities Board (1999b) Shell Canada Limited. Muskeg River Mine Project. Decision No. 99–2. Calgary, Alberta.

Alberta Energy and Utilities Board (1999c) Application by Syncrude Canada Ltd. for Amendment of Approval No. 7550 Proposed Mildred Lake Upgrader Expansion. Decision No. 99–25. Calgary, Alberta.

Alberta Energy and Utilities Board (2004a) Application for Oil Sands Mine, Bitumen Extraction Plant, and Bitumen Upgrading Plant in the Fort McMurray Area. EUB Decision 2004–005. Calgary, Alberta.

Alberta Energy and Utilities Board (2004b) Shell Canada Limited: Application for Oil Sands Mine, Bitumen Extraction Plant, Cogeneration Plant and Water Pipeline in the Fort McMurray Area. EUB Decision 2004–009. Calgary, Alberta.

Alberta Energy and Utilities Board (2006a) Suncor Energy Inc.: Application for Expansion of an Oil Sands Mine (North Steepbank Mine Extension) and a Bitumen Upgrading Facility (Voyageur Upgrader) in the Fort McMurray Area. EUB Decision 2006–112. Calgary, Alberta.

Alberta Energy and Utilities Board (2006b) Albian Sands Energy Inc. Application to Expand the Oil Sands Mining and Processing Plant Facilities at the Muskeg River Mine, Fort McMurray. Decision 2006–128. Calgary, Alberta.

Alberta Energy and Utilities Board (2007) Imperial Oil Resources Ventures Limited Application for an Oil Sands Mine and Bitumen Processing Facility (Kearl Oil Sands Project), Fort McMurray Area. Decision 2007–013. Calgary, Alberta.

Alberta Energy Regulator (2013a) *Alberta Energy Regulator to ensure efficient, comprehensive energy regulation*. Available at: www.aer.ca/documents/news-releases/AERNR2013-24.pdf [Accessed 29.11.2018].

Alberta Energy Regulator (2013b) *Jackpine Mine Expansion Project Joint Review Panel*. Approval No. 9756. Calgary, Alberta.

Alberta Energy Regulator (2014) *CPRS Application – AER Launch*. Available at: www.mtroyal.ca/library/inc/cprs/pdfs/19-05-ALB-14%20Regulator,%20Alberta%20Energy.pdf [Accessed 29.11.2018].

Alberta Energy Regulator (2015) *Alberta's Energy Reserves 2014 and Supply/Demand Outlook 2015–2024*. ST98–2015. Available at: www.aer.ca/documents/sts/ST98/ST98-2015_Infographic.pdf [Accessed 29.11.2018].

Alberta Energy Regulator (2016a) *Hearings and Proceedings*. Available at: www.aer.ca/applications-and-notices/hearings-and-proceedings [Accessed 29.11.2018].

Alberta Energy Regulator (2016b) 'Tailings Status Report' (online) Available at: www.aer.ca/documents/oilsands/TailingsStatusReport_2016.zip [Accessed 10.08.2018].

Alberta Energy Regulator (2017a) 'Alberta Energy Industry Water Use Report – Oil Sands Mining' (online) available at: www2.aer.ca/t/Production/views/AlbertaWaterUseReportMining/Summary?%3Aembed=top&%3AshowShareOptions=true&%3Adisplay_count=no&%3AshowVizHome=no [Accessed 29.11.2018].

Alberta Energy Regulator (2017b) 'Alberta Energy Industry Water Use Report – In-Situ' (online) available at: www2.aer.ca/t/Production/views/AlbertaWaterUseReportInSitu/Summary?%3Aembed=top&%3AshowShareOptions=true&%3Adisplay_count=no&%3AshowVizHome=no [Accessed 18.11.2018].

Alberta Energy Regulator (2018) 'Water Use History for Oil Sands Projects' (online) Available at: http://osip.alberta.ca/library/Dataset/Details/56 [Accessed 18.11.2018].

Alberta Environment (1999) *Regional Sustainable Development Strategy for the Athabasca Oil Sands Area*. Pub No. I/754. Fort McMurray, Alberta.

Alberta Environment Monitoring Panel (2011) *A World Class Environmental Monitoring, Evaluation and Reporting System for Alberta*. Available at: http://abctech.ca/uploads/files/Resources/Final%20Report%20for%20AEMP%20June%202011%20-%20Govt.pdf [Accessed 29.11.2018].

Alberta Federation of Labour (2012) *Danger, Workers at Risk*. Available at: https://d3n8a8pro7vhmx.cloudfront.net/afl/pages/2312/attachments/original/1272469338/WorkersAtRisk_2010Apr.pdf?1272469338 [Accessed 06.06.2018].

Alberta Ministry of Energy (1999) *1998/1999 Annual Report*. Available at: https://open.alberta.ca/dataset/cbd7147b-d304-4e3e-af28-78970c71232c/resource/8c448855-07d7-4d48-9ded-3587fa431671/download/ar1999.pdf [Accessed 01.11.2018].

Alberta Treasury Board and Finance (2018) *Alberta Heritage Savings Trust Fund: 2017–2018 Annual Report* (online) available at: https://open.alberta.ca/dataset/3675e470-646e-4f8a-86a7-c36c6f45471a/resource/1f86ad5d-923c-47d0-816a-063fd6cacbf4/download/2017-18-heritage-fund-annual-report.pdf [Accessed 18.11.2018].

Allen, C., Fontaine, J., Pope, K. and Garmestani, A. (2011) 'Adaptive Management for a Turbulent Future'. *Journal of Environmental Management*. Vol. 92 (5), pp. 1339–1345.

Anaya, J. (2009) *International Human Rights and Indigenous Peoples*. New York, Aspen Publishers.

Anaya, J. (2013) *United Nations Special Rapporteur on the Rights of Indigenous Peoples, James Anaya, Statement upon Conclusion of the Visit to Canada*. Available at: http://unsr.jamesanaya.org/statements/statement-upon-conclusion-of-the-visit-to-canada [Accessed 29.11.2018].

Andersen, M. and Massa, I. (2000) 'Ecological Modernisation – Origins, Dilemmas and Future Directions'. *Journal of Environment and Policy Planning*. Vol. 2 (4), pp. 337–345.

Armitage, D., Plummer, R., Berkes, F., Arthur, R., Charles, A., Davidson-Hunt, I., Diduck, A., Doubleday, N., Johnson, D., Marschke, M., McConney, P., Pinkerton, E. and Wollenberg, E. (2008) 'Adaptive Co-Management for Social-Ecological Complexity'. *Frontiers in Ecology and Environment*. Vol. 7 (2), pp. 95–102.

Athabasca Chipewyan First Nation (2010) 'Athabasca Chipewyan First Nation Advice to the Government of Alberta Regarding the Lower Athabasca Regional Plan'. Available at: https://landuse.alberta.ca/Forms%20and%20Applications/RFR_ACFN%20Response%20to%20LARP%20Panel%20IR%206%20-%20Advice_2014-11-14_PUBLIC.pdf [Accessed 01.11.2018].

Athabasca Chipewyan First Nation (2016) *Written Brief of the Athabasca Chipewyan First Nation to the Standing Committee on Transport, Infrastructure and Communities*. Available at: www.ourcommons.ca/Content/Committee/421/TRAN/Brief/BR8693005/br-external/AthabascaChipewyanFirstNation-e.pdf [Accessed 30.10.2018].

Ayles, G., Dube, M. and Rosenberg, D. (2004) *Oil Sands Regional Aquatic Monitoring Program (RAMP) Scientific Peer Review of the Five Year Report 1997–2001*. Available at: www.andrewnikiforuk.com/Dirty_Oil_PDFs/RAMP%20Peer%20review.pdf [Accessed 30.10.2018].

Bauman, Z. (1989) *Modernity and the Holocaust*. Cambridge, Polity Press.

Beck, U. (1992) *Risk Society: Towards a New Modernity*. London, Sage Publications.

Beetham, D. (1991) *The Legitimation of Power*. London, Palgrave Macmillan.

Beirne, P. and South, N. (2007) 'Introduction: Approaching Green Criminology'. In P. Beirne and N. South (eds.) *Issues in Green Criminology: Confronting Harms Against Environments, Humanity and Other Animals*. Devon, Willan Publishing, pp. xiii–xxii.

Benn, S. (2009) 'Organisations and Society: Sustainability Deconstructed'. In S. Clegg and C. Cooper (eds.) *The Sage Handbook of Organisational Behaviour*. London, Sage Publications, pp. 356–373.

Benton, T. (2007) 'Ecology, community and justice: the meaning of green'. In P. Beirne and N. South (eds.) *Issues in Green Criminology*. Devon, Willan Publishing.

Berger, G., Flynn, A., Hines, F. and Johns, R. (2001) 'Ecological Modernisation as a Basis for Environmental Policy: Current Environmental Discourse and Policy and the Implications on Environmental Supply Chain Management'. *Innovation*. Vol. 14 (1), pp. 55–72.

Berry, J. (1999) 'Aboriginal Cultural Identity'. *The Canadian Journal of Native Studies*. Vol. XIX (1), pp. 1–36.

Beyleveld, D. and Brownsword, R. (2007) *Consent in the Law*. Oxford, Hart Publishing.

Birn K. and Meyer, J. (2015) *Why the Oil Sands? How a Remote Complex Resource Became a Pillar of Global Supply Growth*. Available at: http://on.ihs.com/1MfzvNz [Accessed 03.09.18].

Blaustein, J., Pino, N., Fitz-Gibbon, K. and White, R. (2018) 'Criminology and the UN Sustainable Development Goals: The Need for Support and Critique'. *British Journal of Criminology*. Vol. 58 (4), pp. 767–786.

Boekhout van Solinge, T. (2014) 'Researching Illegal Logging and Deforestation', *International Journal for Crime, Justice and Social Democracy*. Vol. 3 (2), pp. 35–48.

Bonds, E. and Downey, L. (2012) 'Green Technology and Ecological Unequal Exchange: The Environment and Social Consequences of Ecological Modernization in the World System'. *American Sociological Association*. Vol. 18 (2), pp. 167–186.

Bookchin, M. (1982) *The Ecology of Freedom: The Emergence and Dissolution of Hierarchy*. Palo Alto, CA, Cheshire Books.

Bowness, E. and Hudson, M. (2013) 'Sand in the Cogs? Power and Public Participation in the Alberta Oil Sands'. *Environmental Politics*. Vol. 23 (1), pp. 59–76.

Boyd, D. (2012) *The Right to a Healthy Environment*, Vancouver, University of British Columbia Press.

Brogly, J. (2015) *COSIA Performance Update Webcast*. Available at: www.cosia.ca/events/performance-update-webcast/performance-update-2015-webcast [Accessed 06.01.2017].

Burkett, P. (2005) *Marxism and Ecological Economics*. Chicago, Haymarket Books.

Burn, Dr., Dixon, Dr., Dube, Dr., Flotemersch, Dr., Franzin, Dr., Gibson, Dr., Munkittrick, Dr., Post, Dr. and Watmough, Dr. (2011) *2010 Regional Aquatics Monitoring Program (RAMP) Scientific Review*. Available at: www.ramp-alberta.org/UserFiles/File/RAMP%202010%20Scientific%20Peer%20Review%20Report.pdf [Accessed 29.11.2018].

Buttel, F. (2000) 'Ecological Modernisation as Social Theory'. *Geoforum*. Vol. 31, pp. 57–65.

Buttel, F. (2004) 'The Treadmill of Production'. *Organisation and Environment*. Vol. 17 (3), pp. 323–336.

Calgary Homeless Foundation (2014) *Point-in-Time Count Report*. Available at: http://calgaryhomeless.com/wp-content/uploads/2014/06/Winter-2014-PIT-Count-Report.pdf [Accessed 29.11.2018].

Campanella, D. and Bower, S. (2013) *Taking the Reins: The Case for Slowing Alberta's Bitumen Production*. Edmonton, University of Alberta Parkland Institute.

Canadian Association of Petroleum Landmen (2013) *Alberta Energy Regulator*. Available at: www.landman.ca/pdf/2013/AB%20Energy%20Regulator%20Feb%2014%202013.pdf [Accessed 29.11.2018].

Canadian Association of Petroleum Producers (2018a) *Economic Contribution* (online) Available at: www.canadasoilsands.ca/en/explore-topics/economic-contribution [Accessed 29.11.2018].

Canadian Association of Petroleum Producers (2018b) *Statistical Handbook* (online) Available at: www.capp.ca/publications-and-statistics/statistics/statistical-handbook [Accessed 18.11.2018].

Canadian Oil Sands Innovation Alliance (2017) 'Water Project Update with COSIA Tailings and Water Director John Brogly' (online) Available at: www.cosia.ca/node/434 [Accessed 18.11.2018].

Canadian Oil Sands Innovation Alliance (2018) 'Pit Lake Research' (online) Available at: www.cosia.ca/initiatives/water/projects/pit-lake-research [Accessed 17.11.2018].

Candler, C., Olsen, R., DeRoy, S., the Firelight Group Research Co-operative and the Athabasca Chipewyan First Nation (2010) *As Long as the Rivers Flow: Athabasca River Use, Knowledge and Change*. Available at: www.ceaa.gc.ca/050/documents_staticpost/65505/56887/App. 09_ACFN_Community_Report.pdf [Accessed 30.10.2018].

Cannon, M. (2007) 'Revisiting Histories of Legal Assimilation, Racialized Injustice, and the Future of Indian Status in Canada'. *Aboriginal Policy Research Consortium International*. Paper 97.

Carrington, K., Hogg, R. and Sozzo, M. (2015) 'Southern Criminology'. *British Journal of Criminology*. Vol. 56 (1), pp. 1–20.

Carrington, K., Hogg, R., Scott, J. and Sozzo, M. (eds.) (2018) *The Palgrave Handbook of Criminology and the Global South*. London, Palgrave.

Carroll, W. and Little, W. (2001) 'Neoliberal Transformation and Antiglobalization Politics in Canada'. *International Journal of Political Economy*. Vol. 31 (3), pp. 33–66.

Castree, N. (2004) 'Differential Geographies: Place, Indigenous Rights and 'Local' Resources'. *Political Geography*. Vol. 23 (2), pp. 133–167.

Centeno, M. and Cohen, J. (2012) 'The Arc of Neoliberalism'. *Annual Review of Sociology*. Vol. 38, pp. 317–340.

Centre for Indigenous Environmental Resources (2010) *Sagow Pimachiwin: Plants and Animals Used by Mikisew Cree First Nation for Food, Medicine and Materials*. Manitoba, Centre for Indigenous Environmental Resources.

Chang, H.-J. (2003) *Globalisation, Economic Development and the Role of the State*. London, Zed Books.

Chastko, P. (2007) *Developing Alberta's Oil Sands*. Calgary, University of Calgary Press.

Chen, Y. (2009) 'Cancer Incidence in Fort Chipewyan, Alberta, 1995–2006'. *Alberta Health Services* (online) Available at: www.albertahealthservices.ca/rls/ne-rls-2009-02-06-fort-chipewyan-study.pdf [Accessed 30.10.2018].

Cheng, H., Sathiakumar, N., Graff, J., Matthews, R. and Delzell, E. (2007) '1,3-Butadiene and Leukemia Among Synthetic Rubber Industry Workers: Exposure-Response Relationships'. *Chemical-Biological Interactions*. Vol. 166 (1–3), pp. 15–24.

Christoff, P. (1996) 'Ecological Modernisation, Ecological Modernities'. *Environmental Politics*. Vol. 5, pp. 476–500.

Clifford, M. and Edwards, T. (2012) *Environmental Crime* (2nd ed.). London, Jones and Bartlett.

Cobo, J. M. (1986/7) *Study of the Problem of Discrimination against Indigenous Populations*. UN Doc E/CN .4/Sub.2/1986/7.

Cohen, M. (1997) 'Risk Society and Ecological Modernisation: Alternative Visions for Post-industrial Nations'. *Futures*. Vol. 29 (2), pp. 105–119.

Cohen, S. (1998) *Against Criminology*. New Jersey, Transaction Publishers.

Cohen, S. (2001) *States of Denial*. Cambridge, Polity Press.

Colavecchia, M. V., Hodson, P. V. and Parrott, J. L. (2006) 'CYP1A Induction and Blue Sac Disease in Early Life Stages of White Suckers (*Catostomus Commersoni*) Exposed to Oil Sands'. *Journal of Toxicology and Environmental Health Part A*. Vol. 69 (10), pp. 967–994.

Connelly, S. (2007) 'Mapping Sustainable Development as a Contested Concept'. *Local Environment*. Vol. 12 (3), pp. 259–278.

Coulthard, G. (2014) *Red Skin White Masks*. Minneapolis, University of Minnesota Press.

Council of Canadian Academies (2015) *Technological Prospects for Reducing the Environmental Footprint of the Canadian Oil Sands: The Expert Panel on the Potential for New and Emerging Technologies to Reduce the Environmental Impact of Oil Sands Development*. Ottawa, Council of Canadian Academies.

Craik, A. (2016) 'Process and Reconciliation: Integrating the Duty to Consult with Environmental Assessment'. *Osgoode Legal Studies Research Paper Series*. Paper 122.

Cumulative Environmental Management Association (2012) *End Pit Lakes Guidance Document* (online) Available at: http://cemaonline.ca/index.php/news-a-events/cema-press-releases/89-cema-news/press-releases/press-release-articles/196-press-release-cema-delivers-oilsands-mine-end-pit-lake-guidance-document-october-4-2012 [Accessed 17.11.2018].

Cumulative Environmental Management Association (2016) 'Attention' (online) Available at: http://cemaonline.ca/ [Accessed 17.11.2018].

Czech, B. (2013) *Supply Shock: Economic Growth at the Crossroads and the Steady State Solution*. Canada, New Society Publishers.

Daly, H. (1990) 'Sustainable Growth: A Bad Oxymoron'. *Environmental Carcinogenesis Reviews*. Vol. 8 (2), pp. 401–407.

Daly, H. (1993) 'Sustainable Growth: An Impossibility Theorem'. In H. Daly and K. Townsend (eds.) *Valuing the Earth: Economics, Ecology, Ethics*. Cambridge, MA, MIT Press. pp. 267–274.

David, W. L. (1988) *Political Economy of Economic Policy: The Quest for Human Betterment*. London, Praeger Press.

Davidson, D. and Gismondi, M. (2011) *Challenging Legitimacy at the Precipice of Energy Calamity*. New York, Springer.

Davies, P. (2014) 'Green Crime and Victimization: Tensions Between Social and Environmental Justice'. *Theoretical Criminology*. Vol. 18 (3), pp. 300–316.

Davison, A. (2004) 'Sustainable Technology: Beyond Fix and Fixation'. In R. White (ed.) *Controversies in Environmental Sociology*. Melbourne, Cambridge University Press, pp. 132–149.

Delacourt, S. (2015) 'You'll Be Judged by How You Treat Others, Trudeau Cabinet Warned'. *The Star* (online) Available at: www.thestar.com/news/canada/2015/11/12/youll-be-judged-by-how-you-treat-others-trudeau-cabinet-warned.html [Accessed 29.11.2018].

Dillon, P., Dixon, G., Driscoll, C., Giesy, J., Hurlbert, S. and Nriagu, J. (2011) *Evaluation of Four Reports on Contamination of the Athabasca River System by Oil Sands Operations* (online) Available at: www.assembly.ab.ca/lao/library/egovdocs/2011/alen/156416.pdf [Accessed 29.11.2018].

Dobson, S., Lemphers, N. and Guilbeault, S. (2013) *Booms, Busts and Bitumen*. Calgary, Pembina Institute.

Doern, B. and Gattinger, M. (2003) *Power Switch: Energy Regulatory Governance in the Twenty-first Century*. Toronto, University of Toronto Press.

Doremus, H. (2007) 'Precaution, Science and Learning while Doing in Natural Resource Management'. *Washington Law Review Association*. Vol. 82, pp. 547–579.

Dowdeswell, L., Dillon, P., Subhasis, G., Miall, A., Rasmussen, J. and Smol, J. (2010) *A Foundation for the Future: Building an Environmental Monitoring System for the Oil Sands* (online) Available at: http://caid.ca/RepEnvMonOilSan2010.pdf [Accessed 29.11.18].

Downes, D. (1988) 'The Sociology of Crime and Social Control in Britain 1960–1987'. In P. Rock (ed.) *A History of British Criminology*. Oxford, Oxford University Press, pp. 45–68.

Doyle, C. (2015) *Indigenous Peoples, Title to Territory, Rights and Resources*. Abingdon, Routledge.

Dryzek, J. (1997) *The Politics of the Earth: Environmental Discourses*. Oxford, Oxford University Press.

Dryzek, J. (2013) *The Politics of the Earth: Environmental Discourses* (3rd ed.). Oxford, Oxford University Press.

Edwards, J. (2014) 'Oil and Medicine: Alberta MD's gain support'. *Canadian Medical Association Journal*. Vol. 186 (10), pp. E347–348.

Elliot, J. (2013) *An Introduction to Sustainable Development* (4th ed.). London, Routledge.

Energy Framework Initiative (2011) 'Dear Ministers Kent and Oliver' (online) Available at: www.cbc.ca/news/politics/energy-industry-letter-suggested-environmental-law-changes-1.1346258 [Accessed 30.10.2018].

Energy Resources Conservation Board (2009) *The Lieutenant Governor in Council authorises the Energy Resources Conservation Board to grant Amendment F to Approval No. 8535 to Suncor Energy Inc. in the form attached. O.C. 268/2009* (online) Available at: www.qp.alberta.ca/documents/orders/orders_in_council/2009/509/2009_268.html [Accessed 01.11.2018].

Energy Resources Conservation Board (2010) *Tailings reductions operation application (Application No. 1626702)* (online) Available at: www.aer.ca/documents/oilsands/tailings-plans/Suncor_TRO_D074_cover_letter_FINAL.pdf [Accessed 01.02.2018].

Energy Resources Conservation Board (2011) 'Report of the Joint Review Panel: Joslyn North Mine Project, Total E&P Joslyn Ltd, Alberta'. *Decision No. 2011–005.*

Englander, J., Bharadwaj, S. and Brandt, A. (2013) 'Historical Trends in Greenhouse Gas Emissions of the Alberta Oil Sands (1970–2010). *Environmental Research Letters*, Vol. 8 (4). IOP Publishing Ltd.

Evans, J. (2015) 'The Paradox of Plenty: Ending Homelessness in Alberta'. In M. Shrivastava and L. Stefanick (eds.) *Alberta Oil and the Decline of Democracy in Canada.* Athabasca, Athabasca University Press, pp. 313–332.

Fabricius, C. and Cundill, G. (2014) 'Learning in Adaptive Management: Insights from Published Practice'. *Ecology and Society.* Vol. 19 (1), pp. 29–37.

Fawcett, M. (2015) 'The Interview: Alberta Premier on Jim Prentice, Pipelines, First Nations and Why He Didn't Run for Prime Minister' (online) *The Star.* 24 November 2017.

Ferguson, N. (2011) 'From Coal Pits to Tar Sands: Labour Migration Between an Atlantic Canadian Region and the Athabasca Oil Sands'. *Just Labour: A Canadian Journal of Work and Society.* Vols. 17 & 18, pp. 106–118.

Fisher, D. (2002) 'From the treadmill of production to ecological modernisation? Applying a Habermasian framework to society-environment relationships'. In A. Mol and F. Buttel (eds.) *The Environmental State Under Pressure.* Bingley, Emerald Group Publishing Limited, pp. 53–64.

Flanagan (2015a) *Looking in the Mirror: Provincial Comparisons of Public Spending.* Available at: www.parklandinstitute.ca/looking_in_the_mirror [Accessed 29.11.2018].

Flanagan, G. (2015b) *From Gap to Chasm* (online) Available at: www.parkland institute.ca/from_gap_to_chasm [Accessed 29.11.2018].

Fluker, S. (2015) 'The Right to Public Participation in Resources and Environmental Decision-Making in Alberta'. *Alberta Law Review.* Vol. 52 (3), pp. 1–52.

Forrest, M., Lan, Q., Hubbard, A., Zhang, L., Vermeulen, R., Zhao, X., Li, G., Wu, Y., Shen, M., Yin, S., Chancock, S., Rothman, N. and Smith, M. (2005) 'Discovery of Novel Biomarkers by Microarray Analysis of Peripheral Blood Mononuclear Cell-Gene Expression in Benzene-Exposed Workers'. *Environmental Health Perspectives.* Vol. 113 (6), pp. 801–807.

Fort McKay Group (2016) 'Company History' (online) Available at: http://fort mckaygroup.com/about-us/company-history/ [Accessed 10.01.2017].

Foster, J. (1999) 'Marx's Theory of Metabolic Rift: Classical Foundations for Environmental Sociology'. *American Journal of Sociology.* Vol. 105 (2), pp. 266–405.

Foster, J. (2009) *The Ecological Revolution: Making Peace with the Planet.* New York, Monthly Review Press.

Foster, J. (2015) *After Sustainability*, Abingdon, Routledge.

Foster, J. B., Clarke, B. and York, R. (2010) *The Ecological Rift*. New York, Monthly Review Press.

Frank, R., Roy, J., Bickerton, G., Rowland, S., Headley, J., Scarlett, A., West, C., Peru, K., Parrott, J., Conly, M. and Hewitt, L. (2014) 'Profiling Oil Sands Mixtures from Industrial Developments and Natural Groundwaters for Source Identification'. *Environmental Science and Technology*. Vol. 48 (5), pp. 2660–2670.

Freeman, M. (2002) *Human Rights: An Interdisciplinary Approach*. Cambridge, Polity Press.

Fumoleau, R. (2004) *As Long as This Land Shall Last: A History of Treaty 8 and Treaty 11, 1870–1939*. Alberta, University of Calgary Press.

Gibbs, C., Gore, M., McGarrell, E. and Rivers, L. (2010) 'Introducing Conservation Criminology: Towards Interdisciplinary Scholarship on Environmental Crimes and Risks'. *British Journal of Criminology*. Vol. 50 (1), pp. 124–144.

Gibbs, D. (1998) 'Ecological Modernisation: A Basis for Regional Development?'. *Paper presented to the Seventh International Conference of the Greening of Industry Network 'Partnership and Leadership: Building Alliances for a Sustainable Future'*. Rome, 15–18 November 1998.

Gibson, D. (2007a) *Taming the Tempest: An Alternative Development Strategy for Alberta*. Edmonton, Parkland Institute, University of Alberta.

Gibson, D. (2007b) *The Spoils of the Boom: Incomes, Profits and Poverty in Alberta*. Edmonton, Parkland Institute, University of Alberta.

Gibson, G. (2017) *Culture and Rights Impact Assessment* (online) Available at: www.thefirelightgroup.com/2017/05/17/report-release-culture-and-rights-impact-assessment/ [Accessed 13.02.2019].

Gleeson, B. (2006) *Australian Heartlands: Making Space for Hope in the Suburbs*. Syndey, Allen and Unwin.

Gosselin, P., Hrudey, S., Naeth, A., Plourde, A., Therrien, R., Van Der Kraak, G. and Xu, Z. (2010) 'Environmental and Health Impacts of Canada's Oil Sands Industry'. *The Royal Society of Canada Expert Panel*. Ottawa, The Royal Society of Canada.

Gould, D., Pellow, D. and Schnaiberg, A. (2004) 'Interrogating the Treadmill of Production'. *Organisation and Environment*. Vol. 17 (3), pp. 296–316.

Government of Alberta (1930) *Natural Resources Transfer Agreement 1930*. Aboriginal Affairs and Northern Development, Edmonton.

Government of Alberta (1999) *Alberta's Commitment to Sustainable Resource and Environmental Management*. Available at: https://archive.org/stream/albertascommitme00albe/albertascommitme00albe_djvu.txt [Accessed 01.11.2018].

Government of Alberta (2000a) *Oil Sands Conservation Act 2000*. Alberta Queens Printer, Edmonton.

Government of Alberta (2000b) *Energy Resources Conservation Act 2000*. Alberta Queens Printer, Edmonton.

Government of Alberta (2000c) *Alberta Interpretation Act 2000*. Alberta Queens Printer, Edmonton.

Government of Alberta (2000d) *Budget: New Century, Bold Plans, 2000*. Available at: http://finance.alberta.ca/publications/budget/budget1997-2000/2000/fiscal-plan-complete.pdf [Accessed 15.11.2018].

Government of Alberta (2000e) *Pipeline Act 2000*. Alberta Queens Printer, Edmonton.

Government of Alberta (2005) *Alberta's First Nations Consultation Guidelines on Land Management and Resource Development*. Available at: http://indigenous.alberta.ca/documents/2005_Policy_and_Guidelines.pdf?0.40955977142790834 [Accessed 01.11.2018].

Government of Alberta (2006a) *06 Budget: Strengthening Today, Securing Tomorrow.* Available at: http://finance.alberta.ca/publications/budget/budget2006/fiscal-plan-complete.pdf [Accessed 15.11.2018].

Government of Alberta (2006b) *Alberta's 10 Year Strategy: Building and Educating Tomorrow's Workforce.* Available at: https://work.alberta.ca/documents/BETW-strategy.pdf [Accessed 10.01.2017].

Government of Alberta (2007) *Oil Sands Consultations: Aboriginal Consultation Final Report* (online) Available at: https://open.alberta.ca/dataset/a2215ffe-21fc-480a-9b52-a85f480ce911/resource/5f51a275-0f68-4539-a6ab-d5f869903481/download/3952776-2007-oil-sands-consultations-aboriginal-final-report.pdf [Accessed 01.11.2018].

Government of Alberta (2008a) *Launching Alberta's Energy Future: Provincial Energy Strategy* (online) Available at: https://open.alberta.ca/dataset/6f220382-b4ae-43f8-b3f9-7c1230e6700e/resource/e7c2f3d2-7e0d-4774-a463-c54c5450a04e/download/4256197-2009-Launching-Albertas-Energy-Future-Provincial-Enregy-Strategy-2009-08-27.pdf [Accessed 01.11.2018].

Government of Alberta (2008b) *Land Use Framework* (online) Available at: www.landuse.alberta.ca/Documents/LUF_Land-use_Framework_Report-2008-12.pdf [Accessed 01.11.18].

Government of Alberta (2009a) *Responsible Actions: A Plan for Alberta's Oil Sands.* Available at: https://open.alberta.ca/dataset/d1a56e4a-9b36-4068-94ba-dfbc042784c8/resource/4974c0fe-5bdf-4480-9861-4a681ac6d740/download/4284820-2009-OSS-Responsible-Actions-Plan-Albertas-Oil-Sands-2009-02.pdf [Accessed 01.11.2018].

Government of Alberta (2009b) *The Terms of Reference for Developing the Lower Athabasca Regional Plan.* Available at: www.ceaa.gc.ca/050/documents/45582/45582E.pdf [Accessed 01.11.2018].

Government of Alberta (2009c) *Alberta Land Stewardship Act 2009.* Alberta Queens Printer, Edmonton.

Government of Alberta (2009d) *Budget 2009: Building on our Strength.* Available at: http://finance.alberta.ca/publications/budget/budget2009/fiscal-plan-complete.pdf [Accessed 15.11.2018].

Government of Alberta (2010) Oil Sands Tenure Regulation. *Alberta Regulation 196/2010.* Alberta Queens Printer, Edmonton.

Government of Alberta (2011a) *Enhancing Assurance: Report and Recommendations of the Regulatory Enhancement Task Force to the Minister of Energy.* Alberta Queens Printer, Edmonton.

Government of Alberta (2011b) *Shaping Alberta's Energy Future* (online) Available at: www.albertacanada.com/files/albertacanada/ShapingABFuture_Report.pdf [Accessed 29.11.2018].

Government of Alberta (2012a) *Lower Athabasca Regional Plan.* Available at: https://open.alberta.ca/dataset/37eab675-19fe-43fd-afff-001e2c0be67f/resource/a063e2df-f5a6-4bbd-978c-165cc25148a2/download/5866779-2012-08-lower-athabasca-regional-plan-2012-2022.pdf [Accessed 01.11.2018].

Government of Alberta (2012b) *Responsible Energy Development Act 2012.* Alberta Queens Printer, Edmonton.

Government of Alberta (2013a) *The Government of Alberta's Policy on Consultation with First Nations on Land and Natural Resource Management, 2013.* Available at: http://indigenous.alberta.ca/documents/GoAPolicy-FNConsultation-2013.pdf?0.4702485625586763 [Accessed 01.11.2018].

Government of Alberta (2013b) *Response to Aboriginal Consultation on the Lower Athabasca Regional Plan*. Available at: https://landuse.alberta.ca/LandUse%20Documents/Response%20to%20Aboriginal%20Consultation%20on%20the%20Lower%20Athabasca%20Regional%20Plan%20-%202013-06.pdf [Accessed 01.11.2018].

Government of Alberta (2014a) *South Saskatchewan Regional Plan*. Available at: https://open.alberta.ca/dataset/460ac866-4416-4d77-a25a-a02fab85a6ec/resource/8261ce03-aa0f-4621-8e2d-c610a72ac37c/download/south-saskatchewan-regional-plan-2014-2024-february-2017.pdf [Accessed 01.11.2018].

Government of Alberta (2014b) *The Government of Alberta's on Consultation with First Nations on Land and Natural Resource Management*. Available at: http://indigenous.alberta.ca/documents/First_Nations_Consultation_Guidelines_LNRD.pdf.pdf [Accessed 10.01.2017].

Government of Alberta (2015a) *Lower Athabasca Region: Surface Water Quantity Management Framework for the Lower Athabasca River* (online) Available at: http://aep.alberta.ca/lands-forests/cumulative-effects/regional-planning/documents/LARP-SurfaceWaterQuantity-Feb2015.pdf [Accessed 01.11.2018].

Government of Alberta (2015b) *Backgrounder on Alberta's Fiscal Situation* (online) Available at: www.finance.alberta.ca/publications/fiscal/spotlights/2015-0115-Backgrounder-on-Alberta-Fiscal-Situation.pdf [Accessed 10.01.2017].

Government of Alberta (2015c) *Infrastructure. Business Plan: 2015–2018* (online) Available at: http://finance.alberta.ca/publications/budget/budget2015-october/infrastructure.pdf [Accessed 10.01.2017].

Government of Alberta (2015d) 'Total Area of the Oil Sands Tailings Ponds Over Time' (online) Available at: http://osip.alberta.ca/library/Dataset/Details/542 [Accessed 18.11.2018].

Government of Alberta (2016a) *Energy's History in Alberta* (online) Available at: www.energy.alberta.ca/AU/History/Pages/default.aspx [Accessed 01.11.2018].

Government of Alberta (2016b) *Petroleum and Natural Gas Tenure in Alberta*. Available at: www.energy.alberta.ca/Tenure/Documents/TenureBrochure.pdf [Accessed 01.11.2018].

Government of Alberta (2016c) 'Economic Results' (online) Available at: www.albertacanada.com/business/overview/economic-results.aspx [Accessed 15.11.2018].

Government of Alberta (2016d) '2015–16 Annual Report' (online) Available at: https://open.alberta.ca/dataset/7714457c-7527-443a-a7db-dd8c1c8ead86/resource/b7d016f8-1c5a-4724-85d4-b834c343f062/download/goa-2015-16-annual-report-complete.pdf [Accessed 29.1.2018].

Government of Alberta (2016e) *Unemployment Rate (%)* (online) Available at: http://economicdashboard.albertacanada.com/Unemployment [Accessed 29.11.2018].

Government of Alberta (2017) '2016–17 Annual Report' (online) Available at: https://open.alberta.ca/dataset/7714457c-7527-443a-a7db-dd8c1c8ead86/resource/e6e99166-2958-47ac-a2db-5b27df2619a3/download/GoA-2016-17-Annual-Report.pdf [Accessed 29.11.2018].

Government of Alberta (2018a) 'Lower Athabasca' (online) Available at: http://aep.alberta.ca/land/programs-and-services/land-and-resource-planning/regional-planning/lower-athabasca/default.aspx [Accessed 29.11.2018].

Government of Alberta (2018b) 'Historical Royalty Revenue' (online) Available at: https://open.alberta.ca/opendata/historical-royalty-revenue [Accessed 29.11.2018].

Government of Alberta (2018c) '2017–18 Annual Report' (online) Available at: https://open.alberta.ca/dataset/7714457c-7527-443a-a7db-dd8c1c8ead86/

resource/cb1d2565-b262-4746-9499-68e409d9f72c/download/goa-2017-18-annual-report.pdf [Accessed 29.11.2018].

Government of Alberta (2018d) 'Alberta Wage and Salary Survey: Average wages by industry and economic region' (online) Available at: https://open.alberta.ca/publications/alberta-wage-and-salary-survey-average-wages-by-industry-and-economic-region#summary [Accessed 29.11.2018].

Government of Alberta (2018e) 'Unemployment' (online) Available at: http://economicdashboard.alberta.ca/Unemployment [Accessed 29.11.2018].

Government of Canada (1899) *Treaty Texts – Treaty No. 8* (online) Available at: www.aadnc-aandc.gc.ca/eng/1100100028813/1100100028853#chp4 [Accessed 30.10.2018].

Government of Canada (2013) 'The Constitution Acts 1967 to 1982' (online) Available at: http://laws-lois.justice.gc.ca/PDF/CONST_E.pdf [Accessed 01.11.2018].

Government of Canada (2017) *Fiscal Reference Tables* (online) Available at: www.fin.gc.ca/frt-trf/2017/frt-trf-17-eng.pdf [Accessed 18.11.2018].

Government of Canada (2018) 'National Inventory Report 1990–2016: Greenhouse Gas Sources and Sinks in Canada, Part 1' (online) Available at: https://unfccc.int/documents/65715 [Accessed 18.11.2018].

Goyes, D. (2016) 'Land Uses and Conflict in Colombia'. In A. Brisman, N. South and R. White (eds.) *Environmental Crime and Social Conflict*, Abingdon, Routledge, pp. 75–94.

Goyes, D. (2018) 'Green Criminology as Decolonial Tool; A Stereoscope of Environmental Harm'. In K. Carrington, R. Hogg, J. Scott and M. Sozzo (eds.) *The Palgrave Handbook of Criminology and the Global South*, London, Palgrave, pp. 323–346.

Goyes, D. and South, N. (2015) 'Land-grabs, Biopiracy and the Inversion of Justice in Colombia'. *The British Journal of Criminology*. Vol. 56 (3), pp. 558–577.

Goyes, D. and South, N. (2017) 'The Injustices of Policing, Law and Multinational Monopolization in the Privatization of Natural Diversity: Cases from Colombia and Latin America'. In D. Goyes, H. Mol, A. Brisman and N. South (eds.) *Environmental Crime in Latin America: The Theft of Nature and the Poisoning of the Land*. Palgrave Studies in Green Criminology. Springer / Palgrave Macmillan, pp. 187–213.

Grant, J. (2012) *Relying on End Pit Lakes for 'Reclamation' is Reckless* (online) Available at: www.pembina.org/blog/677 [Accessed 17.11.2018].

Grant, J., Angen, E. and Dyer, S. (2013b) *Forecasting the Impacts of Oil Sands Expansion* (online) Available at: www.pembina.org/reports/oilsands-metrics.pdf [Accessed 17.11.2018].

Grant, J., Huot, M., Lemphers, N., Dyer, S. and Dow, M. (2013a) *Beneath the Surface: A Review of Key Facts in the Oilsands Debate*. Calgary, Pembina Institute.

Gregory, R. and Trousdale, W. (2009) 'Compensating Aboriginal Cultural Losses: An Alternative Approach to Assessing Environmental Damages'. *Journal of Environmental Management*. Vol. 90 (8), pp. 2469–2479.

Griffiths, M., Wilson, S. and Anielski, M. (2001) *The Alberta GPI Accounts: Parks and Wilderness*. (online) Available at: www.pembina.org/reports/21_parks_and_wilderness.pdf [Accessed 01.11.2018].

Hajer, M. (1995) *The Politics of Environmental Discourse: Ecological Modernisation and the Policy Process*. Oxford, Clarendon Press.

Hall, M. (2014) 'The Roles and Use of Law in Green Criminology'. *International Journal for Crime, Justice and Social Democracy*. Vol. 3 (2), pp. 96–109.

Hall, M. (2015) *Exploring Green Crime*. London, Palgrave Macmillan.

Halsey, M. (2004) 'Against 'Green' Criminology'. *British Journal of Criminology*. Vol. 44 (6), pp. 833–854.

Halsey, M. and White, R. (1998) 'Crime, Ecophilosophy and Environmental Harm'. *Theoretical Criminology*, Vol. 2 (3), pp. 345–372.

Hansen, J. (2012) 'Game Over for the Climate'. *New York Times*, 10 May 2012.

Harrison, T. (2015) 'Petroleum, Politics, and the Limits of Left Progressivism in Alberta'. In M. Shrivistava and L. Stefanick (eds.) *Alberta Oil and the Decline of Democracy in Canada*. Edmonton, Athabasca University Press, pp. 69–88.

Harvey, D. (2005) *A Brief History of Neoliberalism*. Oxford, Oxford University Press.

Haughton, G. and Counsell, D. (2004) *Regions, Spatial Strategies and Sustainable Development*. London, Routledge.

Hay, P. (2002) *Main Currents in Western Environmental Thought*. Bloomington, Indiana University Press.

Hayden, A. (2014) *When Green Growth is Not Enough: Climate Change, Ecological Modernisation and Sufficiency*. Montreal, McGill-Queen's University Press.

Hierlmeir, J. (2008) 'The Public Interest: What Could it Mean for the ERCB and NRCB?'. *Environmental Law Centre*. Vol. 23 (1), pp. 1–7.

Hill, B. (2016) 'Canada Endorses the United Nations Declaration on the Rights of Indigenous Peoples'. *Global News*, 9 May 2016.

Hillyard, P. and Tombs, S. (2004) 'Beyond Criminology?'. In P. Hillyard, C. Pantazis, S. Tombs and D. Gordon (eds.) *Beyond Criminology: Taking Harm Seriously*. London, Pluto Press. pp. 10–29.

Hillyard, P., Pantazis, C., Tombs, S. and Gordon, D. (2005) ' "Social Harm" and Its Limits?'. In D. Dorling, D. Gordon, P. Hillyard, C. Pantazis, S. Pemberton and S. Tombs (eds.) *Criminal Obsessions: Why Harm Matters More Than Crime* (2nd ed.). London, Crime and Society Foundation, pp. 62–69.

Homeward Trust Edmonton (2014) *2014 Point-in-Time Homeless Count* (online) Available at: http://homewardtrust.ca/wp-content/uploads/2016/12/2014-Edmonton-Homeless-Count.pdf [Accessed 29.11.2018].

Huseman, J. and Short, D. (2012) 'A Slow Industrial Genocide: Tar Sands and the Indigenous Peoples of Northern Alberta'. *International Journal of Human Rights*. Vol. 16 (1), pp. 216–237.

Intergovernmental Panel on Climate Change (2018) 'Global Warming of 1.5°C' (online) Available at: www.ipcc.ch/report/sr15/ [Accessed 30.10.2018].

Jackson, T. (2009) *Prosperity without Growth. Economics for a Finite Planet*. London, Earthscan.

Jacobs, M. (1991) *The Green Economy: Environment, Sustainable Development and the Politics of the Future*. London, Pluto Press.

Kabwe, L., Scott, J., Beier, N., Wilson, G. and Jeeravipoolvarn, S. (2018) 'Environmental implications of end pit lakes at oil sand mines in Alberta, Canada', *Environmental Geotechnics* (online) Available at: https://doi.org/10.1680/jenge.17.00110 [Accessed 17.11.2018].

Kates, R., Parris, T. and Leiserowitz, A. (2005) 'What is Sustainable Development?'. *Environment: Science and Policy for Sustainable Development*. Vol. 47 (3), pp. 8–21.

Kelly, E., Schindler, D., Hodson, P., Short, J., Radmanovich, R. and Nielsen, C. (2010) 'Oil Sands Development Contributes Elements Toxic at Low Concentrations to the Athabasca River and its Tributaries'. *Proceedings of the National Academy of Sciences of the United States of America*. Vol. 107 (37), pp. 16178–16183.

Kelly, E., Short, J., Schindler, D., Hodson, P., Ma, M., Kwan, A. and Fortin, B. (2009) 'Oil Sands Development Contributes Polycyclic Aromatic Compounds to the Athabasca River and its Tributaries'. *Proceedings of the National Academy of Sciences of the United States of America*. Vol. 106 (52), pp. 22346–22351.

Kennedy, M. (2016) 'Dozens of U.S., Canadian Tribes Unite Against Proposed Oil Pipelines'. *National Public Radio*, 23 September 2016.

Kennett, S. (2007) 'Next Steps for Cumulative Effects Management in Alberta's Athabasca Oil Sands Region'. *Canadian Institute of Resources Law*. #96.

King, T. (2012) *The Inconvenient Indian*. Minneapolis, University of Minnesota Press.

Kingsford, R. and Biggs, H. (2012) *Strategic Adaptive Management Guidelines for Effective Conservation of Freshwater Ecosystems in and Around Protected Areas of the World*. Wetlands and Rivers Centre, Sydney.

Kirmayer, L., Brass, G., Holton, T., Paul, K., Simpson, C. and Tait, C. (2007) *Suicide Among Aboriginal People in Canada*. Ottawa, Aboriginal Healing Foundation.

Klinkenberg, M. (2014) 'First Nations Struggle to Save Traditions While Profiting from Boom'. *Edmonton Journal*, 13 March 2014.

Kotz, D. M. (2002) 'Globalization and Neoliberalism'. *Rethinking Marxism: A Journal of Economics, Culture and Society*. Vol. 14 (2), pp. 64–79.

Kovel, J. (2007) *The Enemy of Nature*. London, Zed Books.

Kramer, R. and Michalowski, R. (2006) 'The Original Formulation'. In R. Michalowski and R. Kramer (eds.) *State-Corporate Crime: Wrongdoing at the Intersection of Business and Government'*. USA, Rutgers University, pp. 18–26.

Kulchyski, P. (2013) *Aboriginal Rights Are Not Human Rights*. Manitoba, ARP Books.

Kurek, J., Kirk, J., Muir, D., Wang, X., Evans, M. and Smol, J. (2012) 'Legacy of a Half Century of Athabasca Oil Sands Development Recorded by Lake Ecosystems'. *Proceedings of the National Academy of Sciences of the United States of America*. Vol. 110 (5), pp. 1761–1766.

Lafleur, S. (2018) 'Alberta Deficit Hit $8 Billion Despite Improving Resource Revenues' (online) Available at: www.fraserinstitute.org/blogs/alberta-deficit-hit-8-billion-despite-improving-resource-revenues [Accessed 29.11.2018].

Lahey, K. (2015) *The Alberta Disadvantage: Gender, Taxation and Income Inequality*. Edmonton, Parkland Institute, University of Alberta.

Laidlaw, D. (2016) 'Alberta First Nations Consultation & Accommodation Handbook – Updated to 2016'. Occasional Paper #23.

Laidlaw, D. and Passelac-Ross, M. (2014) 'Alberta First Nations Consultation and Accommodation Handbook'. *Canadian Institute of Resources Law*. Occasional Paper #44.

Lambrecht, K. (2013) *Aboriginal Consultation, Environmental Assessment and Regulatory Review in Canada*. Saskatchewan, University of Regina Press.

Lambrecht, K. (2015) 'Protecting Aboriginal and Treaty Rights in Alberta's Environmental Assessment and Regulatory Review System for Energy Projects'. In S. Berger (ed.) *Key Developments in Environmental Law*. Toronto, Carswell, pp. 103–124.

Larcombe, P. (2012) *A Narrative of Encroachment Experienced by the Athabasca Chipewyan First Nation*. Manitoba, Symbion Consultants.

Lee, R. and Stokes, E. (2005) 'Ecological Modernisation and the Precautionary Principle'. In J. Gunning and S. Holm (eds.) *Ethics, Law and Society*. Aldershot, Ashgate, pp. 103–115.

Lemphers, N. and Woynillowicz, D. (2012) *In the Shadow of the Boom*. Alberta, The Pembina Institute.

Litonjua, M. D. (2008) 'The Socio-Political Construction of Globalization'. *International Review of Modern Sociology*. Vol. 34 (2), pp. 253–278.

Lott, E. O. and Jones, R. J. (2010) 'Review of Four Major Environmental Effects Monitoring Programs in the Oil Sands Region'. *Oil Sands Research and Information Network*. Report #Tr-6.

Low, C. (2009a) 'The AEUB: A Short Chapter in Alberta's Long History of Energy and Utilities Regulation'. *Canadian Institute of Resources Law*. #105–2009.

Low, C. (2009b) 'Energy and Utility Regulation in Alberta: Like Oil and Water?'. *Canadian Institute of Resources Law*. Occasional Paper #25.

Low, C. (2011) 'The Public Interest in Section 3 of Alberta'. Energy Resources Conservation Act: Where Do We Stand and Where Do We Go from Here?'. *Canadian Institute of Resources Law*, Occasional Paper #36.

Lowe, V. (1999) 'Sustainable Development and Unsustainable Arguments'. In A. Boyle and D. Freestone (eds.) *International Law and Sustainable Development: Past Achievements and Future Challenges*. Oxford, Oxford University Press, pp. 19–37.

Lower Athabasca Regional Plan Review Panel (2015) *Review Panel Report 2015: Lower Athabasca Regional Plan* (online) Available at: https://open.alberta.ca/publications/review-panel-report-2015-lower-athabasca-regional-plan [Accessed 29.11.2018].

Lynch, M. (1990). The Greening of Criminology: A Perspective on the 1990s. *Critical Criminologist*. 2 (3–4), 11–12.

Lynch, M. and Stretesky, P. (2003) 'The Meaning of Green: Towards a Clarification of the Term Green and its Meaning for the Development of a Green Criminology'. *Theoretical Criminology*. Vol. 7 (2), pp. 217–238.

Lynch, M., Long, M. and Stretesky, P. (2016) 'A Proposal for the Political Economy of Green Criminology: Capitalism and the Case of the Alberta Tar Sands'. *Canadian Journal of Criminology and Criminal Justice*. Vol. 58 (2), pp. 1–24.

Macalister, T. (2011) 'Canadian Government Accused of Unprecedented Tar Sands Lobbying'. *Guardian*, 4 August 2011.

Macdonald, A. (2012) *Supplemental Social, Economic and Cultural Effects Submission for Shell Canada's Proposed Jackpine Mine Expansion* (online) Available at: www.ceaa.gc.ca/050/documents_staticpost/59540/82080/Appendix_D_-_Part_05.pdf [Accessed 30.10.2018].

Malm, A. (2018) *The Progress of this Storm*. London, Verso Books.

Martuzzi, M. (2007) 'The Precautionary Principle: In Action for Public Health'. *Occupational and Environmental Medicine*. Vol. 64 (9), pp. 569–570.

Maruna, S. and Copes, H. (2005) 'What Have We Learned from Five Decades of Neutralization Research?'. *Crime and Justice: A Review of Research*. Vol. 32, pp. 221–320.

Marx, K. (1976) *Capital*. Vol. 1. London, Penguin.

Marx, K. (1981) *Capital*. Vol. 3. London, Penguin.

Mason, G. (2015) 'Alberta Premier Prentice Warns Deep Cuts Necessary to Avoid Fiscal Ruin'. *The Globe and Mail*, 4 May 2015.

Mawhinney, M. (2002) *Sustainable Development: Understanding the Green Debates*. New York, Wiley.

McCormack, P. (2012) *An Ethnohistory of the Athabasca Chipewyan First Nation*. Edmonton, Alberta.

McGlade, C. and Ekins, P. (2015) 'The Geographical Distribution of Fossil Fuels Unused when Limiting Global Warming to 2°C'. *Nature*. Vol. 517 (7533), pp. 187–190.

McNeil, J. (2017) 'Tailings Ponds: The Worst Is Yet to Come', *Pembina Institute* (online) Available at: www.pembina.org/blog/tailings-ponds-worst-yet-come [Accessed 30.10.2018].

McSheffrey, E. (2016) 'First Nations across North America sign Treaty Alliance against the Oil Sands'. *National Observer*, 22 September 2016.

Michalowski, R. and Kramer, R. (2006) 'The Critique of Power'. In R. Michalowski and R. Kramer (eds.) *State-Corporate Crime: Wrongdoing at the Intersection of Business and Government*. USA, Rutgers University, pp. 1–17.

Mikisew Cree First Nation (2016) *Written Brief of the Mikisew Cree First Nation to the Standing Committee on Transport, Infrastructure and Communities* (online) Available at: www.ourcommons.ca/Content/Committee/421/TRAN/Brief/BR8708926/br-external/MikisewCreeFirstNation-e.pdf [Accessed 30.10.2018].

Milke, M. and Palacios, M. (2015) *Fumbling the Alberta Advantage: How Alberta Squandered a Decade of High Energy Prices* (online) Available at: www.fraserinstitute.org/sites/default/files/fumbling-the-alberta-advantage-rev.pdf [Accessed 29.11.2018].

Millar, G. (2012) *End Pit Lakes: Unresolved Issues* (online) Available at: www.ceaa.gc.ca/050/documents/p59540/83373E.pdf [Accessed 17.11.2018].

Miller, B. (2007) 'Modes of Governance, Modes of Resistance: Contesting Neoliberalism in Calgary'. In H. Leitner J. Peck and E. Shepphard (eds.) *Contesting Neoliberalism: Unban Frontiers*. London, Guilford Press, pp. 223–249.

Miller, J. (1996) *Shingwauk's Vision: A History of Native Residential Schools*. Toronto, University of Toronto Press.

Mills, J. (2017) 'Destabilizing the Consultation Framework in Alberta's Tar Sands'. *Journal of Canadian Studies*. Vol. 51 (1), pp. 153–185.

Milmo, M. (2007) 'The Biggest Environmental Crime in History'. *Independent*, 10 December 2007.

Minor, W. (1981) 'Techniques of Neutralisation: A Reconceptualization and Empirical Examination'. *Journal of Research in Crime and Delinquency*. Vol. 18 (2), pp. 295–318.

Mol, A. (1995) *The Refinement of Production – Ecological Modernisation Theory and the Chemical Industry*. Utrecht, van Arkel.

Mol, A. (2001) *Globalization and Environmental Reform: The Ecological Modernization of the Global Economy*. Massachusetts, MIT Press.

Mol, A. and Spargaaren, G. (2000) 'Ecological Modernisation Theory in Debate: A Review'. *Environmental Politics*. Vol. 9 (1), pp. 17–49.

Moran, A. (2002) 'As Australia Decolonises: Indigenising Settler Nationalism and the Challenges of Settler/Indigenous Relations'. *Ethnic and Racial Studies*. Vol. 25 (6), pp. 1013–1042.

Mouallem, O. (2015) 'The Boom, the Bust and the Darkness: Suicide Rate Soars in Wake of Canada's Oil Crisis'. *Guardian*, 14 December 2015.

Murphy, R. and Clemens, J. (2013) *Reforming Alberta's Heritage Fund: Lessons from Alaska to Norway* (online) Available at: www.fraserinstitute.org/sites/default/files/reforming-albertas-heritage-fund.pdf [Accessed 29.11.2018].

National Energy Board (2016) *Canada's Energy Future 2016: Energy Supply and Demand Projections to 2040*. (online) Available at: www.neb-one.gc.ca/nrg/ntgrtd/ftr/2016/2016nrgftr-eng.pdf [Accessed 30.10.2018].

Nettler, G. (1984) *Explaining Crime* (3rd ed.). New York, McGraw-Hill.

Nikiforuk, A. (2015) *Slick Water: Fracking and One Insider's Stand Against the World's Most Powerful Industry*. Canada, Greystone Books.

Nishi, J., Berryman, J., Stelfox, A., Garibaldi, A. and Straker, J. (2013) *Fort McKay Cumulative Effects Project: Technical Report of Scenario Modelling Analysis with ALCES*. Integral Ecology Group, Victoria.

Notley, R. (2015) *July 7, 2015* (online) Available at: http://indigenous.alberta.ca/documents/Premier-Notley-Letter-Cabinet-Ministers.pdf [Accessed 11.01.2017].

Nurse, A. (2017) 'Criminalising the Right to Hunt: European Law Perspectives on Anti-hunting Legislation', *Crime, Law and Social Change*. Vol. 67 (4), pp. 383–399.

O'Connor, J. (1996) 'The Second Contradiction of Capitalism'. In T. Benton (ed.) *The Greening of Marxism*. London, Guilford Press.

O'Meara (2014) 'Why First Nation Groups Scoring Oil Sands Contracts Is No Longer a Given'. *Financial Post*, 3 July 2014.

Office of the Auditor General of Alberta (2014) *Report of the Auditor General of Alberta*. Edmonton, Office of the Auditor General of Alberta.

Olszynski, M. (2014) 'Environmental Monitoring and Ecosystem Management in the Oil Sands: Spaceship Earth or Escort Tugaboat?'. *McGill International Journal of Sustainable Development Law and Policy*. Vol. 10 (1), pp. 1–44.

Olszynski, M. (2017) 'Failed Experiments: An Empirical Assessment of Adaptive Management in Alberta's Energy Resources Sector'. *UBC Law Review*. Vol. 50 (3), pp. 697–796.

Olszynski, M. (2018) 'Testing the Jurisdictional Waters: The Provincial Regulation of Interprovincial Pipelines'. *Review of Constitutional Studies*. Online Release.

Orwell, G. (1945) *Notes on Nationalism*. Polemic, London.

Parekh, B. (1992) 'The Cultural Particularity of Liberal Democracy'. *Political Studies*. Vol. 40 (1), pp. 160–175.

Parkland Institute (2011) *Unpacking Alberta's Infrastructure Spending* (online) Available at: www.parklandinstitute.ca/unpacking_albertas_infrastructure_spending [Accessed 29.11.2018].

Parlee, B. (2015) 'Avoiding the Resource Curse: Indigenous Communities and Canada's Oil Sands'. *World Development*. Vol. 74, pp. 425–436.

Passelac-Ross, M. and Buss, K. (2011) 'Water Stewardship in the Lower Athabasca River: Is the Alberta Government Paying Attention to Aboriginal Rights to Water?'. *Canadian Institute of Resources Law*. Occasional Paper #35.

Passelac-Ross, M. and Potes, V. (2007) 'Crown Consultation with Aboriginal Peoples in Oil Sands Development: Is It Adequate, Is It Legal?'. *Canadian Institute of Resources Law*. Occasional Paper #19.

Patton, M. (2002) *Qualitative Evaluation and Research Methods* (3rd ed.). London, Sage Publications.

Pearce, F. and Tombs, S. (1997) 'Hazards, Law and Class: Contextualising the Regulation of Corporate Crime'. *Social and Legal Studies*. Vol. 6, pp. 79–107.

PricewaterhouseCoopers (2008) *Strategic and Program Evaluation of the Cumulative Environmental Management Association* (online) Available at: www.andrewnikiforuk.com/Dirty_Oil_PDFs/Price_Waterhouse_Coopers_CEMA%20report.pdf [Accessed 29.11.2018].

Radke, D. (2006) *Investing in Our Future: Responding to the Rapid Growth of Oil Sands Development* (online) Available at: www.assembly.ab.ca/lao/library/egovdocs/2006/alec/158408.pdf [Accessed 29.11.2018].

Rawlinson, K. (2011) 'Mock Trial Finds Tar Sands Spill 'Bosses' Guilty of Ecocide'. *Independent*, 1 October 2011.

Redclift, M. (1987) *Sustainable Development: Exploring the Contradictions*. London, Routledge.

Rifkin, M. (2014) *Settler Common Sense: Queerness and Everyday Colonialism in the American Renaissance*. Minneapolis, University of Minnesota Press.

Roach, R., Collins, J. and Navarro-Genie, M. (2015) *A Good Problem to Have: Lessons for Atlantic Canada from Alberta's Experience with Natural Resource Revenue*. Nova Scotia, Atlantic Institute for Market Studies.

Royal Bank of Canada (2018) *Canadian Federal and Provincial Fiscal Tables* (online) Available at: www.rbc.com/economics/economic-reports/pdf/provincial-forecasts/prov_fiscal.pdf [Accessed 18.11.2018].

Rudel, T., Roberts, T. and Carmin, J. (2011) 'Political Economy of the Environment'. *Annual Review of Sociology*. Vol. 37, pp. 221–238.

Ruggiero, V. (2013) *The Crimes of the Economy: A Criminological Analysis of Economic Thought*. Oxford, Routledge.

Ruggiero, V. (2015) *Power and Crime*. London, Routledge.

Ruggiero, V. and South, N. (2013) 'Green Criminology and Crimes of the Economy: Theory, Research and Praxis'. *Critical Criminology*. Vol. 21 (3), pp. 359–373.

Runge, M. (2011) 'An Introduction to Adaptive Management for Threatened and Endangered Species'. *Journal of Fish and Wildlife Management*. Vol. 2 (2), pp. 220–233.

Sachs, J. (2015) *The Age of Sustainable Development*. New York, Columbia University Press.

Sands, P. (1995) 'Sustainable Development: Treaty, Custom, and the Cross-Fertilisation of International Law'. In A. Boyle and D. Freestone (eds.) *International Law and Sustainable Development*. Oxford, Oxford University Press, pp. 199–208.

Sauchyn, D., St-Jacques, J. and Luckman, B. (2015) 'Long-term Reliability of the Athabasca River (Alberta, Canada) as the Water Source for Oil Sands Mining', *Proceedings of the National Academy of Sciences of the United States of America*. Vol. 112 (41), pp. 12621–12626.

Schattschneider, E. (1960) *The Semisovereign People: A Realist's View of Democracy in America*. Minnesota, Dumfries, Holt, Rinehart and Winston.

Schnaiberg, A. (1980) *The Environment: From Surplus to Scarcity*. Oxford, Oxford University Press.

Scott, M. and Lyman, S. (1968) 'Accounts'. *American Sociological Review*. Vol. 33 (1), pp. 46–62.

Sezgin, Z. (2012) 'Ecological Modernization: A Viable Option for a Sustainable Future?'. *Marmara Journal of European Studies*. Vol. 20 (1), pp. 219–245.

Short, D. (2005) 'Reconciliation and the Problem of Internal Colonialism'. *Journal of Intercultural Studies*. Vol. 26 (3), pp. 267–282.

Shrivistava, M. and Stefanick, L. (2015) 'Introduction: Framing The Debate on Democracy and Governance in an Oil-Exporting Economy'. In M. Shrivistava and L. Stefanick (eds.) *Alberta Oil and the Decline of Democracy in Canada*. Edmonton, Athabasca University Press, pp. 3–30.

Siaroff, A. and Wesley, J. (2015) 'Comparative Voter Turnout in the Canadian Provinces since 1965: The Importance of Context'. *Canadian Political Science Review*. Vol. 9 (1), pp. 147–163.

Simpson, I., Marrero, J., Batterman, S., Meinardi, S., Barletta, B. and Blake, D. (2013) 'Air Quality in the Industrial Heartland of Alberta, Canada and Potential Impacts on Human Health'. *Atmospheric Environment*. Vol. 81, pp. 701–709.

Slowey, G. (2008) *Navigating Neoliberalism: Self-Determination and the Mikisew Cree First Nation*. Toronto, University of British Columbia Press.

Slowey, G. and Stefanick, L. (2015) 'Development at What Cost? First Nations, Ecological Integrity, and Democracy'. In M. Shrivistava and L. Stefanick (eds.) *Alberta Oil and the Decline of Democracy in Alberta*. Edmonton, Athabasca University Press, pp. 195–224.

Smandych, R. and Kueneman, R. (2010) 'The Canadian-Alberta Tar Sands: A Case Study of State-Corporate Environmental Crime'. In R. White (ed.) *Global Environmental Harm: Criminological Perspectives*. Devon, Willan Publishing, pp. 87–109.

Smith, J. (2015) 'Canada Will Implement UN Declaration on Rights of Indigenous Peoples, Carolyn Bennett says'. *The Star*, 12 November 2015.

Snider, L. (2009) 'Accommodating Power: The "Common Sense" of Regulators'. *Social & Legal Studies*. Vol. 18 (2), pp. 179–197.

Somerville, P. (2018) 'Preventing Catastrophic Climate Change'. *Capitalism, Nature, Socialism*. Vol. 209 (3), pp. 110–119.

Sossin, L. (2009) 'The Duty to Consult and Accommodate: Procedural Justice as Aboriginal Rights'. *Canadian Journal of Administrative Law & Practice*. Vol. 23, pp. 93–113.

South, N. (1998) 'A Green Field for Criminology: A Proposal for a Perspective'. *Theoretical Criminology*. Vol. 2 (2), pp. 211–233.

South, N. (2014) 'Green Criminology: Reflections, Connections, Horizons'. *International Journal for Crime, Justice and Social Democracy*. Vol. 3 (2), pp. 5–20.

Spaargaren, G. and Mol, A. (1992) 'Sociology, Environment and Modernity: Ecological Modernization as a Theory of Social Change'. *Society and Natural Resources*. Vol. 5, pp. 323–344.

Spangenberg, J. (2010) 'The Growth Discourse, Growth Policy and Sustainable Development: Two Thought Experiments'. *Journal of Cleaner Production*. Vol. 18 (6), pp. 561–566.

Statistics Canada (2016a) 'Gross Domestic Product By Industry: Provinces and Territories, 2017' (online) Available at: www150.statcan.gc.ca/n1/daily-quotidien/180502/dq180502a-eng.htm [Accessed 29.11.2018].

Statistics Canada (2018b) 'Estimates of the Components of Interprovincial Migration, Quarterly' (online) Available at: www150.statcan.gc.ca/t1/tbl1/en/tv.action?pid=1710002001 [Accessed 18.11.2018].

Statistics Canada (2018c) 'Upper Secondary Graduation Rates, by Sex, OECD, Canada, Provinces and Territories, 2015' (online) available at: www150.statcan.gc.ca/n1/pub/81-604-x/2017001/t/tbla2.1-eng.htm [Accessed 18.11.2018].

Stecyk, K. (2017) 'Environmental Sustainability Versus Economic Interests'. *Journal of Governance and Regulation*. Vol. 6 (4), pp. 7–16.

Stefanick, L. (2015) 'Alberta's Energy Paradigm: Prosperity, Security and the Environment'. In M. Shrivastava and L. Stefanick (eds.) *Alberta Oil and the Decline of Democracy*. Edmonton, Athabasca University, pp. 113–138.

Stelmach, E. (2008) 'Alberta's Engine Drives Canada'. *The Star*, 24 November 2008.

Sterritt, A. (2014) 'Athabasca Chipewyan First Nation Makes the Best of Oil Money'. *CBC News*, 2 April 2014.

Straif, K., Cohen, A. and Samet, J. (2013) 'Air Pollution and Cancer'. *International Agency for Research on Cancer Scientific Publication*. No. 161.

Stretesky, P., Long, A. and Lynch, M. (2013) *The Treadmill of Crime: Political Economy and Green Criminology*. London, Routledge.

Sunstein, C. (2002) *The Paralyzing Principle* (online) Available at: www.heartland.org/sites/default/files/v25n4-9.pdf [Accessed 01.11.2018].

Sykes, G. and Matza, D. (1957) 'Techniques of Neutralization: A Theory of Delinquency'. *American Sociological Review*. Vol. 22 (6), pp. 664–670.

Talbot, J. (2014) 'Chief Medical Officer Shares Updated Fort Chipewyan Report with Community' (online) Available at: www.alberta.ca/release.cfm?xID=3609792C6F042-D7AF-BF59-F07CAA82B9F6BE27 [Accessed 30.10.2018].

Taylor, A. and Friedel, T. (2011) 'Enduring Neoliberalism in Alberta's Oil Sands: The Troubling Effects of Private-Public Partnerships for First Nation and Metis Communities'. *Citizenship Studies*. Vol. 15 (6–7), pp. 815–835.

Taylor, C. (2002) *The Politics of Recognition: An Essay*. Princeton, Princeton University Press.

Taylor-Vaisey, N. (2008) 'Dropping out for Oil'. *Edmonton Journal*, 18 March 2008.

Thompson, D. (2008) *Saving for the Future: Fiscal Responsibility and Budget Discipline in Alberta*. Edmonton, Parkland Institute, University of Alberta.

Thurton, D. (2018) '"We want to be owners": Fort McMurray First Nations and Metis unite on pipelines'. *CBC News*, 15 April 2018.

Tickner, J. and Raffensperger, C. (2003) *The Precautionary Principle in Action* (5th ed.). Oregon, Science and Environmental Health Network.

Timoney, K. (2007) *A Study of Water and Sediment Quality as Related to Public Health Issues, Fort Chipewyan, Alberta*. Alberta, Treeline Ecological Research.

Timoney, K. (2013) *The Peace-Athabasca Delta: Portrait of a Dynamic Ecosystem*. Alberta, University of Alberta Press.

Timoney, K. and Lee, P. (2009) 'Does the Alberta Tar Sands Industry Pollute? The Scientific Evidence'. *The Open Conservation Biology Journal*. Vol. 3, pp. 6–81.

Timoney, K. and Ronconi, R. (2010) 'Annual Bird Mortality in the Bitumen Tailings Ponds in Northeastern Alberta, Canada'. *The Wilson Journal of Ornithology*. Vol. 122 (3), pp. 569–576.

Tombs, S. (2002) 'Book Review: Understanding Regulation?'. *Social & Legal Studies*. Vol. 11 (1), pp. 113–133.

Tombs, S. (2012) 'State-Corporate Symbiosis in the Production of Crime and Harm'. *State Crime Journal*. Vol. 1 (2), pp. 170–195.

Tombs, S. (2017) *Social Protection after the Crisis: Regulation without Enforcement*. Bristol, Policy Press.

Tombs, S. and Whyte, D. (2007) *Safety Crimes*. Devon, Willan Publishing.

Tombs, S. and Whyte, D. (2009) 'The State and Corporate Crime'. In R. Coleman, J. Sim, S. Tombs and D. Whyte (eds.) *State, Power, Crime*. London, Sage Publications, pp. 103–115.

Tombs, S. and Whyte, D. (2015) *The Corporate Criminal: Why Corporations Must Be Abolished*. London, Routledge.

Toth, K. (2018) '"It Hurt": First Nations Leaders' Pipeline Ownership Proposal Comes as Shock to Some'. *CBC News*, 16 April 2018.

Treaty Alliance (2016a) 'First Nation Tribes Sign New Treaty Joining Forces to Stop All Tar Sands Pipelines' (online) Available at: www.treatyalliance.org/wp-content/uploads/2016/09/TAATSE-PR-Treaty-Signing-EN-FINAL.pdf [Accessed 30.10.2018].

Treaty Alliance (2016b) *Treaty Alliance against Tar Sands Expansion* (online) Available at: http://lnib.net/wp-content/uploads/2015/11/Derek-Nepinak-Treaty-Alliance.pdf [Accessed 30.10.2018].

Trescott, J. (2006) 'The Truck Stops Here'. *Washington Post*, 8 June 2006.

Tsalik, S. (2003) *Caspian Oil Windfalls: Who Will Benefit*. New York, Open Society Institute.

Tumbleweed Consulting Ltd. (2008) 'Independent Strategic and Program Evaluation of the Cumulative Environmental Management Association'. Available at: http://environment.gov.ab.ca/info/library/8029.pdf [Accessed 12.01.2017].

Turnbull, D. (2007) 'Maps, Narratives and Trails: Performativity, Hodology and Distributed Knowledges in Complex and Adaptive Systems – An Approach to Emergent Mapping'. *Geographical Research*. Vol. 45 (2), pp. 140–149.

Tuttle, R. (2018) 'Who Says the Oil Sands Is History? New Mine the Size of Cleveland Could Be Blueprint for Survival', *Financial Post*, 11 September 2018.

United Nations (2015) 'Transforming our world: the 2030 Agenda for Sustainable Development' (online) Available at: www.un.org/ga/search/view_doc.asp?symbol=A/RES/70/1&Lang=E [Accessed 01.11.2018].

United Nations Environment Programme (2011) *Decoupling Natural Resource Use and Environmental Impacts from Economic Growth* (online) Available at: www.gci.org.uk/Documents/Decoupling_Report_English.pdf [Accessed 01.11.2018].

United Nations World Commission on Environment and Development (1987) *Our Common Future* (online) Available at: www.un-documents.net/our-common-future.pdf [Accessed 01.11.2018].

University of Manitoba (2014) 'Study Finds Oil Sands Creating 'Perfect Storm' of Danger to Flora, Fauna and People' (online) Available at: http://news.umanitoba.ca/study-finds-oil-sands-creating-perfect-storm-of-danger-to-flora-fauna-and-people/ [Accessed 30.10.2018].

van den Bremer, T. and van der Ploeg, R. (2014) 'Digging Deep for the Heritage Fund: Why the Right Fund for Alberta Pays Dividends Long After Oil is Gone'. *The School of Public Policy SPP Research Papers*. Vol. 7 (32), pp. 1–39.

Veracini, L. (2010) *Settler Colonialism: A Theoretical Overview*. Basingstoke, Palgrave Macmillan.

Veracini, L. (2015) *The Settler Colonial Present*. Basingstoke, Palgrave Macmillan.

Vlavianos, N. (2007) 'The Legislative and Regulatory Framework for Oil Sands Development in Alberta: A Detailed Review and Analysis'. *Canadian Institute of Resources Law*. Occasional Paper #21.

Walker, G. (2012) *Environmental Justice: Concepts, Evidence, Politics*. London, Routledge.

Wall, K. (2015) '"The Sharpest Knives in the Drawer": Visual Culture at the Intersection of Oil and State'. In M. Shrivistava and L. Stefanick (eds.) *Alberta Oil and the Decline of Democracy in Alberta*. Edmonton, Athabasca University Press, pp. 333–362.

Walmsley, C. (2005) *Protecting Aboriginal Children*. Toronto, University of Toronto Press.

Walters, C. J. (1997) 'Challenges in Adaptive Management of Riparian and Coastal Ecosystems'. *Conservation Ecology*. Vol. 1 (2).

Walters, R. (2010) 'Eco Crime'. In J. Muncie, D. Talbot and R. Walters (eds.) *Crime: Local and Global*. Devon, Willan Publishing, pp. 173–208.

Ward, T. and Green, P. (2000) 'Legitimacy, Civil Society and State Crime. *Social Justice*. Vol. 27 (4), pp. 76–93.

Weber, B. (2016) 'Damning Report Finds Alberta Failing Aboriginals on Oil Sands Development'. *The Globe and Mail*, 2 February 2016.
Wheatley, M. (1997) 'Social and Cultural Impacts of Mercury Pollution on Aboriginal Peoples in Canada'. *Water, Air & Soil Pollution*. Vol. 97 (1–2), pp. 85–90.
White, R. (2008) *Crimes Against Nature*. Devon, Willan Publishing.
White, R. (2011) *Transnational Environmental Crime: Towards an Eco-Global Criminology*. Devon, Willan Publishing.
White, R. (2013) 'The Conceptual Contours of Green Criminology'. In D. Westerhuis, R. Walters and T. Wyatt (eds.) *Emerging Issues in Green Criminology*. London, Palgrave MacMillan, pp. 17–33.
White, R. (2018) *Climate Change Criminology*. Bristol, Bristol University Press.
Whyte, D. (2012) 'Between Crime and Doxa: Researching the Worlds of State-Corporate Elites'. *Journal of State Crime*. Vol. 1 (1), pp. 88–108.
Whyte, D. (2016) 'It's Common Sense, Stupid! Corporate Crime and Techniques of Neutralization in the Automobile Industry'. *Crime, Law and Social Change*, Vol. 66 (2), pp. 165–181.
Widdowson, F. and Howardson, A. (2008) *Disrobing the Aboriginal Industry*. Montreal, McGill-Queen's University Press.
Williams, B. (2011) 'Adaptive Management of Natural Resources – Frameworks and Issues'. *Journal of Environmental Management*. Vol. 92 (5), pp. 1346–1353.
Williams, C. (2012) *Researching Power, Elites and Leadership*. London, Sage Publications.
Wilt, J. (2018) 'Are Albertans Collecting a Fair Share of Oil Sands Wealth?'. *The Narwhal* (online) Available at: https://thenarwhal.ca/are-albertans-collecting-a-fair-share-of-oilsands-wealth/ [Accessed 29.11.2018].
Wolfe, P. (1999) *Settler Colonialism and the Transformation of Anthropology*. London, Cassell.
Wolfe, P. (2006) 'Settler Colonialism and the Elimination of the Native'. *Journal of Genocide Research*. Vol. 8 (4), pp. 387–409.
Woolford, A. (2009) 'Ontological Destruction: Genocide and Canadian Aboriginal Peoples'. *Genocide Studies and Prevention: An International Journal*. Vol. 4 (1), pp. 81–97.
Woolford, A. (2013) 'The Next Generation: Criminology, Genocide Studies and Settler Colonialism'. *Revista Critica Penal y Poder*. No. 5, pp. 163–185.
World Health Organization (2013) *Outdoor Air Pollution a Leading Environmental Cause of Cancer Deaths*. Available at: www.iarc.fr/en/media-centre/iarcnews/pdf/pr221_E.pdf [Accessed 30.10.2018].
Wright Mills, C. (1956) *The Power Elite*. Oxford, Oxford University Press.
Wyatt, T. (2016). 'A Comparative Analysis of Wildlife Trafficking in Australia, New Zealand and the United Kingdom'. *Trafficking, Organised Crime and Security*. Vol. 2 (1), pp. 62–81.
York, R. and Rosa, E. (2003) 'Key Challenges to Ecological Modernization Theory'. *Organization and Environment*. Vol. 16 (3), pp. 273–288.

Index

Page numbers in **bold** denote tables, those in *italics* denote figures.

www.ingramcontent.com/pod-product-compliance
Ingram Content Group UK Ltd.
Pitfield, Milton Keynes, MK11 3LW, UK
UKHW022018180926
475701UK00005B/897
* 9 7 8 0 3 6 7 5 3 0 7 9 2 *